How to Stay Afloat in the
Academic Library Job Pool

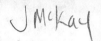

How to Stay Afloat in the Academic Library Job Pool

Edited by Teresa Y. Neely

Foreword by Camila A. Alire

AMERICAN LIBRARY ASSOCIATION
CHICAGO 2011

Teresa Y. Neely is director of access services, University Libraries, University of New Mexico. Most recently she was head of reference at the Albin O. Kuhn Library & Gallery, University of Maryland, Baltimore County; and an adjunct professor at the College of Information Studies, University of Maryland, College Park. She received her MLS and PhD (LIS) degrees from the School of Information Sciences, University of Pittsburgh.

Printed in the United States of America
15 14 13 12 11   5 4 3 2 1

While extensive effort has gone into ensuring the reliability of the information in this book, the publisher makes no warranty, express or implied, with respect to the material contained herein.

ISBN: 978-0-8389-1080-1

Library of Congress Cataloging-in-Publication Data
How to stay afloat in the academic library job pool / edited by Teresa Y. Neely ; foreword by Camila A. Alire.
   pages cm
 Includes bibliographical references and index.
 ISBN 978-0-8389-1080-1 (alk. paper)
 1. Academic librarians--Vocational guidance--United States. 2. Academic librarians--Selection and appointment--United States. 3. Library science--Vocational guidance--United States. 4. Employment interviewing--United States. I. Neely, Teresa Y., 1966-
 Z682.4.C63H69 2011
 023'.2--dc22
                                                                      2010043382

Book design in Avenir and Minion Pro by Casey Bayer.

♾ This paper meets the requirements of ANSI/NISO Z39.48–1992 (Permanence of Paper).

ALA Editions also publishes its books in a variety of electronic formats. For more information, visit the ALA Store at www.alastore.ala.org and select eEditions.

CONTENTS

FOREWORD

As a colleague who delivers workshops on job search strategies for library and information science (LIS) students, I say it is about time a book like this was written! Teresa Neely and her contributor-colleagues have done a great service to new LIS graduates, to graduates who are changing careers, and to librarians who want to move from working in some other type of library to working in an academic library. It's one thing to complain about candidates' performance anytime during the search process; it's another thing to do something about it. That is exactly what Neely and her contributors have done.

As a person who is new to academic librarianship, you will benefit by taking the time to read this book. They have demystified the academic library search process, so please pay close attention.

This book is a *must read* for anyone who wants to work in an academic library as a professional librarian. Everything you need to know about the academic library job search process—ranging from dissecting the job ad to negotiating after the job offer—is included. The contributors left nothing out. Much of what they included (especially in providing the *don'ts* and *what to avoid*) I have expressed over and over as a hiring authority in three university library systems. This book can be validated by any academic librarian who has served on a search committee.

Anyone who reads and follows the advice provided by the authors will have a competitive advantage by understanding what really transpires in the academic library search process and by following the advice offered. The authors provide excellent, real-life examples, many times with a good sense of humor.

I must say that I couldn't put the book down; hence, you can read it in a day's time!

Camila A. Alire, Ed.D.
Dean Emeritus
University of New Mexico &
Colorado State University

CHAPTER 1

WELCOME TO LIBRARY LAND

Teresa Y. Neely

ALTHOUGH THIS BOOK was conceived and written primarily for new library science graduates entering the academic workforce for the first time, those interested in a career change to academic librarianship will also find it useful. Years of experience chairing and serving on search committees, particularly those for entry-level positions in academic libraries, revealed that many newly minted library science graduates need help learning about the process of successfully securing a position in an academic library, or at the least mounting a competitive attempt. From selecting which available positions they qualify for to preparing an application packet, to arriving on campus for the interview, new graduates make mistakes and blunders at every stage; and what is more astounding and frustrating is that they seem oblivious to the impact of their decisions, actions, behaviors, and words.

A marked decrease in available entry-level positions over the years, along with a relatively stable number of new graduates seeking positions in academic libraries, compounds the issue of finding and securing employment in academic libraries.[1] From fall 1996 through fall 2003, the greatest annual increase in American Library Association (ALA)-accredited degrees awarded, according to the Association of Library and Information Science Education (ALISE), was only 6.11 percent, or an increase of 252 degrees awarded in fall 2002. Table 1.1 shows the number of LIS graduates each year, beginning with the 1995–1996 academic school year up to the 2002–2003 school year. Although the number of degrees earned declined four times during the period under review, overall, 35,460 degrees were awarded, which constituted 32.73 percent of total enrollment numbers in LIS programs for the same time period.

On the prospect of jobs in librarianship, the 2008–2009 *Occupational Outlook Handbook* reports that "more than 2 out of 3 librarians are aged 45 or older, which will result in many job openings over the next decade as many librarians retire. However, recent increases in enrollments in MLS programs will prepare a sufficient number of new librarians to fill these positions."[2] Table 1.1 also includes enrollment numbers as reported to ALISE and shows an increase (4,227) in enrollment numbers when fall 1996 and fall 2003 numbers are compared. Enrollment decreased slightly until fall 1999, when numbers dropped by 1,560; rebounding in the next year, numbers climbed steadily, reaching 16,876 in fall 2003. A look at ALISE enrollment numbers between 1980 and 2000 also shows a slight increase in the number of individuals enrolling in LIS programs, confirming, in part, some of the *Occupational Outlook Handbook* predictions.[3]

It has been noted that Stanley J. Wilder's prediction that jobs in libraries would grow as a result of potential retirements by an aged profession have not yet been realized.[4] A review of job advertisements from 2007 and 2008 in chapter 2 of this book reveals that if librarians of retirement age are actually retiring, they generally are not being replaced by entry-level librarians. Poor or limited job-seeking skills, a decrease in the number of entry-level jobs available, plus increased competition from relatively consistent LIS enrollment and graduates, do not make an environment conducive to producing a successfully employed beginning librarian in an academic library. Adding to the competition factor, active job seekers looking for entry-level positions should be aware that, unfortunately, there is no such animal as an entry-level position in academic libraries. Although there are job ads that are advertised as entry-level, or include statements encouraging new graduates to apply, or do not list minimum requirements for work experience, or include language such as "no experience necessary," hiring libraries still need a mechanism to decrease the pools of potential job applicants.[5] This is generally done by listing preferred or desirable (as opposed to minimum) qualifications, and odds are, those qualifications require some level of experience or expertise. ("Minimum qualifications" are those qualifications that are essential, and that the employee must have, while "preferred" or "desirable" qualifications are those that the employer would prefer to see but that aren't required.) In a 1985 study of the requirements for entry-level positions, Sheila Creth and Faith Harders sought "to clarify for both the educators and the graduate library school student the

TABLE **1.1**

LIS enrollment and degrees awarded from ALA-accredited schools

ACADEMIC YEAR	ENROLLMENT	CHANGE FROM PREVIOUS YEAR	DEGREES AWARDED	CHANGE FROM PREVIOUS YEAR IN DEGREES AWARDED
1995–1996	12,649 (fall 1996)		5,271	
Fall 1996– Fall 1997		–169		–203 (–3.85%)
1996–1997	12,480 (fall 1997)		5,068	
Fall 1997– Fall 1998		–321		–44 (–0.86%)
1997–1998	12,801 (fall 1998)		5,024	
Fall 1998– Fall 1999		1,560		22 (0.43%)
1998–1999	11,241 (fall 1999)		5,046	
Fall 1999– Fall 2000		1,886		–93 (1.84%)
2000–2001	13,127 (fall 2000)		4,953	
Fall 2000– Fall 2001		916		–30 (–0.60%)
2001–2002	14,043 (fall 2001)		4,923	
Fall 2001– Fall 2002		1,074		252 (6.11%)
2002–2003	15,117 (fall 2002)		5,175	
Fall 2002– Fall 2003		1,759		
2002–2003	16,876 (fall 2003)			
Total	108,334	(3,585)	35,460	(32.73%) (–96)

Source: ALISE Library and Information Science Education Statistical Report 1997, 1998, 1999, 2000, 2001, 2002, 2003, 2004.

requirements (in addition to the MLS) that academic research libraries have established for beginning librarians." The authors surveyed members of the Association of College and Research Libraries' (ACRL's) Discussion Group of Personnel Officers and found that overwhelmingly, those surveyed "agreed that previous library experience was an important requisite for an entry level position. The majority also indicated that the experience should be in an academic library." The researchers concluded that "the MLS cannot be considered a terminal degree or as the end of the educational process for librarians in the academic research library."[6]

This is a huge revelation, confirmed by Sproles and Ratledge in their 2004 study analyzing job ads. They concluded that "applicants seeking to enter the profession without paraprofessional experience will find themselves at a major disadvantage." The researchers reported on qualities an entry-level librarian would have possessed then, in 2004, but these still seem relevant today in 2010:[7]

- Entry-level librarians will have an ALA-MLS degree.
- They will have a high level of computer/automation knowledge and experience. At a minimum they will be skilled users of the Web, e-mail, desktop computer hardware, peripherals, and software. They may also have a fair degree of basic computer troubleshooting skills and the ability to create relatively complex websites.
- Most will have a significant level of knowledge of, and experience in, their specific area of specialization or interest.
- They will exhibit a high degree of communication ability and interpersonal skills.
- They will have a high degree of diversity awareness and ability to work with others regardless of background.
- They will show evidence of scholarship or scholarly ability.[8]

Like I said, there is no such animal as an entry-level position in academic libraries. These findings should be a monster wake-up call for new graduates and anyone else interested in a career in academic librarianship. In fact, a 2006 survey of the ALA's Spectrum Scholarship recipients found that "the single most predictive indicator of whether a scholar would enter an LIS program was prior experience working in a library." Additionally, "almost 80% of those responding indicated they had experience working in a library either in paid positions or as a volunteer. Nearly 37% of the Spectrum Scholars responding were pursuing degrees in LIS, and 50% indicated academic libraries as the type of organization where they thought they would work initially."[9] How's that for competition?

These findings should impact the way LIS education programs recruit, and also the course and experiential offerings they make available for their students. Ensuring that new graduates have taken the appropriate coursework, but also making sure they have had the opportunity to acquire and master practical library experience, will make them more marketable in today's competitive academic library job market.

THE ACADEMIC SEARCH PROCESS

Unbeknownst to many new graduates, much of the work that goes into recruiting—including developing the position description, reviewing applications for minimum and preferred or desired qualifications, conducting telephone interviews, and winnowing down the pool—is done by committee. A search committee, to be exact. There are a number of published studies and literature on the effectiveness and work of search committees, as well as an abundance of published information and advice for job seekers on applying for academic library jobs and surviving the search process.[10] Additionally, Gregory K. Raschke reminds us that "academic libraries take too long to recruit, to interview, and to hire librarians," an unfortunate by-product of work conducted by committee; thus, applicants should be aware that the process for securing a position in an academic library could, on average, take up to five months, according to a 1987 study by Tedine Roos and Diana Shelton.[11]

Specific search committee practices and procedures vary depending on the library and local practices, the host institution rules, and state and federal laws. Local practices and procedures affect the size and makeup of the search committee; however, a typical committee could include a mix of faculty and staff (depending on the type of positions represented in that library), and some committees encourage or require the inclusion of representation by a person of color. Search committee members can be nominated or appointed, again, mostly dependent on local practice and procedures. What is important to potential applicants is that in many cases, the decision to hire or power to negotiate does *not* usually lie with the search committee, nor with the person to whom the job would report. At the University of New Mexico University Libraries (UNM UL), for example, search committee members do the work and make a recommendation to the dean. The dean considers the committee's recommendation, along with a number of other factors, including feedback from library faculty and staff outside of the search committee, and references provided by the applicant.

The work of the search committee can be grueling and is not for the faint of heart. Between 2005 and 2008, four separate search committees for the UNM UL's resident in research and instruction entry-level position made their way through 449 applications. Table 1.2 shows the number of applications received and the number deemed "bona fide," the UNM term used to describe those applications that remain once the minimum qualification review has been completed. The intent of each of these searches was to hire one resident, and with the exception of the 2008 search, each of these searches resulted in one hire and thus was considered successful.

Once the job description has been written and approved, depending on local practices and requirements for the position level and type, the description is published in library-appropriate publications, posted on websites, and distributed via electronic discussion lists. At the UNM UL, the search committee is involved in the development of a recruitment plan which spells out

TABLE **1.2**

Searches for resident and access services librarian positions at the University of New Mexico's University Libraries

	TOTAL NUMBER OF APPLICATIONS RECEIVED	TOTAL NUMBER OF APPLICATIONS MEETING MINIMUM QUALIFICATIONS
Resident 2005	84	80 bona fide (95.23%)
Resident 2006	137	84 bona fide (61.31%)
Resident 2007	118	66 bona fide (55.93%)
Resident 2008	110	98 bona fide (89.09%)
Subtotal	449	328 bona fide (73.05%)
Access Services 2009	137	94 bona fide (68.61%)
Total	586	422 bona fide (72%)

where the position will be advertised, distributed, and posted. Searches at the UNM UL are assigned a search coordinator who, in the past, was responsible for receiving applications and making them available to the search committee for review. Recently, like many other institutions, the University of New Mexico has streamlined the application process for all position types, and now all applications are accepted through the UNM human resources portal, UNMJobs. Much of what was done on paper is now being done online. This should speed up the search process considerably.

OVERSTEPPING BOUNDARIES

Some practices from nonacademic job searches do not translate well to the world of academia. As I write this chapter, I am cochairing the search for a faculty librarian for the access services department. My experience with this search, and others, provides a number of examples of what applicants should *not* do in the pursuit of an academic position. For example, I was e-mailed directly by an applicant who wished to provide additional information for her application, even though she had already submitted her application via the UNMJobs online system. Another applicant decided to snail mail her application to me directly, even though my name was not listed on the job advertisement, and instructions to applicants directed them to visit the UNMJobs online system to apply for the position. Unfortunately for this potential applicant, her application was never seen by the search committee because she did not follow posted instructions. Although I applaud applicants for taking the initiative to review the job description for the title of the person they would be reporting to, and then tracking down that person's name and contact information, it is nevertheless disconcerting to receive direct e-mails and telephone calls from applicants who believe it is acceptable to communicate directly with their potential supervisor. Although communicating in any way with applicants for an available position at UNM is not illegal, and may be handled differently on other campuses, it is, in the grand scheme of things, not appropriate and I would personally recommend it be avoided at all costs. At UNM, searches are confidential until applicants are invited to campus, and an offer is extended and accepted. At that point, anyone can have access to the names of those who apply for a particular position. Down the road, if an individual is not selected for the position or perhaps even an interview, and they have knowledge that the successful candidate had the "inside" track with the search chair, the legal implications are too many to contemplate.

OPEN UNTIL FILLED

That said, depending on the number of applicants for a particular position, the search committee may begin their work prior to the "closed" or "best consideration" date posted on the job advertisement, particularly if the applicant numbers are large. At this point, their work involves confirming the minimum or required qualifications for the position, a practice called "bona fides" at UNM, as noted previously. In general, if you meet or exceed the preferred or desired qualifications, this is a good thing! It ensures you a place beyond the bona fides process, although there is some research that questions the effectiveness of search committees in advancing candidates who meet minimum and maximum qualifications, particularly when candidates make it difficult for search committees to locate the required information in their cover letters or curricula vitae.[12] Most importantly, if you do not meet *each* of the minimum or required qualifications, the search committee is unlikely to review or discuss your remaining qualifications. Job descriptions list minimum qualifications for a reason. These are the minimum qualifications established for being hired into a particular position. For entry-level positions in academic libraries, there is often one consistent requirement: the ALA-accredited MLS degree by the time the position begins.[13] There may be additional minimum requirements in job advertisements, categorized by Sproles and Ratledge as "personal abilities," such as

- ability to work with others/diversity awareness
- public service commitment
- supervision or leadership ability
- interpersonal skills, such as oral and written communication skills
- ability to participate in scholarship and professional development[14]

It should be noted that in the authors' experience at UNM, most search committees cannot and will not base their decision on personal characteristics such as the fact that you "love Mexican food," or you "hope to learn to speak Spanish," or that you "have always been interested in Native Americans so you read fiction books." These are real examples voluntarily offered during telephone interviews or in cover letters for the resident searches mentioned earlier.

Next, the search committee will need to apply some sort of weighting or ranking to the preferred qualifications, depending on the job duties and responsibilities. This ranking could include a point system or a numerical value; it will vary from library to library. These rankings are important and are generally determined by the preferred qualifications and how important they are if held by the successful hire. Table 1.2 shows that the four resident searches yielded a total of 449 applicants. Once bona fide status had been established, 328 applicants remained, which made up approximately 73 percent of the total number of applicants for these four searches. These numbers show that for these searches, before qualifications beyond the minimum applications had been discussed or applied, more than 25 percent of the pool had been eliminated. These findings are relatively low compared to the case studies presented by Womack, where she reported that 61 percent of applicants for Case Study One did not meet the minimum requirements for a position; 78 percent did not meet the minimums for Case Study Two; and in Case Study Three, 62 percent did not meet the minimums.[15] Meeting the minimum qualification requirements and heeding the results of the research findings reported earlier from Creth/Harders and Sproles/Ratledge will position applicants well for an entry-level position in today's tough academic library job market. Applicants must realize that once they've reached bona fide status, however, the process begins anew, with all qualified candidates on a level playing field as preferred qualifications are weighted or ranked.

The remaining chapters of this book address and discuss major aspects of the academic search process. Chapter 2 presents the results of a content analysis of job ads published in *American Libraries* and *College and Research News* in order to determine the current availability of entry-level positions, as well as examine any trends in job advertisements for entry-level academic library positions. In chapter 3, Sever Bordeianu and Christina M. Desai impart the art of reading and deciphering a job advertisement, and how to use it to write your cover letter. In chapter 4, Sarah L. Stohr shares with readers "how to compile an application packet that doesn't make the search committee want to kill you." I believe this title speaks for itself. Chapter 5 explores the use and misuse of online tools and social networking during the job search process. Chapter 6 deconstructs the telephone interview process, along with advice on things you probably shouldn't say or do during the interview. In chapter 7, Daniel Barkley offers a discussion of what to expect during the on-campus interview. Sarah L. Stohr coauthors chapter 8 with Bruce Neville and examines the do's and don'ts of preparing and making a presentation during the on-site job interview. Chapter 9 discusses job offers and negotiations and is coauthored by Neely and Evangela Q. Oates. Silvia Lu rounds out this volume with chapter 10, "The Eight-Month Marathon: From Library School to New Librarian," which brings everything together.

It is absolutely possible to apply for and get offered a professional library position in an academic library without the advice provided in this book. However, we hope the advice and information provided here increases your odds for success. Enjoy the journey.

Notes

1. Rachel Holt and Adrienne L. Stock, "The Entry-Level Gap," *Library Journal* 130, no. 8 (2005): 36–38.
2. U.S. Department of Labor, Bureau of Labor Statistics, "Librarians," in *Occupational Outlook Handbook, 2008–09 Edition,* http://www.bls.gov/oco/ocos068.htm (accessed December 9, 2009*).*
3. Teresa Y. Neely, "Minority Student Recruitment in LIS Education: New Profiles for Success," in *Unfinished Business: Race, Equity, and Diversity in Library and Information Science Education,* ed. Maurice B. Wheeler (Lanham, MD: Scarecrow, 2005), 108.
4. Penny M. Beile and Megan M. Adams, "Other Duties as Assigned: Emerging Trends in the Academic Library Job Market," *College and Research Libraries* 61, no. 4 (2000): 336–47. See also Stanley J. Wilder, "The Age Demographics of Academic Librarians: A Profession Apart," *Journal of Library Administration* 28, no. 3 (1999): 1–84.
5. David W. Reser and Anita P. Schuneman, "The Academic Library Job Market: A Content Analysis Comparing Public and Technical Services," *College and Research Libraries* 53, no. 1 (1992): 49–59.
6. Sheila Creth and Faith Harders, "Thirty Academic Research Libraries Report Their . . . Requirements for the Entry Level Librarian," *Library Journal* 105, no. 18 (1980): 2168–69.
7. Claudene Sproles and David Ratledge, "An Analysis of Entry-Level Librarian Ads Published in *American Libraries,* 1982–2002," *Electronic Journal of Academic and Special Librarianship* 5, nos. 2–3 (2004): n.p.
8. Ibid.
9. Loriene Roy and others, "Bridging Boundaries to Create a New Workforce: A Survey of Spectrum Scholarship Recipients, 1998–2003," American Library Association, 2006, www.ala.org/ala/aboutala/offices/diversity/spectrum/spectrumsurveyreport/BridgingBoundaries.pdf (accessed December 9, 2009). See also Teresa Y. Neely and Lorna Peterson, "Achieving Racial and Ethnic Diversity among Academic and Research Librarians: The Recruitment, Retention, and Advancement of Librarians of Color: A White Paper," Association of College and Research Libraries, 2007, www.ala.org/ala/mgrps/divs/acrl/publications/whitepapers/ACRL_Achieving Racial.pdf (accessed December 9, 2009).
10. Phillip C. Howze, "Search Committee Effectiveness in Determining a Finalist Pool: A Case Study," *Journal of Academic Librarianship* 34, no. 4 (2008): 340–53; Kay Womack, "Applying for Professional Positions in Academic Libraries: Meeting Minimum Requirements," *Journal of Academic Librarianship* 23, no. 3 (1997): 205–9.
11. Gregory K. Raschke, "Hiring and Recruitment Practices in Academic Libraries: Problems and Solutions," *Portal: Libraries and the Academy* 3, no. 1 (2003): 53–67; Tedine J. Roos and Diana W. Shelton, "The Cost of Hiring an Academic Librarian," *Journal of Library Administration* 8, no. 2 (1987): 81–91.

12. Womack, "Applying for Professional Positions"; Howze, "Search Committee Effectiveness."
13. Creth and Harders, "Thirty Academic Research Libraries"; Reser and Schuneman, "Academic Library Job Market"; Sproles and Ratledge, "Analysis of Entry-Level Librarian Ads."
14. Sproles and Ratledge, "Analysis of Entry-Level Librarian Ads."
15. Womack, "Applying for Professional Positions," 206–8.

CHAPTER 2

ENTRY-LEVEL JOBS IN ACADEMIC LIBRARIES

Teresa Y. Neely with Kathleen B. Garcia

THE ORIGINAL IMPETUS for this book came from the experiences of search committee members for the University of New Mexico's resident in instruction and research services position. The resident position was designed specifically for entry-level librarians, defined by the University Libraries as recent graduates of ALA-accredited library and information science programs with no prior experience. This chapter is designed to show those destined for academic librarianship the paucity of entry-level positions, in hopes that the information will motivate applicants to put their best foot forward. As universities throughout the country experienced budget cuts, and UNM in particular underwent a hiring "pause" in 2009, the reality of readily available entry-level positions profession-wide seemed to become a myth, even as library and information science programs continued to produce MLS/MLIS graduates at a steady rate. Additionally, there is very little evidence that the advice provided in the published literature for job seekers at all levels is actually being heeded. According to Kay Womack in her 1997 article:

> Although William Fietzer has reported that a common complaint of people involved in academic library searches is that "too many patently unqualified people apply" and others have noted that these

individuals waste their time and have even advised them not to apply, many applicants either do not take these points seriously or do not understand their importance.[1]

The original research presented in this chapter updates and confirms published research analyzing job ads directed towards entry-level academic librarian job seekers, and examines the minimum requirements and expectations, skills, and experience levels demanded by these job ads. It will also provide those seeking employment in academic libraries with an updated profile of the trends in the academic library employment market via an examination of available job advertisements.

REVIEW OF THE LITERATURE

There is a robust body of research analyzing job descriptions for positions in libraries covering a range of specialties, including Latin American and Caribbean studies, information systems, information technology skill sets, electronic resources, and cataloging.[2] More pertinent to this study are Reser and Schuneman's 1992 study comparing job advertisements for public services and technical services positions, and Beile and Adams's 2000 replication of that study.[3] Although some of these studies do address, in part, entry-level positions, there are far fewer published studies which focus primarily on entry-level positions in academic libraries.[4]

Sheila Creth and Faith Harders's 1979 study was undertaken "to give a profile of the hiring practices at academic libraries" that was representative of the population they surveyed. The researchers queried members of the ACRL Discussion Group of Personnel Officers, and the responses received represented a 67 percent (30 out of 45) return rate. Although only two of the responding libraries in the sample required it, previous (nonprofessional) experience in a library was identified as an important qualification for entry-level positions. In addition to nonprofessional work experience, other qualifications addressed in the survey were foreign languages, second master's degrees, and undergraduate studies.[5]

Foreign languages were only required by four of the responding libraries, with most of the sample reporting it was "very important or helpful" in cataloging first, followed by "some reference positions." Candidates with foreign language abilities were considered to have stronger qualifications that would allow them to "maintain greater flexibility throughout their careers." While only one library in the sample required a second master's degree, it was required for some subject specialist and branch librarian positions. Most surveyed listed this qualification as preferred, and while some didn't list it as a qualification, having the degree "strengthened applications." One respondent noted that "in general, it is a good indicator of promise in scholarship and subject mastery required for promotion and tenure." Respondents indicated "a growing trend to use the second degree as a screening device when reviewing all applications." The second master's degree was also a qualification that would make the holder more competitive "as they advanced in their careers," as similarly noted for foreign language abilities. Interestingly, in terms of undergraduate studies, those responding "consistently agreed that it was not the subject but the quality of the educational experience that counted."[6]

In 1992 Reser and Schuneman published their content analysis of 1,133 job ads appearing in three publications in 1988, comparing public services and technical services positions, in order to examine and document differences between the two divisions. They believed these differences might shed "new light on the recruitment problems concerning technical services." After eliminating duplicate ads and applying the criteria for their particular methodology, each ad was coded into various classifications. In this study, entry-level position information was revealed in the category labeled "work experience." Ads were classified "work experience required," "work experience preferred/desired," or "no work experience or none stated." To be included in the latter category, "announcements (1) had no work experience mentioned in the advertisement; (2) had a statement specifying that no experience was necessary; or (3) were labeled 'entry level.'"[7]

The researchers found that the majority of job ads, 579 (51.1 percent), required work experience; followed by 353 (31.2 percent) which preferred work experience. The remaining 201 (17.7 percent) job ads required no experience or none was stated in the ads.[8]

In the category of "minimum salary," the researchers found that 316 (28 percent) of the job ads contained a salary range, while 960 (85 percent) published a minimum salary in the job ads.[9] It's difficult to determine how many job ads, if any, did not list salary information because the number of ads reported that did list some salary information (960 plus 316) exceeded the number of job ads analyzed—1,276 vs. 1,133. The researchers used the minimum salary figure listed to determine the mean, including the lower range of those listing a salary range. The job ads were divided into three subgroups for comparison:

- "Cataloging and reference positions without administrative duties have mean salaries that are nearly identical."

- Cataloging and reference positions "with administrative duties . . . average more than $1,200 more per year."
- The mean minimum salary for heads of public services was more than $4,400 higher than technical services heads.[10]

Of possible interest to experienced librarians seeking to move into academic librarianship are the study findings on the differences between technical services and public services positions:

- Technical services position advertisements require more computer skills and previous work experience and are more than twice as likely to require foreign language skills.
- Public services candidates are expected to have more advanced degrees.
- Minimum salaries advertised for the two groups are nearly equal for lower-level positions, but public services salaries rise faster as administrative responsibilities grow.[11]

In 2000 Beile and Adams replicated Reser and Schuneman's 1992 study, adding systems positions in addition to the public services and technical services categories. The researchers analyzed 900 job advertisements appearing in four publications in 1996. Like the 1992 study, Beile and Adams's findings are of interest "to librarians and administrators interested in learning more about the academic library job market."[12] When findings from the two studies are compared, Beile and Adams report a decrease of nearly 20 percent in the number of available job advertisements overall.[13]

Twenty percent (181) of the 900 job ads in this study required no work experience and were identified as entry-level, slightly more than the nearly 18 percent coded as such in the 1992 Reser and Schuneman study. Nearly 23 percent (205) of the ads listed work experience as preferred, and 57 percent (514) required work experience.[14]

Replicating Reser and Schuneman, Beile and Adams used the minimum salary listed in the job ads for their analysis, including the lower end of those with a range. As anticipated, they found that job ads for electronic services advertised higher salaries, with a mean salary $1,700 higher than positions in technical services and $1,831 higher than those in public services. Positions requiring experience listed higher mean salaries ($32,875) than entry-level positions ($28,971). Only a slight difference in salary, less than $900, was indicated between positions preferring experience ($28,090) and those requiring none ($28,971).[15] Interestingly, Beile and Adams did not address this difference in their discussion.

In comparing their 1996 data analysis findings to Reser and Schuneman's data from 1988, the researchers reported:

- Salaries for cataloging without administrative duties were almost $1,000 greater than those for reference positions without administrative duties, up from being nearly identical in 1988.
- Salaries for systems positions without administrative duties were listed on average at $3,719 more than for reference positions, and at $2,823 more than for cataloging positions without administrative duties. Systems positions were not analyzed in 1988.
- Reference positions with administrative duties were listed on average at $1,794 more than similar cataloging positions, up slightly from the $1,200 reported in 1988.
- Division head positions for technical services were listed at $387 more than heads of public services positions, significantly less than the $4,400 difference reported in 1988. Heads of electronic services positions, on average, were listed below heads of technical services positions by more than $750.

In addition to the decrease in the number of positions advertised, the researchers reported:

- The decreases in position volume were found mainly in technical services positions. Cataloging positions in particular experienced the most dramatic loss.[16]
- Specialist positions are growing. "The number of job titles analyzed within the public services division increased from six in 1988 to eleven in 1996. Branch managers, collection development, government documents, music, and special collections positions were . . . added to the positions of reference, head of public services, instruction, circulation, interlibrary loan (ILL), and other public services as reported by Reser and Schuneman. The number of job titles under technical services was the same in both studies."[17]
- There was increased demand for computer skills from 1988 (40.5 percent) to 1996 (66.9 percent).[18]
- There was an increase in the acceptance of degrees other than the ALA-accredited MLS, primarily to fill systems positions. Although public and technical services positions continued to require the ALA-accredited library degree in well over 90 percent of job advertisements, this qualification was present in only three-fourths of the electronic services advertisements.[19]

In their 2004 study Sproles and Ratledge hypothesized the following:

- Over time, employers required more experience and knowledge that could not always be gained from library school.
- On-the-job experience before obtaining a professional degree was almost mandatory.
- The number of entry-level jobs was decreasing.[20]

The researchers analyzed jobs over a twenty-year period in five-year intervals, from 1982 to 2002, totaling 2,613 positions. Analyses resulted in 1,441 (55 percent) unique ads for entry-level positions published in *American Libraries*. Job ads meeting the researchers' definition of "entry-level" were analyzed for required qualifications only. The first and second hypotheses were found to be valid. However, results for the third hypothesis proved to be mixed. Although the total number of published ads decreased over time, the researchers reported that "the number and percentage of entry-level ads remained relatively constant." The data revealed that "employers in the later years of the study increasingly sought to hire more well-rounded and experienced entry-level applicants than in earlier years, while keeping the actual number of entry-level positions constant." Their findings also confirmed that "entry-level positions have changed over time," which fits nicely with the expectations of employers over time represented in the first hypothesis.[21]

Sproles and Ratledge also found that "experience gained on the job either before or while obtaining a professional degree does appear to be almost mandatory in order to qualify for most of the advertised positions," confirming the findings of Creth and Harders twenty-five years earlier.

Only average salary information for reference, cataloging, and systems positions was reported for this study. Systems librarian salaries averaged higher (7 percent higher on average) than reference or cataloging positions; and systems librarian salaries enjoyed the biggest increases in average salaries. Over the course of the years studied, reference librarian salaries were less than those for technical services librarians, except for 1997.[22]

Unique to other studies, Sproles and Ratledge sought to capture what they called "personal abilities":

- ability to work with others/diversity awareness
- public service commitment
- supervision/leadership ability
- interpersonal skills, such as oral and written communication skills
- ability to participate in scholarship and professional development[23]

After further analyses of these personal abilities, Sproles and Ratledge reported

- increased demand for diversity awareness and working well with others—51 percent of ads required these by 2002
- increased support for public service commitment, particularly for reference positions
- supervision/leadership skills reached a peak in 1997, and were most likely to be required by technical services positions
- increased importance of interpersonal skills—nearly two-thirds of ads required these skills by 2002
- increased demand for professional activities, from zero listing in 1982[24]

In 2008 the School of Information Sciences' Curriculum Committee at the University of Tennessee, Knoxville (UTK) posted the "most frequent qualifications required for select entry-level positions in LIS" on the School of Information Sciences website. Committee members reviewed position advertisements from four publications over a three-month period at the end of 2007. With a pool of ninety-eight entry-level job ads, 85 percent required the ALA-accredited master's degree, and 59 percent required personal abilities, including "excellent interpersonal, verbal/written communication, organizational, and analytical skills." Twenty-one percent required "web scripting languages HTML, XHTML, CS, PHP, XML, JavaScript, PERL, OWL," and 19 percent required "web development skills, wireframes."[25]

Experience at the reference desk, in academic libraries, in library instruction, strong customer services skills, and a commitment to public service all fell between 13 and 19 percent of the job ads. Working among change in a team environment, ability to manage multiple projects, foreign language skills, excellent leadership skills, knowledge about metadata formats, and ability to meet promotion and tenure requirements all fell around 12 percent and lower.[26]

THE NEELY AND GARCIA STUDY

The study undertaken by Neely and Garcia analyzed job advertisements published in 2007 and 2008 in two publications, *College and Research Libraries News* and *American Libraries*. These publications were targeted because they were used in the previously discussed studies. Additionally, the authors believed the bulk of job advertisements for positions in academic libraries would be found in these two publications. This study focused solely on positions from academic libraries; thus ads for positions in public libraries, at library associations and organizations, in school library media centers (K–12), at state and local government libraries, and for employment in LIS education programs were excluded from this study. For the purposes of this study, "entry-level" is defined as positions that require no practical experience beyond the acquisition of the MLS degree or an acceptable equivalent. The definition of "entry-level" closely resembles that used in the 2004 Sproles and Ratledge study:

- Ad says "entry-level," or recent graduates are encouraged to apply
- "No mention of required profession experience" in minimum requirements
- "No experience or duties impossible for entry-level librarians to gain (i.e., supervising other professionals, administrative experience, substantial progressively responsible experience)"[27]

Positions were coded "yes" if they met the definition above, "no" if they did not meet the definition, and "n/a" if the printed advertisement did not contain enough information to code it yes or no.

Findings

A total of 552 unique job ads appearing in the two publications were identified for the time period under review. Three hundred sixty job ads (65.22 percent) were published in 2007 and 192 (34.78 percent) were published in 2008, a more than 30 percent decrease in unique job advertisements for the two years. One hundred sixty-four ads (29.71 percent) were published in *American Libraries,* and the remaining 388 (70.28 percent) appeared in *College and Research Libraries News,* confirming the authors' belief that the majority of published job ads for positions in academic libraries would be found in *College and Research Libraries News.*

Data for each ad was captured at the state level, with the 552 job ads representing forty-six states, Canada, and Beirut, Lebanon. Table 2.1 shows the distribution according to the four geographic regions used by the ALA-APA Salary Survey.[28] Previous studies used the geographic regions from the ALA Survey of Librarian Salaries (Reser and Schuneman, 1992; and Beile and Adams, 2000), which underwent a name change with the 2005 edition, when it began to be published cooperatively with the ALA Allied Professional Association.

Each position was analyzed for entry-level qualifications as defined in the 2004 Sproles and Ratledge study. Forty-nine (8.87 percent) positions were coded yes and designated as known entry-level positions; 422 (76.44 percent) were coded no, and the remaining 81 (14.67 percent) were coded n/a. Table 2.2 shows the geographic distribution of the job ads coded as entry-level positions.

Nearly 30 percent (14) of the forty-nine positions indicated entry-level status by stating it outright, or indicating a two- to three-year cap on degree acquisition. The latter was routinely assigned to resident and diversity fellowship positions. The entry-level language was similar to that described by Sproles and Ratledge, but for some cases, the position wasn't really entry-level because the requirements and job "duties were impossible for entry level librarians" to acquire and master.[29] For example, an ad for a health sciences librarian position included the statement, "Applications from entry-level candidates with the appropriate subject background will be considered." A minimum requirement for that position, however, was "significant knowledge of nursing and allied health disciplines." An ad for a reference and instruction services librarian indicated, "Entry level candidates are welcome to apply and should highlight their potential for success in this position," along with "ready knowledge of general reference, fine and performing arts, government information sources" listed as minimum requirements. Adding a statement that encourages

TABLE **2.1**

Positions advertised by region in the Neely and Garcia study

REGION	NUMBER OF POSITIONS	REGION'S SHARE OF TOTAL POSITIONS (IN PERCENTAGES)
North Atlantic	139	25.18%
Great Lakes and Plains	140	25.36%
Southeast	97	17.57%
West and Southwest	174	31.52%
Canada	1	0.18%
Lebanon, Beirut	1	0.18%
Total	552	99.99%

entry-level candidates to apply without adjusting the minimum requirements sends mixed messages to potential candidates. Care and attention to detail must be taken to ensure that the job ads we publish to recruit for positions are clear and unambiguous.

The low number of entry-level positions identified in this study is extremely sobering. It is possible that some of the eighty-one positions coded "n/a" in the current study could fall into the entry-level category; however, without the complete job descriptions to analyze, we cannot say how many of those would have made the cut. Incidentally, the addition of all eighty-one to the entry-level category in this study would only increase the percentage of entry-level positions to just under 24 percent.

The previously discussed studies reported larger numbers of positions overall, as well as larger numbers of entry-level positions. Table 2.3 shows the data collected to date from the current and previously discussed studies. Between 1982 and 2008, with one of four publications constant, only 36 percent of the 5,198 job ads analyzed were identified as entry-level positions.

TABLE **2.2**

Entry-level positions advertised by region in the Neely and Garcia study

REGION	NUMBER OF POSITIONS	REGION'S SHARE OF TOTAL POSITIONS (IN PERCENTAGES)
North Atlantic	5	10.20%
Great Lakes and Plains	13	26.53%
Southeast	8	16.32%
West and Southwest	23	46.93%
Total	49	100%

Positions by Job Title

Table 2.4 shows the distribution of entry-level ads by position title in the Neely and Garcia study. Like other studies discussed in this chapter, the majority of the positions advertised were in public services. More than 75 percent of the positions coded as entry-level were reference and instruction, including information literacy jobs, access services, web services, and e-learning (a job ad that focuses on Web 2.0 technologies and social networking tools). Resident/library fellowship positions, representing more than 10 percent of the entry-level positions identified in this study, typically fall under public services. Because these positions are generally all entry-level in nature, as well as short-term, however, they were categorized separately for this study. Technical services positions represented more than 6 percent of the population, followed by the archivist category, which included one archivist and a position titled librarian-digital and requiring "demonstrated understanding of current trends and issues regarding digital collections and services," and preferring "relevant experience in an academic library or cultural heritage preservation organization," and "knowledge of metadata schemas and digital capture standards/methodologies." This position was coded as entry-level because the job ad included the statement, "New graduates with digital library coursework are encouraged to apply."

Education—Required

As was expected, the majority of the entry-level positions, nearly 90 percent (44), required the ALA-accredited master's degree in library and information science. Eleven of those positions, less than 25 percent, would accept either the ALA-accredited master's degree or an (international) equivalent degree.[30] There were five job ads with no educational requirements listed.

Interestingly, some positions included requirements in addition to the MLS degree. The government documents position listed in table 2.4 required a "BS in a social science discipline" *and* the ALA-accredited MLS *or* an MS in a social science discipline plus related professional experience in an academic or research library or a government documents depository. The librarian-digital position required either the ALA-accredited MLS or an ALA-accredited information science degree.

Other positions included educational requirements with conditions. One position required a second master's degree in a subject area in addition to the MLS, one required a subject master's degree for tenure, one required an additional advanced degree for appointment as an assistant professor, and two

TABLE **2.3**

Entry-level positions in academic libraries

RESEARCHERS	YEAR JOB AD WAS PUBLISHED	PUBLICATIONS[1]					TOTAL JOBS	ENTRY-LEVEL JOBS	PERCENTAGE OF JOBS THAT WERE ENTRY-LEVEL ONES
		AL	C&RL News	Chronicle of H. Edu.	LJ	JASIST Jobline			
Sproles and Ratledge (2004)	1982	X					421	231	55%
Sproles and Ratledge (2004)	1987	X					774	452	59%
Reser and Schuneman (1992)	1988	X	X	X	X		1,133	201	17.7%
Sproles and Ratledge (2004)	1992	X					517	266	51%
Beile and Adams (2000)	1996	X	X	X	X		900	181	20.1%
Sproles and Ratledge (2004)	1997	X					492	284	58%
Sproles and Ratledge (2004)	2002	X					409	208	51%

UTK SIS Curriculum Committee (2008)[2]	2007	X	X[3]	X	X	N/A	98*	N/A
Neely and Garcia (2010)	2007	X	X			360	25	6.94%
Neely and Garcia (2010)	2008	X	X			192	24	12.5%
Total						5,198	1,872	

[1] AL = American Libraries; C&RL News = College & Research Libraries News; Chronicle of H. Edu = Chronicle of Higher Education; LJ = Library Journal; JASIST Jobline = Journal of the American Society for Information Science and Technology online service for job seekers.

[2] UTK SIS reviewed three months of job ads in 2007.

[3] UTK SIS listed ACRL News as source. It is presumed they are referring to C&RL News, as ACRL News does not appear to include job advertisements in the online version or the printed version.

* 98 entry-level positions not included in total or total calculation of percentages.

required twenty-four baccalaureate credits in addition to the MLS for appointment at the librarian II level. For appointment at the librarian IV level, a second master's degree in a subject area in addition to the MLS was required.

Education—Preferred

Few of the entry-level positions in this study required educational qualifications beyond the ALA-accredited master's degree. Nearly 80 percent (39) of entry-level positions did not list preferred educational qualifications. Fluency in a second language was preferred in two of the job ads. Preferred education varied among the remaining positions with few surprises, with the exception of one that preferred "thorough education or experience." As could be expected, most were subject-based, and several would accept education or experience:

- additional advanced degree (listed in two ads); second master's preferred; second degree or experience in subject specialty
- undergraduate or graduate degree in political science, public affairs, or a related social sciences field
- education or experience in position-related subject areas

TABLE **2.4**

Positions advertised by job title in the Neely and Garcia study

JOB TITLE	NUMBER OF POSITIONS	PERCENTAGE OF TOTAL JOBS
Reference and Instruction	37	75.55%
Diversity/Resident/ Fellowship	5	10.20%
Technical Services	3	6.12%
Archivist	2	4.08%
Government Documents	1	2.04%
Systems Librarian	1	2.04%
Total	49	100.03%

- liberal arts college background
- science background; advanced or undergraduate degree in a life science
- graduate coursework related to the interplay between media, culture, and society (preference given)

Required and Preferred Experience

Turning to required experience, the nature of an entry-level position, as defined by this book, is that no experience is required. However, many entry-level job ads analyzed in this study required experience beyond the MLS degree. Required and preferred elements were categorized into categories. Tables 2.5 and 2.6 show the required and preferred qualifications and personal abilities.

As to be expected, based on the majority of public service positions indicated in table 2.4, reference experience was the most frequently required qualification, appearing in more than 16 percent (8) of job ads. The information literacy/instruction/teaching category appeared in more than 12 percent (6) of ads, followed by experience in academic librarianship (8.16 percent [4]). In the preferred qualifications, the information literacy/instruction/teaching category appeared in more than 26 percent (13) of the job ads, followed by computer and web skills (18.36 percent [4]) and reference experience (16.32 percent [8]).

In terms of personal abilities, the public and customer service-oriented category appeared in nearly 30 percent (14) of the job ads analyzed, closely followed by the team player category (26.53 percent [13]). Diversity was required in more than 16 percent (8) of the job ads, followed by the independent worker category (12.24 percent [6]).

Salary

Salary data comparable to that discussed in studies previously was not gathered for this study. More than 65 percent (367) of the job ads did not list a salary range or minimum salary. Less than 8 percent (44) of the job ads included a salary range, and the remaining 25 percent (141) listed a minimum salary. The salaries for the 552 positions ranged from a low of $9,000 to a high of $100,000.

Of the forty-nine entry-level positions, salary was not listed for more than 50 percent of the job ads (28). A minimum salary was listed for sixteen ads (32.65 percent), and a salary range was listed for the remaining five job ads (10.20 percent). Using the lowest salary on those ads that included a range, as in previously discussed studies, entry-level salaries ranged from a low of $32,640

TABLE **2.5**

Required and preferred qualifications for entry-level positions in the Neely and Garcia study

QUALIFICATIONS	REQUIRED	PREFERRED
Academic librarianship	4	3
Access services	0	1
Collection development	1	3
Computer and web skills	3	9
Digitization	0	3
General (knowledge of library systems)	1	0
Government information	1	0
Integrated library systems	0	5
Information literacy/instruction/ teaching	6	13
Library experience	0	3
Marketing experience	0	1
Outreach/liaison work	3	4
Presentation and facilitation skills	2	1
Productivity software	1	0
Program development	0	3
Public/customer service (experience)	2	2
Publishing and scholarly activity (record)	0	4
Reference experience	8	8
Subject knowledge and collections	3	5
Supervisory experience	0	1
Technical services	0	3

TABLE **2.6**

Required and preferred personal abilities for entry-level positions in the Neely and Garcia study

PERSONAL ABILITIES	REQUIRED	PREFERRED
Diversity	8	0
Leadership skills	4	0
Meeting tenure-track requirements	2	0
Professional development	6	2
Service-oriented (public/customer)	14	3
Team player	13	2
Independent worker	6	2

for public services librarians in Hawaii to a high of $57,060 for a web services librarian position. Both of these salaries appeared at the low end of a range.

Discussion

Clearly, the findings from this study reveal a significant decline in the number of available entry-level positions in academic libraries, as is represented in the published literature. Table 2.3 shows us that the decline over the past twenty-eight years has been significant, ranging from a high of 59 percent in 1987 to a low of just over 6 percent in 2007. There are gaps in coverage, and although there was only one common data source used by all researchers, *American Libraries,* other factors were not consistent. In any case, the lack of available entry-level positions is something the profession cannot continue to ignore, particularly when we're faced with a steady stream of LIS graduates ready to enter the academic library job force.

It's difficult to generalize or make comparisons to previously discussed studies due to the size of the entry-level population in the current study, as well as the differing purposes for each of the studies. However, a more descriptive view of the data provides advice to job seekers as well as employers.

WHAT THE DATA REALLY TELLS US

The findings from the review of job advertisements for this study are somewhat revealing and, overall, incredibly disappointing. I can only imagine how frustrated job seekers would be from the very beginning of their job searches because the amount and depth of information provided in the advertisements reviewed varied wildly. As I reviewed ad after ad, I was struck by what was routinely *not* included, and thus, I felt compelled to clarify for job seekers and employing institutions my list of things job seekers should expect to see in a job ad for professional library positions in academic institutions. (For comparison, see figure 2.1 for the job description of an access services librarian position, posted in 2009 by the UNM UL.)

Position Title

At the very least, job ads should include the title of the position. For many ads, it was necessary to read through all of the detail to find out what "librarian I" or "assistant librarian" meant. It was clear that many of the reviewed positions were posted using the official position title or rank; it would be helpful, however, if the position was advertised using something more descriptive, such as "reference and instruction librarian," or "cataloging librarian." These may seem more generic, but job seekers will know right away if this is a position they are interested in applying for.

City and State

The name of the hiring institution, along with the city and state, is extremely helpful to include when advertising for professional positions. Geographic information is important to job seekers at any stage of their careers. While analyzing these job ads, I frequently found myself using Google to find out where the position was located, as it was not included in many of the ads. Community colleges frequently omitted the city and state in their ads. For some positions where the name of the institution is obvious, say, the University of New Mexico, or Texas A&M University, it was immediately clear where this position was—or at least which state. However, I was stumped by listings for Lafayette College, Murray State University, Johnson County Community College, and Eureka

FIGURE **2.1**

Job advertisement for access services librarian position, University of New Mexico University Libraries, 2009

ACCESS SERVICES LIBRARIAN

The University of New Mexico Libraries (UL) has an opening (Position #0803056) for an Access Services Librarian. This is a full-time, 12-month, non–tenure-track faculty position. The faculty rank will be Lecturer III. The desired start date is January 4, 2010. The annual salary is negotiable from a minimum of $40,000 and includes full benefits.

Position Description

The successful candidate will work in a team-oriented and highly electronic environment, provide support and leadership to Access Services projects and initiatives including but not limited to collection management and inventory, collection development, and coordinating a combined reference and circulation service point that primarily serves undergraduates. The successful candidate will have a working knowledge of print and electronic information sources, strong interpersonal skills, and outstanding analytic and problem-solving skills for initiating plans and carrying out projects. This position reports to the Director of Access Services. The successful candidate will participate in faculty governance as detailed in the UNM Faculty Handbook.

Education and Experience

Minimum Requirements:
> Master's degree earned by the start date from an ALA-accredited Library/ Information Science program.
> 2 years reference desk experience, library information desk experience, or circulation desk experience in an academic or public library.

Preferred (Desired) Qualifications:
> One year classroom library instruction or other teaching experience.
> One year desk experience in a combined service setting.
> One year desk experience providing reference in an academic or public library.
> Experience leading and completing projects.

CONT.

FIGURE 2.1 (CONT.)

Experience with developing and implementing training programs.
Coursework or experience working with government documents.
Demonstrated motivation to learn new technologies.
Bilingual (Spanish-English) speaking skills.
Experience working with culturally diverse populations.
Excellent oral and written communication and interpersonal skills.
Demonstrated strong commitment to excellent customer service.

Primary Duties

Provide public services at a combined service point (reference and circulation) on a schedule which includes evenings and weekends.
Provide support and leadership for Access Services initiatives and projects.
Participate in library technology problem-solving, implementation, and applications.
Participate in library orientation and bibliographic instruction as appropriate.
Provide effective and timely supervision of any assigned employees, including training, career development, and performance management.
Participate in faculty governance meetings, as appropriate, and in library management meetings, as required.

Environment

The UL Facilities and Access Services Unit is responsible for maintaining safe, secure, inviting facilities for the UL, which includes four libraries on the main UNM campus in Albuquerque. Access Services includes circulation and general reference services, a 24/5 facility, InterLibrary Loan and express document delivery, electronic reserves, LIBROS online catalog support, and physical collection maintenance. The University of New Mexico Libraries is a member of the Association of Research Libraries, the Greater Western Library Alliance, and the New Mexico Consortium of Academic Libraries and leads the LIBROS Consortium that hosts the shared catalog for fourteen academic libraries in New Mexico. The UL contains over 2 million volumes and includes four branch libraries: Centennial Science and Engineering Library; Fine Arts & Design Library; Parish Memorial Library (management and social sciences); and Zimmerman Library (education and humanities). Planning is currently underway in Zimmerman Library for the implementation of a Learning Commons with a Combined Service Point as the centerpiece. Zimmerman Library also houses the Center for Southwest Research and Special Collections. The UL is a regional library in the Federal Depository Library Program.

UNM enrolls nearly 26,000 students and employs 2,800 faculty and 4,400 staff. UNM offers 103 baccalaureate degrees, 75 master's degrees, and 45 doctoral degrees/professional degrees. The University of New Mexico is a Tier I Research Institution and a Hispanic-Serving Institution. UNM attracts a culturally diverse student population and has strong academic and research programs concerned with the Southwestern United States, indigenous studies, and Latin America.

The University of New Mexico is located in Albuquerque, New Mexico. Albuquerque is ranked number one in creativity among medium-sized cities in Richard Florida's book *Rise of the Creative Class*. Albuquerque is an ethnically diverse city with a rich culture and history located within minutes of the Sandia and Manzano mountain ranges, which provide opportunities for hiking, biking, rock-climbing, and skiing.

To Apply

Please visit UNMJobs at http://unmjobs.unm.edu/.

Deadline

The search will remain open until the position is filled. For best consideration, complete applications should be received no later than October 7, 2009.

UNM's confidentiality policy ("Disclosure of Information about Candidates for Employment," UNM Board of Regents' Policy Manual 6.7), which includes information about public disclosure of documents submitted by applicants, is located at http://www.unm.edu/~brpm/r67.htm.

The University of New Mexico is an Equal Employment Opportunity/Affirmative Action Employer and Educator.

College located in Pennsylvania, Kentucky, Kansas, and Illinois, respectively. As an experiment, state-level data was recorded for all positions, and whether the state name or abbreviation appeared in the job ad was noted for the 192 job ads published in 2008. State information was provided in the job ads for 135 positions (70.31 percent). This means that 30 percent of the job ads did not include a state in the position description. Employers would do well to shell out the bucks to add the two-letter state abbreviation, at the very least, in posted job ads.

Too Much Detail

Several of the job ads had quite extensive descriptions about the hiring library, often featuring the name of the library more prominently than the institution. Given that ad costs are probably based on the number of words, it would be wise for hiring institutions to prudently edit out those details, especially if they're not directly related to the position, unless the successful candidate would actually be working in that particular building. Detailed descriptions of relevant collections are certainly appropriate when the position includes collection management, curator, or archival responsibilities, but these descriptions could also be pruned down, thereby allowing more space to publish information like salaries, cities, and states.

Not Enough Detail

More than 65 percent of the total job ads reviewed did not list a minimum salary or a salary range. Surely, the hiring library had some salary figure in mind when they made the decision to advertise. At the very least, listing a salary range is much more helpful to job seekers than including "salary commensurate with experience and education," or "competitive salary." Given the range of what is considered competitive in certain states, there is no logical way for an applicant to even guess what the salary is prior to applying. Given that it is advised in this book and in other sources that an applicant not ask about salary before an offer is made, this puts the applicant at a disadvantage from the beginning, and might deter candidates from applying for your position. The more information that can be shared ahead of time, the more your position will get noticed, and this, I believe, will lead to an increased pool of applicants. Unless you are not listing a salary because it is quite low, you're increasing the chances of a failed search and are perhaps losing candidates when you are unable to negotiate the salaries offered for similar positions at other institutions.

As an example, for whom do you think this job ad was written?

> Instruction Librarian: The University of Somewhere University Libraries invites applications for the position of Instruction Librarian. This faculty position, reporting to the Head of the Instruction Department, will serve as a Libraries' liaison to the University's general education program, the University College, the Honors College, student affairs offices, and athletics programs. The incumbent will contribute significantly to the planning, development, provision, and assessment of strategic information literacy initiatives for undergraduates. He or she will conduct specialized instruction for targeted populations as well as general library resource instruction sessions. This librarian will take the lead in evaluating the print and electronic collections with the greatest impact on general education, both serial and monographic, and in making recommendations to purchase resources relevant to curriculum and research needs. In addition, the incumbent will provide general reference assistance

to library patrons in person, on the telephone, and electronically through e-mail and instant messaging. For more information, please visit www.library.somwhere.edu/employment.html.

There's a lot going on in this job ad, and if the reporting line hadn't been included, I would have thought this was a department-level position. As it is written, I'm not really clear about whom they are targeting. There are no qualifications listed to give me a sense of the skills and experience needed to be successful in the position, and of course, there is no minimum salary or range listed.

Minimum or Required Qualifications and Preferred or Desired Qualifications

I think the lack of distinction between *minimum* and *preferred* qualifications confounded me the most in the total pool of job ads reviewed. Some ads jumbled them all up in one sentence or paragraph, and others left them out altogether. Again, it is most likely fiscally prudent for hiring libraries to refer job seekers to their websites, where there is much more detail about the position. However, advertisements which do not clearly delineate what is *required* from what is *desired* for a particular position force job applicants to visit the website just to find out if the job is worth their time, or if they even qualify for the position.

The Entry-Level Card

For most job ads, it was easy to determine which jobs were considered entry-level and which were not. As noted previously, for the analysis done for this chapter, the primary criterion used was the ALA-accredited master's degree (MLS or MLIS), and most positions listed this as a required educational qualification. However, after that was determined, it was a bit challenging to make the determination based on the contradictory language in the job ads. For example, one ad for "librarian–digital" required, in addition to a recently received ALA-accredited MLS, a demonstrated understanding of current trends and issues regarding digital services. This same ad listed as job responsibilities: build and sustain appropriate digital collections, cultivate cooperative relationships with others, and work with library teams, departments, or vendors to identify digital projects, collections, and/or digital services. Although these responsibilities appear to me to be beyond the scope of an entry-level position, the ad encouraged "new graduates with digital library coursework" to apply.

Here is an example of the problems contradictory language in job ads can cause:

> U of Somewhere is seeking an entry-level librarian to assume a leadership role for the United States federal depository library, state, and international documents collections ... *REQUIREMENTS:* BS in a social science discipline, MLS from an ALA-accredited program.

My assumption as a job seeker would be that my BS in accounting would disqualify me from this entry-level position. When you begin to add requirements or exceptions to the job advertisement, the position is technically no longer entry-level.

Excessive Abuse and Misuse of "Demonstrated," "Knowledge of," and "Interest in"

The use of such language as "interest in," "knowledge of," and "demonstrated ability to" could also fall into the personal ability category in that it might be difficult to provide evidence to confirm their presence in a candidate, and thus make it even more difficult to quantify as an objective measure of evaluating a candidate's qualifications.

The word "demonstrated" is obviously the go-to word for all levels and all things in the job ads. As noted previously, Sproles and Ratledge identified skills that fall into the "personal abilities" category as those that are difficult to quantify. However, this study found the term "demonstrated" used excessively and in situations where quantification was actually possible, if not overly difficult, particularly in "entry-level" positions. For example, how would you rank

- demonstrated interpersonal and organizational skills
- demonstrated commitment to diversity and understanding of the contributions a diverse workforce brings to the workplace
- ability and interest in instruction
- ability to provide services required by the position [my personal favorite]
- a working knowledge of emergent technologies that are critical for library development, such as wikis, "media-casting," RSS, and other digital capabilities
- Applications from entry-level candidates with the appropriate subject background will be considered (desired qualification is "advanced or undergraduate degree in a life science")
- up-to-date computer and web skills

- … welcomes applicants who are knowledgeable about and interested in working within a cross-cultural learning environment
- The successful candidate will have background and qualifications to make a significant contribution to the library and the teaching and learning environment
- Affinity for small liberal arts colleges would be advantageous.

These are all statements taken from entry-level job ads analyzed for this study. Librarians new to the profession or new to academic librarianship have an uphill climb when trying to land a position. Increasingly, it seems as though everyone is conspiring against them, including the very institutions that profess to want to hire them. A more concerted effort from employers to do a better job of developing position descriptions and crafting job ads could go a long way toward making applicant pools richer and available positions more appealing and truly competitive.

Notes

1. Kay Womack, "Applying for Professional Positions in Academic Libraries: Meeting Minimum Requirements," *Journal of Academic Librarianship* 23, no. 3 (1997): 205. See also William Fietzer, "World Enough, and Time: Using Search and Screen Committees to Select Personnel in Academic Libraries," *Journal of Academic Librarianship* 19, no. 3 (1993): 150; Carol MacAdam, "Job Hunter's Workshop: How to Find and Land the Right Job, and Survive the Transition," *Serials Librarian* 25, nos. 3–4 (1995): 357; Anna Therese McGowan and Lynn K. Siemers, "Steps to a Job Interview," *Medical Reference Services Quarterly* 4, no. 4 (1985/1986): 67; and Suzanne T. Larsen and Joan S. McConkey, "Applying for Professional Positions," *College and Research Libraries News* 56, no. 6 (1995): 415.
2. See Jesús Alonso-Regalado and Mary K. Van Ullen, "Librarian for Latin American and Caribbean Studies in U.S. Academic and Research Libraries: A Content Analysis of Position Announcements, 1970–2007," *Library Resources and Technical Services* 53, no. 3 (2009): 139–58; Peter A. Todd, James D. McKeen, and R. Brent Gallupe, "The Evolution of IS Job Skills: A Content Analysis of IS Job Advertisements from 1970 to 1990," *MIS Quarterly* 19, no. 1 (1995): 1–27; Janie H. Matthews and Harold Pardue, "The Presence of IT Skill Sets in Librarian Position Announcements," *College and Research Libraries* 70, no. 3 (2009): 250–57; Michael L. Bradford and others, "Education and Electronic Resources (ER) Librarianship: How Library School Programs Are Meeting the Needs of the ER Librarian Position," *Collection Management* 32, nos. 1–2 (2007): 49–69; Abdus Sattar Chaudhry and N. C. Komathi, "Requirements for Cataloging Positions in the Electronic Environment," *Technical Services Quarterly* 19, no. 1 (2001): 1–23; and Sylvia D. Hall-Ellis,

"Cataloger Competencies . . . What Do Employers Require?" *Cataloging and Classification Quarterly* 46, no. 3 (2008): 305–30.

3. David W. Reser and Anita P. Schuneman, "The Academic Library Job Market: A Content Analysis Comparing Public and Technical Services," *College and Research Libraries* 53, no. 1 (1992): 49–59; Penny M. Beile and Megan M. Adams, "Other Duties as Assigned: Emerging Trends in the Academic Library Job Market," *College and Research Libraries* 61, no. 4 (2000): 336–47.

4. Sheila D. Creth and Faith Harders, "Thirty Academic Research Libraries Report Their . . . Requirements for the Entry Level Librarian," *Library Journal* 105, no. 18 (1980): 2168–69; Claudene Sproles and David Ratledge, "An Analysis of Entry-Level Librarian Ads Published in *American Libraries*, 1982–2002," *Electronic Journal of Academic and Special Librarianship* 5, nos. 2–3 (2004): n.p.

5. Creth and Harders, "Thirty Academic Research Libraries," 2169.

6. Ibid.

7. Reser and Schuneman, "Academic Library Job Market," 53.

8. Ibid., 54.

9. Ibid., 55.

10. Ibid., 56.

11. Ibid., 49.

12. Beile and Adams, "Other Duties as Assigned," 336.

13. Ibid., 338.

14. Ibid., 342.

15. Ibid., 343–44.

16. Ibid., 344.

17. Ibid., 338, 344.

18. Ibid., 345.

19. Ibid.

20. Sproles and Ratledge, "Analysis of Entry-Level Librarian Ads," n.p.

21. Ibid.

22. Ibid.

23. Ibid.

24. Ibid.

25. School of Information Sciences Curriculum Committee, "Most Frequent Qualifications Required for Select Entry-Level Positions in LIS," www.sis.utk.edu/careers/resources/qualifications (accessed September 15, 2009).

26. Ibid.

27. Sproles and Ratledge, "Analysis of Entry-Level Librarian Ads."

28. American Library Association, "ALA Survey of Librarian Salaries Now Has State-Level Reporting and Includes Smaller Public Libraries," www.ala.org/Template.cfm?Section=archive&template=/contentmanagement/contentdisplay.cfm&ContentID=103777 (accessed March 31, 2010).

29. Sproles and Ratledge, "Analysis of Entry-Level Librarian Ads."

30. The American Library Association's policy on foreign credentials states: "The master's degree from a program accredited by the American Library Association (or from a master's level program in library and information studies accredited or recognized by the appropriate national body of another country) is the appropriate professional degree for librarians." Although the ALA "does not conduct evaluations of transcripts or credentials or make recognition decisions," nor does it recommend an agency for independent evaluation of credentials or endorse any evaluation results, it does list the United Kingdom, Australia, and New Zealand as countries that "have been identified as having 'formal' accreditation processes and an individual who has received his/her degree from an institution in one of these countries is considered acceptable for employment in the United States." See American Library Association, "Foreign Credentials Evaluation Assistance Employer Information, http://ala.org/ala/education careers/employment/foreigncredentialing/foremployers/index.cfm (accessed March 31, 2010).

CHAPTER 3

HOW TO READ A JOB AD

Seeing the Obvious, and
Reading between the Lines

Sever Bordeianu and Christina M. Desai

THE JOB AD: YOUR FIRST CONTACT WITH YOUR NEW JOB

Interpreting the job ad is key to your new job. Most institutions are required by law to advertise jobs in the professional literature as well as in select local and regional publications, such as the state library association's newsletter, publications of special interest groups such as minority professional associations, and possibly the local newspaper. Consequently, libraries advertise their job openings in a variety of publications and Internet resources. If you are new to the profession, by the time you are ready to graduate, your graduate school should have provided you with access to most of these resources. If you are an experienced librarian, you will already have the skills to find most of these sources for learning about job openings at libraries around the country and the world. Your first step toward getting a new job is to find these ads, and decode them properly. This will help you respond appropriately and improve your chances of getting an offer.

Which sources you decide to use to find out about job openings will depend on the type of library you are interested in. While some publications list jobs for academic, public, and special libraries, many resources specialize in one type of library; for example, *College and Research Libraries News* publishes primarily positions in academic libraries, while *American Libraries* lists available positions in academic, public, and school libraries, associations, and library education. Many of the ads you find in published sources may be available online prior to the publication cycle of the journal. For example, job ads appearing in these two titles are also published in the employment section of the American Library Association website (http://joblist.ala.org). State and national library associations, ALA member organizations, such as the ACRL (Association of College and Research Libraries), individual libraries, and academic library consortiums are good examples of online sources for job ads. Additionally, you will undoubtedly receive job ads via electronic discussion lists, as well as from your library graduate school, so depending on the type of position you are seeking, you may choose to subscribe to certain discussion lists, and add relevant blogs and wikis to your job search toolkit.

At first you will want to try a variety of sources, but you will come to prefer one or two, either because of the coverage or, for online sources, the usability of the interface. Checking online sources is a must since the application process is time-consuming; you will want to learn about any openings as soon as possible to give you more time to prepare your application. Most sites allow you to customize your search based on type of library, level of position, and geographic location. Once you familiarize yourself with several job lists, and decide which ones you like best, you will want to check them regularly. Many sites post new jobs daily. While you may not have time to check the sites every day, it's important to check them at least once a week.

Job ads will usually indicate a specific deadline by which the application process closes. Some will indicate that the position will remain open until filled, but often these ads will include a date by which applications will receive first or "best" consideration. Most deadlines for applications are about thirty days from the time of the posting, but there are many instances when libraries, due to special circumstances, give shorter deadlines. Generally, missing a deadline for an application automatically disqualifies you from consideration. Hiring practices are governed by law, and posted deadlines cannot be changed at will. Even in ads stating that the "position will remain open until filled," the library needs to set certain working deadlines in order to proceed with reviews, interviews, and the hiring process. If many good applications are received by the best consideration date, the library may not even look at applications received after that date. Therefore, the date for best consideration should be taken seriously.

In general, job ads require that you submit a letter of interest or a cover letter addressing your qualifications for the job, a resume or curriculum vitae

(CV), and a list of references. In some instances, particularly for city or county library jobs, including some community colleges, you must obtain and submit an official application. These libraries will not accept a cover letter and resume in lieu of the official application. While most libraries verify transcripts during the interview or hiring process, some require that you submit official transcripts at the time of the application. For this reason, it is important that you read the job description carefully, so that you do not disqualify yourself by missing one of the required steps. Currently, many libraries are moving toward requiring applicants to apply online, following practices at the institutional level. If so, read the instructions carefully. You may not have a chance to resubmit or update your online application. When starting this process, you may want to consult with mentors, past professors, or library school advisors for the best and most efficient way to evaluate the job lists and interpret the position descriptions. These advisors may have a good sense of how well your qualifications and interests match the opening.

EVALUATING THE JOB DESCRIPTION: SEEING THE OBVIOUS

There are job openings and maybe you qualify. Fantastic! But before printing out more copies of your resume and stocking up on stamps, consider this: applying for jobs is a lot of work. Half-hearted attempts will not work. If you are new to the field, remember that this is no longer a classroom exercise; you are about to enter the real world. You must do some research on the organization and the place. Applying for a job is a two-way process. You want to evaluate your future employer as rigorously as your future employer will evaluate you. In this process, the employer has the advantage, because they have done this numerous times and have vast experience. Going into the process with the right preparation will increase your chance of getting the right job at the right library. So consider . . .

What Type of Job Is It?

You don't want to waste your time reading every job ad every time. And as we've learned from the job ad analysis in the previous chapter, not every job ad will be comprehensive, and you may need to devote valuable time to tracking down the complete job description so that you can make a decision about applying. Some positions will not interest you, others you won't qualify for, and quite a few will be in parts of the country where you would prefer not to ost job ads are structured similarly, so a quick scan will easily eliminate those jobs of no interest. The rest you will need to read more carefully. When you first start looking for jobs, it may be educational to read a variety of job ads carefully, but as you become a more experienced job seeker, you will be looking for the following features: type of job (technical services or public services, for example), type of institution (academic, public, special), and geographic location. Usually, this entails reading the beginning and the end of the job ads first, as most post the position type and institution at the beginning of the ad, and give the location at the end. Once you've decided that this job is of interest, you can review the details to decide if you qualify, and if you would indeed be willing to take this job.

Do You Qualify?

Academic institutions follow strict guidelines to ensure that there is no discrimination in hiring based on race, creed, or gender. They are expected to hire the candidate who is best qualified, and they must be able to show that the chosen candidate best meets the requirements stated in the job ad, in order to ensure that qualified minority candidates have not been passed over. Qualifications in the ad may be divided into two categories: required and preferred or desired. The required qualifications may be set low to assure the largest pool of candidates. Or they may be set high, if the job search is either for a high-level, specialized position or for an entry-level position for which a very large number of applicants would otherwise qualify. The preferred qualifications are used to bring the best-qualified candidates to the top of the pool. Do not waste your time applying if you do not meet the minimum or required qualifications, because you will be eliminated from the pool at the outset. "Required" means what it says: the successful candidate *must* meet these minimums. If the job requires a second master's degree and yours is still in progress, you do not qualify.

If the second master's degree is preferred but not required, you may be seriously considered. Include information about your progress toward the degree. If a certain number of years of experience is required, be explicit about dates in your resume. Do not expect the hiring body to guess whether your "2008–2009" experience included two whole years or one academic year, whether it was part-time or full-time, or if the preferred qualification was a major or minor part of your job. Preferred qualifications may become, in effect, required qualifications if the position is an entry-level job for which there are likely to be many qualified applicants, such as a position as a reference librarian in the humanities. If you are thinking of applying for such a position, you will need to meet almost all of the preferred as well as all of the required qualifications. If the position is harder to fill, you may get by with fewer preferred qualifications.

Do You Want to Go There?

This may seem obvious, but be sure you would be willing to seriously consider accepting the position if offered. There are many facets to this question. Consider the geographic area, the institution, and the type of job you will be applying for. It may be tempting to apply for a job just to get the experience or to get your foot in the door, but if you are not serious about moving to that particular geographic area, working in that specific environment, or doing the job for which you are applying, you will be wasting your time, and in the long run, it may have a negative impact on your career. You may be encouraged by friends or relatives to apply for the sake of gaining practice in interviewing. However, bear in mind that the hiring process costs a lot of money and time. It is unethical and unfair to apply for a job which you have no intention of accepting. Hiring institutions risk losing serious candidates by interviewing those who are not serious, even if they are qualified. If the hiring institution offers you a job and you decline, other viable candidates may have accepted other positions in the meantime. If you need practice interviewing, contact your university's placement office or enlist the help of friends or coworkers. There are better and cheaper ways to learn interviewing skills.

Location is often the last thing on the applicant's mind, but be realistic about your willingness to live far from familiar places, family, and friends. Some experts advise that it should be the first criterion when making a job decision. If you move to a geographic area where you are not happy because of climate, distance from home, culture, or other subjective reasons, you may be less motivated to do your best on the job. It may not be as easy to relocate after your first job as you may think. You'll be happier in the job if you are happy in the general location. This can affect your performance, and can influence how smoothly your career progresses and, ultimately, how successful you will be professionally. Since choosing a geographic location is a personal preference, there is no formula for choosing the right location, but geography should be a factor in choosing which job you will consider and which you will not.

Do You Want to Do That?

Upon being booted out into the real world after graduation, or after leaving another job for whatever reason, you may feel that any job is worth taking. But be patient. While it is understandable that most applicants view entry-level positions as simply getting their foot in the door, you should try to make your first job a meaningful, satisfying, and useful step toward achieving your ultimate long-term career goal. If this is not your first job, it is even more important to choose openings that match your interests and skill set. You cannot assume that applying for and accepting a specific position will automatically open up a multitude of other possibilities at the institution. Be prepared to perform the job duties as stated in the job ad. Libraries in general have very limited resources and little flexibility in the number of positions they can offer. Often, they can only hire for a specific, approved need. At academic libraries, professional-level hiring must be approved at the dean or director level or above. Departments are in competition for resources with other units within the library and with other departments within the university. Generally, libraries advertise for the types of jobs and positions they really need filled. Given the difficulties most academic libraries have in getting permission to fill vacancies, expect that what you see in the job ad is what you will be doing on the job. Furthermore, administrators have a vested interest in making the organization work and in moving it forward; the position for which they are hiring is part of this broader goal. Often, the hiring plan must advance not only the library's goals, but those of the college or university president or chancellor as well.

Having said all this, it is still wise to consider your chances for advancement in the organization. If the position involves tasks you consider below your level of education or experience, it is fair to ask during the interview what the possibilities for advancement would be. It is not advisable to ask at that point about your chances of moving to a totally different position within the organization. This signals to the employer that you would probably not be happy in the advertised position. Furthermore, your next position will depend largely on what you do in your current position or what you have done in previous positions. If you have been a reference librarian exclusively, your chances of being hired as a cataloger for your next job are slim. If you are a reference librarian who wants to become a cataloger, try to gain some relevant experience as part of your current position, even if it is low-level or volunteer work. Employers try very hard to gauge interest, and will use your previous experience, projects, and coursework as indications of your interests and strengths. So don't take just any job!

Another consideration is faculty status. Most librarians enter the profession with a strong desire to serve the researching public. If the opening is a tenure-track faculty position, do you understand what that means? Faculty rank and tenure status differ among libraries. Most require some effort in the area of research and publication. This could range from a few state- or national-level presentations to a stipulated number of peer-reviewed journal articles. If you take on a tenure-track position that requires published research, are you willing to put in the time and effort, much of it in the evenings and on weekends, outside of regular working hours? Faculty positions are not nine-to-five jobs; faculty are expected to do the work until the work is done. In addition to research and publication, tenure-track faculty are often expected to perform national service activities. If this is the case, understand that you may have to foot much of the bill for travel to meetings and conferences. Realize that you will be expected to participate in committee work and possibly be expected to advance to leadership positions in professional organizations. Library faculty positions vary widely in the criteria for achieving tenure. Check the library's website or ask the search coordinator for information on tenure requirements before applying if you are not sure you want to do serious research or participate in service activities. Each library is unique in its requirements, but generally you can assume that a position which is not tenure-track will have fewer requirements to publish or perform professional service activities than one that is tenure-track. Nonfaculty academic librarians usually do not have stringent publication or service expectations during the probationary period. If you would prefer to spend more time with your patrons, and the tenure track does not appeal to you, there are many prestigious academic libraries where librarians are not on the tenure track. If your goal is to contribute to research in the field or to advances in the profession through service, administration, or technological innovation, then tenure-track positions may be right for you.

Consider also the type of library you prefer. The professional environment in a large PhD-granting academic library is quite different from that in a small liberal arts college library. Similarly, academic libraries are very different from public libraries, while special libraries can be very unique and varied. The type and size of library you will be working in can vary greatly, and different types of libraries can have vastly different environments, each presenting its own challenges and rewards. But more importantly, each will require that you use specific sets of skills. So if the job is solo director of a special library, for example, are you willing to do all the mundane as well as more challenging administrative tasks, answer to the (sometimes disgruntled) public or governing board, and work with a limited budget? Would you be happy being on-call at all times, and could you adapt to being without the company of colleagues? Would you be ready to step into a job in which you would be responsible for the entire operation, public as well as technical services, and would you enjoy it? There are steps you might take to help you decide such questions. Find out if the previous occupant is willing to share her knowledge of the day-to-day functioning of the library. Is there documentation for procedures and policies, or would you have to start from scratch? Does starting from scratch appeal to you? Similar questions apply to other library types. Medical library jobs may put you at the beck and call of busy physicians; law and corporate libraries may restrict you to a narrower range of questions; urban libraries may expose you to a wide variety of community patrons, some of them not really interested in serious research. Academic libraries may require you to be on various committees and get involved in service to the university, which can leave less time for your job as a selector or reference librarian. While no setting will be perfect, be realistic about your personality and your intellectual interests.

Does This Job Fit Your Long-Term Plans and Goals?

Again, do not apply for every job for which you qualify. Consider the job you are applying for in the context of your long-term goals. If your ultimate goal is to become a library administrator someday, for example, then experience in all aspects of library work will be helpful. But you will want to look for a library in which innovation is a possibility and in which your ideas for new projects and services are not automatically shot down. You will not become an administrator by simply maintaining the status quo and doing as you are told. If your goal is to move toward an administrator position, you need to take on more administrative and supervisory responsibilities whenever opportunities arise. As in other areas, experience is essential for someone who wants to advance up the administrative ladder, and the best way to gain experience is to take advantage of or create leadership opportunities. Do not wait for the promotion you want before you take on new responsibilities. While you may not see immediate rewards such as a change in job title, pay, or job description by following this course, in time this experience will become an asset and will be recognized. And if, on the other hand, the organization is not ready to move with the times, you will not be happy there and your employer will not be happy with you.

Reading between the Lines: What Certain Phrases Really Mean

Like all professions, librarianship has its specialized jargon in which generic terms have special meanings, and which those with experience recognize and use. Professional jargon changes with time, as new technologies and practices are introduced, and older terms fall out of favor. The job ads in particular are full of words that are rich in meaning and that need to be properly understood in order to interpret the job description. More importantly, understanding the terminology will enable you to reply intelligently to the job ad in your letter of application, and to address the specific requirements of the job description. Using this terminology appropriately in the right context will give you an advantage in the application and interview process, and will make communication with the search committee clearer. Here are some common terms and phrases you may see in job ads.

"Electronic" = you gotta love it. There are few libraries remaining that still long for the days of paper card catalogs or manual research and processing. You must be able to demonstrate familiarity with, and appreciation for, the latest electronic resources and tools. And know your acronyms!

"Changing environment" = anything from a new electronic resource to physical renovation to organizational turmoil. The phrase "changing environment" is becoming a cliché in libraries, since change occurs constantly. It refers to either technological or physical or administrative changes. It may refer to the latest social networking software as applied in the library, or the newest collection of e-books. On the other hand, it may be a code word for staff reorganization, fire, flood, budget cuts, political controversy on campus, or some other calamity. Today there are probably few libraries not experiencing at least one of these conditions; you must be able to show your adaptability. If this phrase is part of the job ad, and it probably will be, try to find out what form the change is taking in that particular library.

"Challenging" = hard. "Challenge" is often a code word for "problem." But don't admit that something is hard. Don't use the word "problem." Every challenge or problem must be viewed as an opportunity. This may sound like doublespeak, but in fact the ability to adjust to unpleasant changes by coming up with creative solutions is one of the most prized qualifications for any position. In fact, no one appreciates the employee who focuses solely on the problems and sees no possibilities for change or solutions. Why would any administrator hire such a person?

"Enthusiastic" = energetic, hard-working. Again, a positive attitude and a solid record of accomplishment are important to a successful application. In addition to on-the-job activity, you might mention outside activities. If you have no professional job experience, think about other arenas. Did you participate in extracurricular activities in graduate school or participate in faculty research projects? Go to conferences? Take advantage of opportunities to gain practical experience by, for example, volunteering at your local library or spearheading a book drive? Are you active in your community? These are all examples of enthusiasm and willingness to engage.

"Communications and interpersonal skills" = speaking and writing skills and the ability to get along. This may sound like fluff, but is a real requirement for most professional jobs. Do not slight this aspect of your qualifications.

Speaking skills are evaluated during the telephone interview and the on-site interview, if you make it that far in the process. Writing ability is demonstrated by your publications and by the letter you write as part of your application. For this reason, the letter may be even more important in getting you the job than your resume. Faced with dozens, possibly hundreds of applications, search committee members are more likely to remember an interesting, well-written, grammatically correct letter than a dry CV listing position titles, dates, and duties. "Interpersonal skill" refers to your ability to get along with others. Hopefully your letters of recommendation will address this crucial element. However, you should also demonstrate this ability by such evidence as promotions, committee assignments and chairships, and collaborative projects. Collaboration is one of the current buzzwords, and one of the ways employers gauge these skills.

"Flexibility" = the organization is going through lots of changes. The job you accept may in time bear little resemblance to the job you end up doing. Many libraries are seeing huge shifts in human resource allocation—more outreach activities, and more staff in new and emerging functions and services such as electronic resource management, web development, digitization, expanded resource sharing, and donor development. These demands often come at the expense of traditional positions. Academic librarianship is no longer a job for introverts who love books. It is important for your future employer to see that you are open to learning, working with others, and performing new tasks. Do not convey the impression that you are rigid, and that only one way is the right way. In today's work environment, flexibility is a necessity, not a luxury.

"Research" = publications and presentations. In academic libraries, research leading to publication or presentation in the field of library science or information technology is usually expected; however, many academic institutions allow publication or creative works in any field. Some even encourage research in a nonlibrary discipline, particularly if you collaborate with academic faculty in that department. This fosters ties between university faculty and the library and bolsters your research skills and credibility among academic faculty.

"Ability to meet tenure requirements" = a record of publication and service. This can also simply mean evidence that you can (and preferably do) research. If you have not published yet, conference presentations count toward this expectation as evidence of scholarship. There will also be service requirements. Service in this context does not mean public service. Rather, it refers to service to the profession; for example, serving on library association committees or statewide initiatives. Besides publication and service, librarianship is the third criterion for tenure here at UNM UL. This refers to your day-to-day job, and is

usually weighted most heavily in the tenure decision. However, without at least some publications and service, you are not likely to achieve tenure. A denial of tenure means you cannot stay in the position; you will have to find another job. If you simply want to focus on librarianship, in an academic library, you would be better off applying to libraries where librarians do not have faculty status.

"Patron-oriented" = you're a yes man (in the good sense of the word). If your first response to a patron request is usually no, if you never bend a rule, if you judge the motives or sincerity of your patrons, you may not be ready for twenty-first-century librarianship. If, on the other hand, you are always interested in putting patron needs first and finding better ways to serve the public, and if you never show impatience, disrespect, or condescension toward patrons (even difficult or rude patrons), this attitude will come through. Though librarians may joke among themselves about "problem patrons" and even refer to known characters by less than flattering names in the privacy of the staff lounge, in good libraries you will find that their actions belie these attitudes and tell quite a different story. Truly free, unbiased, and egalitarian services to all are necessary to maintaining libraries that are both relevant and viable. The first step in this direction is a positive attitude, even in the face of adversity.

"References" = letters from higher-ups or professors who will say nice things about you. References from coworkers or coauthors do not count. A good reference from your supervisor (current or previous) counts most heavily. Choose references who can speak to *specific* aspects of your work and your achievements, who know you well, or who supervised you. If possible, include professionals from outside your organization; for example, people you worked with on a state or national committee or perhaps a community group. You should be confident that your references will speak or write honestly about you. Your new employer is more interested in hearing the truth than in a glossy recommendation that does not tell much. Before listing someone as a reference, be sure to ask that person if he would agree to serve as a reference, and consider how enthusiastically that person responded. Often, an unresponsive or weak reference can convey a negative impression, even if nothing specifically negative is said about you. An overly enthusiastic reference does not necessarily help much either. So be sure to use as references people who know you and your work, and are able to address your specific strengths and weaknesses.

"Ability to work with a diverse population" = proven record of working with minorities and other diverse groups. Being a nice, open-minded people person is not enough. If you have ever worked with cultural, racial, or linguistic minorities in any previous position, say so. You cannot assume the search committee will recognize that the year you spent working in a certain remote village

teaching ESL or setting up a library there was evidence of experience working with a culturally diverse population. You must highlight it in your cover letter. In fact, do not assume the search committee knows anything at all about you or the settings where you've worked. If you have experience assisting people with disabilities, using adaptive software, meeting web accessibility standards, and so on, be sure to mention it. If you have developed instructional techniques or materials for individuals with differing learning styles, make it known. Specific experience will get you much farther than interest or good intentions. Be sure not to embellish your experience. Open-mindedness is obvious from how one writes and talks about these issues. Overstatements are easily detected and are detrimental to the applicant. Hiring bodies are aware that not every single individual can have extensive experience with every aspect of diversity. What matters is that the applicant is able to show her capacity and willingness to work in these environments effectively.

DECONSTRUCTING THE JOB DESCRIPTION

Learn the latest jargon of library organizations; for example, terms like access services, discovery services, information literacy theories, information or learning commons, metadata and digital initiatives, and position titles like electronic resources manager, web librarian, systems librarian, information literacy coordinator or librarian, library liaison, and usage or data trends analyst. Some of these are established terms, and others are new names for slightly different or totally new positions. The job description should give you a good idea of what the job entails, but it may be necessary to view the library's organizational chart (often available on the library's website) to get an idea of where you will fit into the chain of command and to whom you will report. If this chart is not available on the Web, be sure to ask for it at the interview. You may also ask for a brief outline of the organizational chart if you are selected for a phone interview.

Make a Grid—They Will

Again, following strict guidelines set by the campus office of equal opportunity, search committees in academic institutions must show that all qualified candidates have been seriously considered. Words in the ad like "dynamic leader" and "enthusiastic collaborator" are not empty phrases. The search committee members must be able to rate you on each of the terms in the job's required and preferred qualifications. Search committees typically make a grid to tabulate and evaluate qualifications and expertise. Various criteria are often weighted, based on their importance to the job. The grid makes it easy to compare candidates and spot weaknesses. Table 3.1 is a simplified example of such a grid.

Think carefully how you may match your experience to each required and preferred qualification. Also try and match your experience and current position to the level of the job: if you have never supervised anyone, don't apply for a job as head of a large cataloging or acquisitions department. While you may not weigh each criterion exactly as the search committee will, creating your own grid will still give you a fair idea of how your education and work experience will fare against the job description.

WRITING THE COVER LETTER

The cover letter is the first impression you make on the search committee. It shows how you communicate, how you present yourself, how you organize your thoughts, and how good you are at conveying information. It is immediately obvious to a reader whether you are using the same generic letter for all positions, or you have tailored this letter to this position. It's also obvious if the letter was done in haste. This conveys whether or not you are really interested

TABLE **3.1**

Simplified example of a grid used to evaluate job applicants' qualifications

QUALIFICATION	TAMARA	JOE	DELORES	MANUEL
Dynamic leader	X		X	X
Enthusiastic collaborator	X	X	X	
Second master's degree		X	X	X
Publications	X			X
Supervisory experience	X		X	X

in the position. The letter also gives an impression of who you are as an individual: thoughtful and precise, long-winded and unorganized, direct, ambiguous, honest, boastful, or repetitive. Be careful about tooting your own horn. State your accomplishments simply and clearly and they will speak for you.

Address each required and preferred qualification in your letter. It is very important that you use the same terminology used in the job ad, and that you address each required qualification in your letter, because in this process, an omission could be interpreted as a lack of that particular qualification. As already mentioned, lacking a required qualification automatically excludes you from the qualified pool, and eliminates all chances of being considered for the job. Generally, search committees do not go back to a candidate to ask for clarification (doing so could give that candidate an unfair advantage), so be sure that you do not disqualify yourself by omitting important information. Similarly, overstating your role or qualifications could also eliminate you from the pool, because any overstatement you made will certainly become evident as the evaluation progresses.

Make the letter long enough to give readers a picture of your career to date, with some specific examples of projects you either initiated or worked on and skills you have acquired. The more senior the position, the longer the letter should be, but even for an entry-level position, the letter should summarize relevant experience. You can't expect search committee members to remember every detail in every resume; the letter is your chance to make an impression. It should also give readers an idea of what you are like, what you enjoy, and why you are interested. Avoid including information that is purely personal or irrelevant to the position that you are applying for. Be direct and to the point. Committee members will not appreciate having to guess what your experience is, or what your role was in a project. Avoid vague terms like "participated in" that don't tell how or what you contributed. Avoid summaries and bulleted lists of projects, services, or tasks that do not reveal your role in completing them. The easier you make it for a reviewer to understand your qualifications and experience, the better it will reflect on you as an applicant, as a communicator, and ultimately as an employee.

Understanding Which Skills Meet Which Requirements

Once you have clearly addressed the required qualifications, translate your experience into terms of the preferred qualifications. Often an applicant fresh out of library school has relatively little experience in a library setting. In this situation, it is appropriate to use the skills you have acquired from your work history in nonlibrary environments to address preferred qualifications. For example, if public service experience is required and you don't have public service experience in a library, highlight other jobs you've held in which you dealt with the public; for example, as a bank teller, call center or help desk assistant, or waitress or cashier. If you've held any of these jobs, you've probably dealt with the public on its good days and bad; knowing how to handle angry customers can be a real asset. In your letter, you need to make a reasonable case for why the experience you are describing would be relevant in a library setting. In your interview, be ready to give examples of how you dealt with difficult customers. If you are applying for a position involving technical skills, be ready to cite instances of technical problem-solving with individual end users or with the organization-wide system. If a technical job entails working with the public or coworkers, be sure to highlight your ability to work well with people as well as with machines. For example, if the position calls for web design skills, perhaps you might relate your experience observing users struggling with commercial database interfaces or your experience teaching these databases, along with citing the design of your own personal web page. Experience with relational database software, spreadsheets, or the organization of information may be gained in a corporate setting. Selection and buying for a bookstore could arguably give you some understanding of collection development. Perhaps it was some of these experiences that led to your interest in librarianship, a fact quite likely to interest a hirer as evidence of your commitment.

Use the Same Terminology as That Used in the Job Ad: Apply That Jargon to Your Experience

Bear in mind that search committees may be dealing with dozens or even hundreds of applicants. If the committee is looking for an applicant strong in collaboration, for example, make it easy to find that qualification in your letter by using the same wording. Think about your readers and how they will fill out the grid as they read your letter and resume. An aesthetically well-organized letter, using terminology that the committee members will be looking for, will help your application rise to the top. Clarity will not only give a good impression of you as a professional, but will make it easier for evaluators to rate you and your skills. If a search committee is evaluating a large pool of applicants, those with ambiguities and question marks will automatically rate lower than those who present no ambiguities.

What Not to Say

Keep personal information out of your application. Do not emote about how much you love books and have always wanted to be a librarian. Ditto about the wonderful librarian who inspired you as a child. Do not inquire about job opportunities for your spouse or partner. This is appropriate only *after* you've been offered the job and are in the midst of negotiating. Show your interest in the job, not the location. You do not need to mention that your significant other just got a job in the area to explain why you want to move a thousand miles from your current location to apply for this job. (If this is the case, however, you may want to let it slip, if and when you reach the interview stage, as an indication that you would indeed accept the position if offered.) Above all, do not express dissatisfaction with your current position, boss, or coworkers. This could be taken as a sign that you are hard to get along with. Negative comments about your current boss, your current job, or your current library reflect negatively on you. Keep your application positive and professional. You may discuss problems in the abstract, and how you handled them, but do not make them personal. Nobody wants coworkers who are disgruntled or negative.

Finishing Your Letter

Make sure you finish the letter on a positive, forward-looking note. Do not be overly enthusiastic about the job or the library, and do not exaggerate your experience and abilities. If your letter was done thoughtfully, these will be obvious. It should be clear that you have done some background research on the institution where you are applying which shows that, based on what you have found, you would make a good match. Provide a working e-mail address that you check regularly, and a working phone number that would give you some privacy when answering any questions or setting up an interview, especially if you do not want it known in your current position that you are looking for a new job. And don't forget to thank the committee for considering your application, and add that you would be happy to answer further questions. Finally, proofread, proofread, proofread.

CHAPTER 4

COMPILING AN APPLICATION PACKET THAT DOESN'T MAKE THE SEARCH COMMITTEE WANT TO KILL YOU

Sarah L. Stohr

PICTURE IT: it's a Friday afternoon, around 3:30 p.m. The search committee for the position for which you've applied is huddled around a table, sorting through the piles of application materials they've received for the position. The members of the search committee have had a long week and they want nothing more than to go home as quickly as possible. They've received eighty applications for a single job and have a huge amount of work ahead of them as they try to sort out who meets the minimum qualifications for the position. They are using a checklist of minimum and preferred qualifications to keep track of the status of each applicant and are taking notes on the application packets they view. In short: now is not the time to get on their bad side.

The search committee's first real interaction with you comes from your application packet. The old adage that "you never get a second chance to make a first impression" is particularly true when it comes to applying for a job. In the case of most academic library jobs, the first impression your would-be employer gets of you is through the application packet you submit for the position. Think about that late Friday afternoon search committee when you compile your application packet. You want them to be able to easily discern what makes you a qualified candidate; more specifically, you want to make it easy for them to understand exactly why you meet the minimum qualifications and any preferred qualifications for the job. Your goal should be to compile a packet that gives the search committee everything they've asked for in the job announcement. If you put together an application packet that doesn't address the specific job for which you are applying, don't be surprised if you aren't selected to be interviewed.

If you are serious about landing a job, each time you submit an application it must be organized, well thought out, and contain every single piece of information that the employer has asked for. This sounds like a lot of work (and it is), but the good news is that if you read the job announcement carefully, you will know *exactly* what you need to do in order to get through to the next stage of the application process. A typical job announcement will describe the position and make it clear what the person hired will be expected to do. It will list the minimum qualifications that the employee must have and will also list qualifications that the employer would prefer to see but that aren't required. Your job as an applicant is to show the search committee how you meet the minimum qualifications, how you meet any preferred qualifications, and to show them that you are qualified to perform the duties as described in the announcement.

Due to the human resources rules that search committees must follow, there is typically a very easy way to determine who moves on to the next round of the application process. Applicants who demonstrate that they meet all of the minimum qualifications for a position usually move forward. If you do not meet the minimum qualifications for a position, you should not expect to hear back from the search committee. In fact, it is probably wiser to save your time and keep looking for positions for which you qualify rather than spend your time applying for a position you can't get. If, on the other hand, you can show the search committee that you meet the minimum qualifications and any of the preferred qualifications, you are very likely to move on to the next stage of the application process.

In academic librarianship, you'll typically have two tools at your disposal with which to highlight your qualifications for a position: the curriculum vitae and the cover letter. You'll find that the bulk of job announcements will ask you to apply by submitting these items. Knowing how to use the curriculum vitae and the cover letter properly will help ensure that your application is one that the committee appreciates.

YOUR CURRICULUM VITAE

A curriculum vitae, or CV, is similar to a resume, except it is usually longer, with much more specific information (like what you've published, grants you've received, courses you've taught). It is a standard application device used in academia. If you've never seen a CV, do a Google search and you can find thousands of examples. Or ask friends or mentors if you can see a copy of their CV to get an idea of what one looks like. If you are a young librarian or new to the profession, your CV will be short and read much like a resume—don't worry about that. Anyone reading the CV of a professional new to the field will understand that it takes years to fill a CV with content.

What you need to be concerned with is making sure that as much of your CV as possible can be interpreted by the search committee as being relevant to the job for which you are applying. How do you do that? Again, go back to the job announcement and look closely at the job description and the qualifications. Then think about your previous jobs or experiences and consider how they relate to what the employer is looking for. If you're applying for a reference job, for instance, and you worked at a job where you did both reference and cataloging, you can mention your cataloging experience in your CV, but what the search committee really wants to know about is your reference experience. Use your CV to highlight your previous work experience and explain how it might relate to the position for which you are applying.

Make sure that your CV includes all relevant dates when you were employed at a particular institution. List the starting and ending months and years. Many positions for which you apply will have minimum qualifications of "x-number of years in public services" or "x-number of years of teaching experience." In order for the committee to establish that you qualify with the minimum amount of experience, they need to be able to easily calculate the number of years of experience you have. Make it easy for them to find this information in your CV. Even if you make this information crystal clear in your cover letter, the search committee will still want to confirm those statements with an actual position listed in the CV, with the years of experience easily discernible.

You may need to create several different versions of your CV to have on hand if you are applying for a variety of jobs (i.e., public service jobs *and* jobs in technical services). You may even find that you need to rework your CV for each position to which you apply. This is time-consuming, but if you really are interested in a job, you need to make sure that each piece of information you submit to the search committee aligns with the qualifications they are seeking in an employee. Think about it: if you are asked to submit only a CV and a cover letter, you are being judged based solely on what you put into those two documents. You need to make each as perfect as you possibly can every time.

YOUR COVER LETTER

A cover letter is a letter of introduction that explains your qualifications for the position to which you are applying. Ideally, your cover letter should be about pages in length; it shouldn't take more than that to address all of the qualifications for most positions. Format your cover letter like you would a business letter; if you're unsure of how it should look, there are thousands of examples online.

You only need to do one thing with your cover letter: address the minimum and preferred qualifications as listed in the job announcement. The search committee does not want to read your life story in your cover letter; they want you to cut to the chase and make it easy for them to understand how you meet the qualifications for the job. Similarly, don't think that a one-line e-mail with your CV attached will suffice as a cover letter. When you are crafting your letter, imagine the checklist the committee will be using to grade you. The checklist will include all of the minimum qualifications listed on the job announcement and all of the preferred qualifications. Make it as easy as possible for the committee to check off the items that they are looking for on your application materials. To that end, avoid the following in your cover letter.

Personal Details

Do not write about how you need to get a new job because your fiancé lives across the country and you want to be together. That sort of information is irrelevant to the search at hand (and it is almost guaranteed that a member of the search committee is going to do a dramatic reading of that portion of your cover letter for the other committee members). Religion, health issues, and hobbies fall into this category as well (unless they are somehow relevant to the job for which you are applying, i.e., you're applying to work in a special collections department known for its cookbook collection and you are interested in cooking).

Unnecessary Details

This happens a lot when people use one generic cover letter for every job for which they apply. You want every piece of information you include in your cover letter to be relevant to the position at hand. If you are applying for a job that requires you to have taken a government documents course, then by all means write in your letter that you've taken one. If, on the other hand, you are applying for a job that does not ask that you have taken a government documents course and doesn't mention government documents anywhere in the job description or announcement, don't mention it in your cover letter. You're just making the committee read information that isn't relevant to what they are looking for.

Stretching the Truth

Do you want to apply for a job that requires you to have library instruction experience, but your experience is limited to what you've learned in graduate school about instruction? Don't lie or try to fool the committee—the truth will come out during the search. Instead, write something in your letter like: "While I don't have experience conducting library instruction sessions, I have taken a library instruction course and am familiar with the best practices in designing effective instruction for students. Additionally, I have x-years experience working with students one-on-one at a busy reference desk at an urban university research library." While that may not be enough to get you past the initial minimum qualification test, it will at least make the search committee stop to discuss whether or not you meet the minimums, which isn't necessarily a bad thing.

Making the Committee Guess or Hunt

If a minimum qualification for the job you want to apply for is having one year of reference experience, be explicit—tell the search committee you have one year of reference experience. You can write: "I have one year of reference experience working for the Funtown Library in Funtown, NM." If, on the other hand, you write: "I have reference experience working for the Funtown Library in Funtown, NM," the search committee will then have to go back to your CV to verify that you worked at the Funtown Library for at least one year. Make it easy for the committee and be direct when addressing any qualifications that require you to have had a specific number of years of experience. It is also a good idea to make sure that the experience you claim in your cover letter can be verified in your CV, so that the search committee does not find any incongruence between the two documents.

Having a Computer Proofread Your Draft

Do not rely on spell-check to weed out all of the errors that may be lurking in your application materials. Spell-check has no problem allowing you to say you've worked at the "pubic" library instead of the "public library." Read and reread your materials before submitting them, and, if possible, have someone you trust proofread for you. There is no excuse for misspelling your own name or the name of the institution you are applying to on your cover letter, an error I've seen on more than one occasion as a search committee member.

OTHER APPLICATION MATERIALS

If the employer wants copies of references, transcripts, or letters of recommendation, they will list that information in the job description, too. If you aren't asked in the job announcement to submit transcripts, references, or other materials, don't. Remember—it's 3:30 on a Friday afternoon and the search committee wants to go home rather than sift through materials they didn't ask for. What's more, including transcripts or other materials when they have not been asked for makes it appear that you haven't bothered to read the job announcement to see which materials should actually be included in your packet.

References. Sometimes you will find that you are asked to include references with your application packet. You may be asked to include reference letters or simply submit the names of your references. If you are asked to give the names of references, give the search committee the name, address, phone number, and e-mail address of your reference. This way, the committee can contact the reference using whichever medium they prefer. While it should go without saying, remember to choose people who can and will actually give you a good reference. If you've been fired from a previous position and your former boss doesn't have great things to say about you, do not include him or her as a reference. If a reference has asked you to remove his or her name from your reference request, please do so; similarly, if it's been a while since you've spoken with a reference, contact that person to make sure he or she is still willing to sing your praises. If you're an excellent employee but your current boss is slightly diabolical and you can't be sure what he may say in regard to your employment, leave him off of the list! It is perfectly acceptable and legal to ask the search committee to not contact your current supervisor unless you are a finalist in a search. In a search that has many qualified and capable applicants, recommendations may be critical in determining who gets the position—don't leave your chances up to anyone who may be a potential liability.

The best references are those who can actually speak to your qualifications and skills or who have firsthand knowledge of why you would be an excellent choice for the job. The committee wants to hear from people who can speak about your actual skills and your ability to perform the duties of the position. The committee does not want to hear from your best friend, your pastor, or your brother-in-law about what a great person you are. Keep your references professional, not personal. Don't forget to give your references a heads-up so that they know they may be contacted in regard to you and the position. It's courteous to send them a copy of the job description and your CV as well, so that they can have those as a frame of reference should they be called upon to speak with the committee. (See figure 4.1 for a list of questions that are typically asked of references.)

Transcripts. Transcripts are occasionally asked for at the beginning of the application process but typically are requested in the latter stages of the interview process. If you are asked to submit official transcripts as part of the application and the application is due the first of January, you may not get priority consideration if your transcripts arrive late, because technically, your application would be considered incomplete. To be safe, always have official transcripts in your possession, because ordering them from your college or university can often take several weeks. You will then be prepared whenever the committee asks for them. Unofficial transcripts are also sometimes requested or accepted temporarily in lieu of official transcripts; just make sure that if official transcripts are needed, official transcripts are what you send. You can always check with the search coordinator or contact individual listed in the job description if you have questions as to whether an official copy is what is needed.

MAKING YOUR APPLICATION PACKET STAND OUT

The easiest way to make your application stand out in the pool is to be as meticulous as you can in putting it together. Pay attention to every small detail of your application. In addition to crafting superb cover letters and CVs, don't

---

FIGURE **4.1**

Questions for references

1. In what capacity do you know the candidate? Please describe your experiences working with this candidate.

   a. As a follow-up, did you observe evidence of leadership and/or initiative?

2. Can you speak to the candidate's ability to deal with fast-paced change or perform in a fast-changing environment?

3. Can you speak to the candidate's strengths, if any?

4. Can you speak to the candidate's weaknesses, if any?

5. Are there any additional comments you would like to make?

forget about how you present the materials to the committee. If you have to submit a paper copy of your application materials, make sure that the quality of the printing is excellent. When you mail your application, make sure that all materials are neatly arranged in an envelope. Avoid staples and use paper clips if you need to hold anything together, so that the committee can easily organize items once they are received. If you are submitting materials electronically, give your files names that make them easy to identify (for instance, StohrCV or Stohrcoverletter). If you are able to submit electronic documents in the format of your choosing, consider submitting them as PDFs so you can be sure that when the search committee prints them out they are formatted as you intended them to be. If you are submitting Microsoft Word documents online to a human resource site that automatically converts them to PDFs, be sure to review these documents post-conversion. The gibberish that can result from the conversion could be misconstrued by the search committee as the applicant's lacking basic technological skills.

CONCLUSION

The hardest part about compiling a job application is the time it takes to do it properly. If you are really interested in landing a job in an academic library, you must make sure that all of the materials you submit to the search committee prove your interest. Don't forget that if you fail to address even one of the minimum qualifications listed in a job description, your application may find its way to the reject pile. Opportunities to fix your application once you've been rejected are not common, since typically what the committee lets one person do, they would have to let every rejected applicant do. Demonstrate to the committee that you are detail-oriented by paying close attention to the requirements set forth in the position description. Show them that you value their time and effort by making it as easy as possible for them to discern whether or not you belong in the applicant pool. When a search committee is looking at dozens of applications, they will appreciate being able to easily pick out who should move forward to the next round of interviews. And when it is easy for the search committee to move forward, it will also take less time for someone—hopefully you—to be hired.

CV AND COVER LETTER RESOURCES

UC Berkeley's CV Information: https://career.berkeley.edu/Phds/PhDCV.stm.

Academic Cover Letter Sample from The OWL at Purdue: http://owl.english .purdue.edu/owl/resource/639/02/.

Medical Library Association CV Guidelines: www.mlanet.org/academy/cv.html.

University of Colorado CV Instructions: http://ucblibraries.colorado.edu/internal/fac/V.D.5_cv.pdf.

University of Michigan School of Information Resume and Cover Letter Writing Guide: http://si.umich.edu/careers/docs/2008–09_SI_Career_Resume_CL_Guide.pdf.

CHAPTER 5

YOU HAVE THE RIGHT TO REMAIN SILENT THROUGHOUT THE INTERVIEW PROCESS

Teresa Y. Neely

IN HIS STAND-UP comedy routine "They Call Me 'Tater Salad'" and in his book *I Had the Right to Remain Silent . . . but I Didn't Have the Ability,* comedian Ron White tells the story of how he got his nickname, Tater. He also tells us about his inability to remain silent in his interactions with the police after being "thrown out of a bar in New York City."[1] It is appropriate at this point in this book to have a discussion about common sense. Or rather, the prudent use of such. As we reflect on our experiences chairing and serving on search committees, we are struck by the similarities between Ron White's situation and the seemingly noninebriated decisions and actions of individuals applying for jobs in academic libraries.

There is something about pseudo-anonymity that leads some of us to do or say things or make decisions that we would not otherwise make, unless, perhaps, we were Ron White and charged with "Drunk . . . in . . . Public." These are decisions that could impact our ability to be successful in acquiring a job, not solely in academia, but in other professions as well. As a graduate student in the final semester of library school, I was a bit worried about landing a position. I worked on my curriculum vitae and wrote letters that highlighted my skill set and experiences. I did not realize, however, that the hip-hop music and cheeky message on my answering machine were sabotaging my efforts. Finally, someone told one of my references to tell me to change the message on my answering machine. And I did so. Today, many of us no longer have landlines and rely on our cell phone as the primary method of contact via telephone. Have you checked your message lately? When someone calls you, what do they hear? Is it a professional message that you would let your grandmother listen to, or is it a cute or borderline offensive message recorded by your favorite artist or actor? Is the message intelligible? Is there music? How long does it play? Will the caller momentarily forget who they were calling, and why? Will they be offended by the music clip or message, or will they be dancing around to the beat and then jolted back to reality at the beep?

More so than telephone calls, the use of e-mail is fairly widespread in the conduct of search committees these days. What is your e-mail address? Is it something cute or something not so cute? Generally speaking, if you must express yourself or your love of something, it is probably a good idea to maintain a separate professional e-mail address that is not sexually suggestive or, again, borderline offensive.

The popularity of electronic discussion lists, blogs, wikis, and other social networking tools has significantly decreased, or enhanced, that six degrees of separation between us and our fellow library colleagues. There is a small body of literature that reminds us to exercise common sense and caution in what we post on electronic discussion lists and blogs, or on our Facebook and MySpace pages. Technically, assuming your privacy settings limit the information you post to your "friends," you should be okay. However, I have seen or been privy to posts on discussion lists of which I am not a member and have read information posted on pages where I was not a "friend." A general rule of thumb is once you type it up, e-mail it, post it (including video and audio clips and digital pictures), blog it, or speak it, it's out there, never, ever to be taken back. "Even if you do use the privacy settings, don't forget that your friends know more people than just those mentioned on your own friends list—and that it's easy for private information to become common knowledge."[2] "So such things as photos and detailed descriptions of a drunken weekend posted in one's blog and hateful or threatening comments posted in another person's blog could easily be discovered by a future employer conducting a simple background check, for example."[3]

A candidate invited to interview for one of the four resident searches posted to a new librarian electronic discussion list complained about how hard it was to get an interview at an academic institution. This made its way back to me because one of the individuals on that discussion list happened to be a member of the search committee and became increasingly uncomfortable with the postings from this candidate. Like I said, it's a small world. You can never be too careful.

A recent CareerBuilder survey reported that "45 percent of employers . . . use social networking sites to research job candidates, a big jump from 22 percent last year."[4] Social networking sites and search engines used by employers include

- Facebook, used by 29 percent
- LinkedIn, used by 26 percent
- MySpace, used by 21 percent
- Blogs, used by 11 percent
- Twitter, used by 7 percent[5]

"Thirty-five percent of employers reported that they have found content on social networking sites that caused them not to hire the candidate. Examples of objectionable information include"

- provocative or inappropriate photographs or information
- content about drinking or doing drugs
- bad-mouthing previous employer, coworkers, or clients
- poor communication skills
- discriminatory comments
- lies about qualifications
- confidential information from previous employer[6]

The occurrence of "communication skills" in this list is interesting and kind of a slippery slope. Informal communication is the norm for many of these social networking tools, using shorthand language and texting protocols. However, we must be careful with the language we use while participating in these forums. I have been surprised more than once at the use of profane and inappropriate language by "friends" who were "friends" with their bosses or their bosses' boss! The work relationship doesn't change once you go virtual. If you wouldn't say it in front of grandma, you probably shouldn't type it for the world to see.

When these lapses in judgment and, perhaps, in common sense are juxtaposed with the "personal abilities" noted previously in academic library job ads, you get justifications cited by recruiters in the CareerBuilder survey "supporting their decisions to make a hire":

- Profile provided a good feel for the candidate's fit within the organization (50 percent)
- Profile supported candidate's professional qualifications (39 percent)
- Candidate showed solid communication skills (35 percent)
- Candidate was well-rounded (33 percent)
- Candidate was creative (28 percent)

- Other people posted good references about the candidate (19 percent)
- Candidate received awards and accolades (15 percent)[7]

According to the survey, "the industries most likely to screen job candidates via social networking sites or online search engines include those that specialize in technology and sensitive information: information technology (63 percent) and professional and business services (53 percent)."[8] Academic libraries fall squarely in the midst of these industries.

Although there is some evidence that the use of social media can be an advantage in the job search, "most experts recommend keeping your professional life on a site like LinkedIn, or possibly Twitter. Information that is deeply personal—photos from your family picnic, your raves about a new pair of shoes—should be kept separate on another site, such as Facebook." It's clear from the CareerBuilder survey that employers are not discriminating about which sites they use to research candidates, so it is up to you as an individual looking for a job to make decisions that will not jeopardize your chances at success.[9]

Additionally, there is evidence that information, albeit incorrect and not posted by you, can derail a job search. A law student at Pennsylvania State University had a job offer rescinded from an office where he had clerked. "His soon-to-be employer took the offer back because the candidate had affiliated himself with a website that disparaged female law students, even though the student himself had not posted any offensive remarks. A year and a half later, the student, now a Penn grad, is still looking for work."[10]

Although behavior before, during, and after the job interview process may not get you arrested or lead to a prison sentence, it may very well cost you an opportunity for gainful employment. Some things to remember:

Practice confidentiality on your end of the job search. Don't whine and complain out loud to anyone about your prospects—you don't know who is listening. Behavior you practice in public forums may reveal things about your work habits and preferences that can help you or be used against you in the job search process.

Practice professionalism. That funny, hot, sexy, or, on the other side, highly religious, God-fearing gospel song that sounds so cute as your ringtone is not appropriate for your voice mail or answering machine when you're seeking a job or in the process of interviewing. Also, the message you recorded that you thought was funny probably isn't. If your cell phone *is* your primary phone, you might want to resist the urge to entertain your callers.

The academic job search process is a confidential affair on-site. The library profession, however, like many others, is relatively small. Someone always knows someone when you least expect it.

The academic interview process can be long and drawn out. While you're waiting to hear back, be conscious of your actions and behavior.

When posting on electronic discussion lists or social networking sites, you never know who is lurking, or who is "friends" with whom. Be careful of what you post and to what mediums. Library folk also have accounts on social networking sites and participate in electronic discussion lists.[11]

Behavior at conferences and internships. Be aware that the person sitting next to you at a program or committee meeting or in the same room might be a future employer or might work at the place you have applied. Also be aware that once you apply for a position, someone at that institution might ask someone they know at *your* institution about you. The library world is a small one, and meetings and programs at library professional conferences are even smaller.

Using connections to find jobs and make contacts is generally not the best way to job search because of all the unknowns. You never know what relationship your "hookup" has with the human resources department or the individuals in charge. It is never a good idea to try to get a position through someone you know. The best way to get your application noticed and on the right desk is to submit it the right way, through the appropriate process.

Notes

1. *They Call Me "Tater Salad,"* DVD, performed by Ron White (Chatsworth, CA: Image Entertainment, 2004); Ron White, *I Had the Right to Remain Silent . . . but I Didn't Have the Ability* (New York: Penguin Group, 2006), 268.
2. David Emin, "Don't Count on Privacy on Facebook," *Media Week* no. 1224 (September 8, 2009): 17.
3. Cynthia G. Wagner, "Blabbing on Your Blog," *Futurist* 40, no. 4 (2006): 7. See also travels, "Profiles on Social Networking Sites Prove Hazardous for Job Seekers: Social Networking Sites Can Get You Hired, Fired, Reprimanded or Denied a Job," Associated Content, www.associatedcontent.com/article/1388145/profiles_on_social_networking_sites.html (accessed September 16, 2009).
4. "Nearly Half of Employers Use Social Media to Research Candidates," *HR Focus* 86, no. 12 (2009): 8.
5. Ibid.
6. Ibid.
7. Ibid.
8. Ibid.
9. Cindy Kibb, "Social Networking Media Enhances Your Job Search," *New Hampshire Business Review* 31, no. 24 (2009): 12. See also Rachael Eccles, "Link in, Get Hired," *Corporate Meetings and Incentives* 28, no. 11 (2009): 12–16.
10. Hope Viner Sanborn, "Go Google Yourself!" *ABA Journal* 93, no. 8 (2007): 56.
11. Wagner, "Blabbing on Your Blog," 7.

CHAPTER 6

THE PHONE INTERVIEW

Take Your Best Foot Out of Your Mouth and Put It Forward

Teresa Y. Neely with Monica Etsitty Dorame

ABOUT TELEPHONE INTERVIEWS

The telephone interview could possibly be the most overlooked and misunderstood part of the job search process. Either you're really good at it or really bad at it. There is often no in-between. At the University of New Mexico University Libraries, once search pools have been confirmed as bona fide, and the review of the preferred qualifications completed, the search committees then had the task of determining which of the candidates would be selected for a telephone interview. Because the pools for some of these searches were so large, the telephone interviews become much more critical, since it is not economical or efficient to invite fifteen to twenty candidates to campus for an interview. Nearly twenty candidates had telephone interviews for the UNM UL's 2009 access services librarian position.

It's important to realize that the recruitment and hiring process is a phased approach, with at least three distinct opportunities for advancement to the next level. This may vary from institution to institution, but basically the process begins with a pool made up of the entire group that applied for the position. All applicants are considered equal until the application of minimum and preferred qualifications. Once that process is completed, the remaining applicants become the eligible pool for telephone interviews. This is the second opportunity for success, since all applicants are considered equal until the first telephone interview is completed. Based on the performance of applicants during the telephone interview, the pool for the on-campus interview is developed.

SCHEDULING THE TELEPHONE INTERVIEW

In chapter 7, Daniel Barkley provides an overview of the on-campus interview and includes a discussion on scheduling that interview. The process for the telephone interview is remarkably similar. At the UNM UL, the search coordinator contacts those applicants selected for a telephone interview, usually via the e-mail address the applicant has provided. Applicants are given multiple times and dates from which to choose. It is generally understood, at least on the part of the search coordinator and the search committee, that if those times and dates don't work, the applicant will let the search coordinator know, so more time slots can be identified. This particular aspect rarely goes as smoothly as we hope. Generally, recent graduates, including applicants for the resident searches at UNM, first stumble on the telephone interview by exhibiting an inability to manage their schedules.

Despite having an agreed-upon time and date when we might call, we have called individuals who were driving in their cars, or who were on a reference desk and answered, "Hello, this is reference, how can I help you?" We've called individuals where the phone was busy or dead, and those where we've left messages because, well, no one answered. In the case of the latter, either the applicants did not let us know that their plans had changed or they exercised poor time management. They may or may not realize that they kept a group of search committee members waiting, particularly when the applicants had no intention of making that particular interview. On at least one occasion, the candidate said, "I should probably stop what I'm doing and pay attention." Up until that point, we had no idea she was multitasking or whatever she was doing. Bottom line, it's okay to ask for alternate telephone interview times and dates, and in fact we prefer that you do, rather than us calling and calling, trying to reach you, and then wondering what happened, and if you're okay.

If you happen to be residing in a country that is different from the one you are interviewing for, it is a good idea to provide the search coordinator with the country code so that your telephone interview won't be delayed. It might seem unnecessary to add this, but you must also demonstrate your awareness of time zones and that you recognize that they are different. If you don't know what 3:00 p.m. MST means, please don't assume it is the same as your time zone, just with different letters. Please ask, as this is the most inexcusable reason to miss your telephone interview.

HOW TO PREPARE FOR THE TELEPHONE INTERVIEW

You should prepare for the telephone interview as if it were an in-person interview. On-site interviews are generally not conducted at service desks or in vehicles, so you should probably not do those things during your telephone interview. You should find a quiet place, preferably with a landline and no interruptions like barking dogs, jackhammering, or crying babies, if at all possible. Even today, with the incredible advances in mobile technology, cellular phones do weird things. They make you sound like an alien, like you are in a tunnel, or like you have hung up on the search committee each time you stop speaking. Despite their ubiquitous nature, cell phones continue to be problematic in the interview setting, as was evidenced during the telephone interviews conducted in November 2009 for the access services librarian position.

You should also make sure your answering machine is professional and music-free, just in case we have to leave a message. It's just good professional behavior to do this, since you are seeking a professional position.

Also, make sure you do your homework: look at the library's website, read their latest news or updates, and find out what's going on where they are. In April 2006 UNM UL's Zimmerman Library suffered a devastating fire, with significant loss to collections and physical damage to the basement, where the fire occurred. We were due to begin our telephone interviews for the 2006 resident position the day after the fire. We only delayed telephone calls by one day, since most of us did not have an office to work from. In any event, when given the opportunity to ask us questions, only one candidate asked us about the fire.

As part of your preparation for the telephone interview, review the job description closely, particularly the job responsibilities and the preferred or desired qualifications. This should give you some insight into the questions you might be asked.

Virtually everything you do and say can be used in the determination of whether or not your telephone interview was successful, and whether you should be invited to campus for an interview. *Everything.* So, for example, when you make the decision to use a cell phone, and it sounds like you've hung up on us when you're not talking, we're writing, "candidate seemed to cut out throughout the interview," but we're probably thinking, "poor choice for telephone interview." When you sound as if you have just woken up or are ready to go to sleep, we're writing, "candidate exhibited low energy throughout the interview." The following are examples from our committee's most recent search, and consist of comments we made in addition to the candidates' responses to the questions we asked:

- Mr. X didn't really seem prepared for the interview and had difficulty keeping to topic. Although he seemed thoughtful, he also seemed to have trouble separating his current position, where there appears to be conflict between faculty and staff, from the position he was applying for.
- Ms. X seems to be extremely service-oriented, but she projected low energy during the telephone interview and appeared to be on a cell phone, which made it difficult to hear her sometimes.
- Mr. X's interview started out poorly and finished poorly, since he basically just wants to move to Albuquerque. Although he has at least twenty years of library experience, his responses to our questions made him seem a bit dated and not forward-thinking.
- Ms. X is very archives-focused. Her primary experience is in archives, as were the majority of her examples. She was very talkative, using lots of details for her responses, and often answered our questions with questions, so much so that we ran out of time and had to skip one of the questions (the only candidate where we had to do so), to keep to our schedule.
- Ms. X seemed direct and able to confront issues head-on. She has a strong customer service orientation and likes helping and learning. Her interview started off strong but dropped off with the fourth question, which was about covering an overnight shift.

It's clear from these comments that the evaluation process for the telephone interview is not limited to the questions themselves, but takes into account the interview as a whole. Candidates should understand that their fate lies in their hands at this stage of the recruitment process.

- Ms. X was very well prepared for her telephone interview. She understood all of the questions and was ready to answer right away.
- Ms. X seemed thoughtful, likeable, and adaptable, and admitted when she didn't know something.
- Ms. X had a good telephone interview. She seems competent and patron-oriented, with an interest in technology.
- Ms. X was articulate, energetic, enthusiastic, positive, and expressed a sense of humor during her interview. Her responses were very complete.

It is important to keep in mind that these are only partial statements from the summaries, which actually run sixteen pages and cover eighteen candidates. There were candidates with good interviews; however, as mentioned before, it is not practical to bring in for an in-person interview every candidate we interview over the telephone, so the questions we ask over the phone must assist us in further narrowing the pool.

DEVELOPING QUESTIONS FOR THE TELEPHONE INTERVIEW

In our experience, some applicants seem thrown by the telephone interview questions. We do not believe in squandering our limited time with candidates on questions we already know the answer to. For example, if experience at a reference desk or library instruction is required, don't expect to be asked about those things during the telephone interview, or at least you shouldn't, since presumably you've already passed that hurdle.

In our experience, the telephone interview is a good way for us to determine your ability to communicate orally and to think on your feet, and it is also a good way for us to glean more in-depth information about your skill set and your fit for the job. Often, the preferred qualifications and information from the job duties are used to develop telephone interview questions. We have found that the questions that tell us about the applicants' project management and problem-solving experience, as well as their public service experiences, particularly with difficult or unhappy patrons, provide a wealth of information. Keep in mind that the search committee isn't trying to trip you up here. You should look for clues to possible questions in the job description, and for information the search committee hasn't been privy to before. (Figure 6.1 contains a list of questions used for a telephone interview by the UNM UL in 2009.)

KEEPING IT LEGAL

Faculty search committees are guided by laws and human resource regulations in the conduct of searches. There are things we can ask and things we can not ask. This is why it is critical for search committees to focus specifically on the job duties, the requirements, and the qualifications for positions. Examples of things we can legally ask you about include questions about your

- educational background
- experiences that qualify you for this job
- licenses and certifications for this job
- your willingness to travel

FIGURE **6.1**

Telephone interview questions

1. Please describe your role in a project you were involved in that you are particularly proud of.

   a. *(Possible follow-up question: What leadership characteristics contributed to the success of the project?)*

2. Please describe an encounter with a difficult patron or coworker and how you handled it.

   a. *(Follow-up: What did you learn from the experience?)*

3. Which of your previous jobs has been most challenging for you, and what techniques did you use to overcome (or meet) the challenges? (Note to search committee: could be a positive challenge that is met, or negative challenges that are overcome.)

4. A University Libraries location is open 139 hours a week, including a 24/5 service at one of the four branch libraries on campus. How would you respond to being asked to cover a shift that falls between 8:00 p.m. and 8:00 a.m.?

5. What role do you see yourself playing in the development and implementation of a learning commons?

6. What new technologies do you think hold the most promise for academic libraries in developing training programs?

7. What professional goals have you established for yourself for the next five years?

8. What has been your favorite past position and why?

9. Do you have any questions for us?

- the name(s) on your work records
- whether you have the legal right to work in the United States
- whether you are available for overtime

Although there are things we cannot ask, most of these are also things we don't really want to know, particularly during the telephone interview. It is important for the candidate to stay focused and on task during the telephone interview. The "inability to hold water," as the Neely family calls those of us who cannot keep secrets, should not be unleashed during the telephone interview. Examples of things that candidates can't seem to keep to themselves include the following.

Their age and/or date of birth. And it's not necessary for candidates to put these facts on their CV either. Have you heard of ageism? It can apply to those who are youthful in age, as well as those of us who are more seasoned, and so search committees should make every effort to avoid evaluating candidates based on their age, whether young or old.

Whether they have pets and/or children, how many, and how old they are. We're sure that they're cute, but the telephone interview is really not the place to introduce us to them.

Their sexual orientation. Honestly, we really do not want to know this, and candidates might also consider asking their references to not "out" them during the reference check, because this happens too.

Their religious beliefs or the church they attend. We're sure that religion is very important to some candidates, but we are not hiring them to work at the church or for the church. Academic libraries are generally nondenominational, unless they are part of a church-affiliated institution. We can work with anyone from any religious background. Sharing this information will not give a candidate a leg up.

Their maiden name or their marital status. This information goes right up there with a candidate's children and pets.

The name, and occupation, and health condition of their spouse or partner. We're sure the New Mexico air is just what a candidate's spouse needs for that upper respiratory issue, but we're not physicians.

Any physical impairments or disabilities that would prevent them from performing the job for which they are applying. We understand that candidates want to be open and honest and disclose fully any issue that they think might be relevant. But their broken arm, leg, toe, or any preexisting condition is not relevant. Especially now that we have health reform in the United States. Additionally, Title I of the Americans with Disabilities Act lists these additional prohibited questions:

- Have you ever been hospitalized? If so, for what condition?
- Have you ever been treated by a psychiatrist or psychologist? If so, for what condition?
- Is there any health-related reason that you may not be able to perform the job for which you are applying?
- How many days were you absent from work because of illness last year?
- Are you taking any prescribed drugs?
- Have you ever been treated for drug addiction or alcoholism?[1]

And for the record, we're not interested in the answers to these questions either.

The following questions were used for the telephone interviews for several of the UNM UL resident searches:

How will your personal characteristics, qualities, and other experiences outside of librarianship aid you in this position? Because this position required no experience, we wanted to find out how other aspects of the candidates' lives had prepared them for the position. Our advice to any applicant is to keep it professional and remember the job you are applying for. You would be surprised at the responses we received for this question. The amount of personal information shared in response to this question boggles the mind. In fact, it was in response to this question that an applicant said she had always been interested in Native Americans so she read fiction books.

What technologies do you think hold the most promise for libraries? Most responses to this question were Web 2.0, blogging, wikis, social networking, and very little else. Few applicants were able to adequately describe these things, but everyone knew the "right" responses to give. We learned virtually nothing and decided to rewrite the question for subsequent searches.

What kinds of people do you find it most difficult to work with, and what do you do to improve the situation? In responding to this question, keep it professional and above the waist; this is not the time to get personal and name individuals, or to air out a long-standing dispute with a previous or current coworker. In general, it is not a good idea to trash your former or current boss and colleagues to your potential boss and colleagues.

How do you communicate most effectively, and why do you think so? Responses to this question were surprising in that many of them did not specify the categories of oral, written, or electronic communication. Rather, a review of summaries prepared after telephone interviews for several years of searches revealed that some candidates simply ignored the question; others had trouble understanding it, so the question had to be repeated or restated.

Describe a problem you have faced, professionally or personally, and how you resolved it. Generally, steer clear of references to color, race, ethnicity or nationality, alcohol or drugs, and your deeply personal trials and tribulations that may reveal too much about your potential behavior at work. In our experience at the University of New Mexico, responses tended toward negative comments about populations (e.g., Native Americans) and issues (e.g., reservations, trading posts) native to New Mexico. However, be aware that similarities also exist in other states with regard to native populations and local issues. It is a good idea to be aware of this when answering these types of questions so as not to offend anyone on the search committee or lessen the chance for an on-site interview or job offer.

How would your coworkers describe you? Don't self-evaluate. During one telephone interview, the candidate appeared to be having an extremely low-energy day. She talked long and slowly and it was physically exhausting to listen to her. When asked this question, she finally got around to responding: "They would say I'm energetic," in the same long and slow manner in which she had answered previous questions. In this case, the response itself was in direct contrast to the way the candidate delivered it. It's a good idea to strive for a positive, upbeat tone of voice during the telephone interview. This indicates to the search committee that you are energetic, engaged in the process, and interested in the position.

Do you have any questions for us?

- Don't ask the obvious. During introductions at the start of the interview, one of the search committee members introduced herself: "Hi, I'm Megan, the current resident." At the end of the interview, when the candidate was asked if she had any questions for the search committee, she asked, "Have you had this position before?" It's important to pay attention when the committee calls and introduce themselves. They are not just search committee members, they are potential colleagues. Make an effort to jot down the names and position titles if at all possible in order to avoid a blunder like the one described here. Asking a question that has already been answered may indicate to the search committee that you are not taking the interview seriously, or that you are just not interested enough to pay attention. Also, writing down their names and titles will help when you write the committee afterwards to thank them for the interview.
- Don't keep asking for a permanent job when you clearly know it's not permanent.
- Don't ask about things that are in the job description or information that has already been provided to you unless you need further clarification.
- Don't take this as an opportunity to negotiate or continue to sell yourself for the job.

Please have questions to ask us. Ask us anything about the position, the location, the management style, what we like about where we work, something you read about on the website. Not having any questions makes you look unprepared and not interested.

- Do ask about
  - the timeline for the hiring process and next steps
  - the expected start date
  - the work environment and job expectations
  - who will be your supervisor, if it has not already been stated in the position description

- appropriate job level questions
- support for professional development

When asked if you have questions for the search committee, remember to do the following.

Steer clear of anything that might be offensive or inappropriate. Do not shock the committee with your responses. Generally, unless asked, race, ethnicity, and religion should not be discussed.

If you are not familiar with something, don't talk about it as if you are an authority. It's okay to say "I don't know" or to ask for further clarification; but it is generally fairly obvious when someone is not an authority on a particular topic.

Think before we call, and then, think again before you speak. Know the difference between countries and the states of the United States. (Seriously, we aren't joking about this one.) Know the name of the institution where you have applied for a position. Know the difference between fiction and nonfiction.

Be conscious of time; don't talk too much or too little. Some of our interviews have lasted seven minutes, and some have lasted more than fifteen. In some cases, we have had to ask candidates to stop talking. It's not a good sign when the search committee has to shush you, literally.

Don't project low energy.

Use humor if appropriate.

Don't antagonize or become angry with the committee, especially if you don't tell them why. At the beginning of one telephone interview, the search committee chair introduced herself to begin the interview: "Hello, this is Teresa Neely from the University of New Mexico. How are you today?" The response came in a distinctly surly tone, "Oh, yeah, nice to talk to you again." The candidate remained angry at me, or us—we never figured out who—for the rest of the telephone interview. I still don't know where I met her, if I ever did.

Close out the interview and follow up. Once the telephone interview is complete, it is appropriate to thank the search committee members for selecting you and giving you the opportunity to interview with them. As noted above, your chances of getting an on-campus interview after the telephone interview rest almost entirely on you and the effort you put forth to prepare for the telephone interview. We strongly encourage you to read this chapter as many times as you feel necessary. In fact, make a point to read it prior to every single telephone interview you are invited to participate in. It can't hurt your chances any more than if you decided to wing it and go it alone.

Note

1. Iseek jobs, "Legal Interview Questions," www.iseek.org/jobs/legalquestions.html (accessed April 1, 2010).

CHAPTER 7

LIVE AND IN-PERSON
Get Ready to Meet the Entire Library Family

Daniel Barkley

CONGRATULATIONS, YOU'VE MADE it to the final round—the Interview. You're almost there. Obviously, you did well during the initial stages of the filtering process to have made it this far. At this point you should really want this job. If you are having any doubts at this juncture, it's permissible to withdraw your name from consideration. There is no shame in doing so, nor should there be. Don't waste your time or the time and expense of those who want to meet you. If you're using this interview to hone your interviewing skills, visit a part of the country you have no strong desire to live in, or if you have family opposing a move to the potential job site, say adios and find a position in a location that suits you.

If you're 100-percent certain that this is the job and the location where you want to begin your career in academic librarianship, then it's time to prepare for the final steps that will get you there. There is much to do prior to the on-site interview besides selecting the shoes and accessories that best highlight the suit on which you've spent so much money. Now is the time to think about questions that should and should not be asked, prepare your presentation (should one be required), and, most importantly, consider how you want to present yourself to your potential new family.

By now you should have a "feel" for the job duties and requirements, the atmosphere, and a few of your new "family" members. They've certainly gotten to know you from your application materials, the phone interview, and information from your references. Hopefully, you used your telephone interview to ask some questions of the search committee, not only about the job but also about the people, the challenges, the library's strategic plans, and the expectations they have of you.

The library family is just that—a family of individuals who are connected by the DNA helix called work. Yes, they work together, hopefully well, and some even play together. There is probably a crazy uncle somewhere in the basement whom they want you to avoid. Do so. As with any family, there are going to be people and situations that don't blend well together. It's good to get a feel for these situations during the interview process, as well as asking your potential colleagues some questions about how folks get along in the workplace. At the same time, remember you are not meeting the Addams or Munster families, or your in-laws. You are applying for a job in academic librarianship, possibly your first—it's a bit like dating, only more serious—and you definitely don't want to suffer rejection at first sight.

Be yourself. Be sincere, succinct, and pertinent. Don't try to be the class clown, or a stand-up comic. Having a sense of humor is important, but being knowledgeable about the job requirements is crucial.

Best of Luck!!

SCHEDULING THE IN-PERSON INTERVIEW

The key component is to be flexible. You are unlikely to be the only candidate the library is interviewing. This alone can create a set of challenges, many of which you probably aren't aware of. Each interview situation is different; one potential employer may want to bring in candidates as quickly as possible, scheduling them almost next to each other, one on one day, another on the very next. Another employer may schedule candidates to be interviewed around holiday or semester breaks, professional meetings (e.g., ALA conferences), or other campus or professional events. Thus far, you are viewed with high esteem; don't ruin it by being so inflexible that scheduling a shuttle launch to the international space station would be less challenging than arranging an interview time with you.

What to Expect

Depending on the size of the library, its organizational structure, and other key components such as staffing, you will receive a call, or perhaps an e-mail, requesting your presence for a face-to-face interview. If you receive a phone call, remain calm, listen carefully to what the person is saying, and respond appropriately. Do take notes and ask for a follow-up e-mail to confirm for your official record. It might not be a good idea to depend on your memory of the phone call at this point.

Unless the interview is local, you will be scheduled for a round-trip flight from your point of origin, as well as a stay at a nearby hotel. As noted earlier, try and be as flexible as possible with your flight and hotel arrangements. The more flexible you are, the easier it becomes for those making the arrangements. Don't forget that you are now under the microscope. You don't want to start in the red with the administrative assistant. Don't underestimate her importance in the library family. She can become your best friend, or one of your most formidable opponents. You may have preferences as to times of departure, airline, and hotel, but if at all possible, don't let your preferences sabotage this important first step. Also, realize that this is your first academic library position, possibly at entry-level, so don't expect to stay at the Ritz Carlton or fly first class.

Regardless of the length of your flight and place of rest, there are a number of questions that are appropriate and necessary to ask. For example, if you feel you need a full day of rest prior to your interview, ask if you can arrive a day or two earlier than your scheduled interview. It's quite all right to ascertain if you can extend your stay a day or two after your interview. Mention that you are more than willing to pay for the additional days. And *expect* to pay for those additional days.

In many ways, coming in earlier or staying later indicates to the library family that you are, indeed, quite interested in and serious about this job. This is essential, should you have a family. Bringing the spouse and children demonstrates the sincerity of your desire to work at this location. It also provides your real family with an opportunity to look around for houses, schools, recreational activities, and other pertinent family needs. If you are unable to bring the family along, do prepare questions about housing, school districts, and other things relevant to your family situation.

Once you finalize your travel plans, the next set of questions is vitally important to your success. You need to know if a presentation is required, how long the interview will last (e.g., one day or more), the complete interview itinerary, and any other interview-related questions you might have. If you haven't already located this information (and you should have already done this), ask for the electronic location of the library's mission statement, strategic plan, budget, organizational chart, and any other related institutional information you feel is relevant.

Don't be difficult in your travel plans, rude in your posing of questions, or dismissive or impertinent in your tone or tenor over the phone (or electronically). Don't ask questions regarding salary or benefits or any other compensation components. Now is not the time—the opportunity to discuss these issues will appear when you are the successful candidate.

Do be cooperative, flexible, and easygoing. Do understand that arranging every aspect of your visit is a challenge for the employer. Do remember that those at the potential job location have adjusted their hectic lives to fit you into their day or have committed their entire day to your interview. You want to fit into their day, and not expect them to fit into yours.

THE ON-SITE, JOB INTERVIEW MARATHON

And what a marathon it will be! You need to be able to go the distance. You have prepared yourself to some degree, and you know some of the family through the initial interview process—members of the search committee, the administrative assistant who arranged your flight and hotel and provided other information, and others you may have researched prior to your arrival. It's now go time—from the time you set foot on the ground and are met at the airport until the time you finish and someone drops you off at the hotel or the airport—and you need to shine.

You don't have time for fatigue, jet lag, a restless night, too much caffeine, or any other physical or mental obstacles. The spotlight is on you, whether you like it or not. You are performing two roles, but with many acts. You are not only being interviewed by almost everyone in the library family, you are also interviewing them to make sure this truly is the job you want.

By now you know whether or not a presentation is part of the interview. If it is, this will be your first opportunity to meet a number of library personnel who have yet to do more than read your cover letter and resume and make time to attend your presentation. A word of advice: if your presentation is to be delivered within a specified time frame (e.g., twenty-five minutes), don't run over. Nothing hurts an interviewee more than running long on her presentation. Hopefully, you have practiced this presentation several times—alone with a stopwatch, as well as in front of friends, family, advisors, or other trusted individuals. More advice on the presentation can be found in chapter 8.

A Very Rigorous Day

It's not just the day of the interview that will be rigorous. Chances are, regardless of when you arrive, you might have dinner with members of the search committee and others from the library family the night before the interview. Every word you speak, every gesture, mannerism, and facial expression will be judged by those attending, sometimes consciously and sometimes unconsciously. Dinner may seem like an innocuous and easygoing evening, but the folks from the family are on the clock and are observing you. This is your first make-or-break opportunity.

It's tough to try to be relaxed, calm, and easygoing. You're going to be nervous and that's okay. But do try to relax, be genuine, and be yourself. Let the shining star personality that got you this far come out further. Ease your way into the conversation even though questions will be coming at you from everyone at the table.

The questions may range from why you want the job to how many pets you own. Someone will probably ask you if you have a hobby, about your favorite foods, and other non–work-related topics. The family is attempting to put you at ease, but also to get to know you. Let them. Unless you're in the Federal Witness Protection Program, or you're a former contestant on an *American Idol* audition show, you have nothing to hide.

It's difficult to get personal without revealing too much. This part of the interview process is like wearing a bathing suit—you can reveal as little or as much as you like. Try to keep that appendectomy scar hidden for the time being. Once you get the job, you can tell folks whatever you want, but please remember basic decorum.

The day of the interview is really the next *huge* challenge. Again, from the time you are retrieved from your hotel until you are back there, you are the focus of almost everyone's attention. You will likely have a full agenda, and there will be only a few moments when you will be alone—like bathroom breaks. Avail yourself of those whether you have to go or not.

During the course of the day you will meet a variety of people. Some of these people you will encounter multiple times during your visit. Others you may see once in a meeting or presentation and perhaps again as you are taken from point to point. It's likely that you will be given a tour of the library, other branch libraries if appropriate, and possibly the campus. You are going to meet a slew of people. You may be able to remember everyone's name, but don't be too concerned if you can't. You may meet someone in the morning, and not see them again until a late afternoon break or dinner. Not remembering everyone's name is not the end of the world, unless of course, it's your immediate supervisor-to-be or the library dean or director. The library family understands.

Your day will include answering the same questions multiple times. The questions will come from a variety of library family members. The questions may or may not be stated the same way, and there may be a few people who will ask you the same question repeatedly. Like a good Boy or Girl Scout, *be prepared.* Answering a question one way in the morning, and contradicting yourself by answering it differently in the afternoon is generally a no-no, and will be remembered by the person who asked it and by all who heard it at both encounters.

Your day may also include a variety of meetings that fall outside the library. Depending on the size of the university, and the position you are applying for, you may have meetings with teaching faculty who serve on a library committee, academic deans or chairs, the provost, or perhaps even the president of the institution. The smaller the campus, the more likely you are to meet upper administration. Impressing these individuals is as important as impressing the library family.

You should expect similar questions throughout your interview day that can run the gamut from "How was your dinner last evening?" to "Why do you want this job?" to "What fascinates you about our campus, institution, city, or area?" You may also hear questions similar to those asked during the phone interview.

Interview Dress Etiquette

Wear clothing that is suitable to the area and climate you are visiting. It's strongly encouraged that you purchase a new set of interview clothes, if at all possible, or at least select clothing that fits well and that you are comfortable in. Regardless of gender, nothing shouts out success like a new business suit or outfit. Don't show up in clothing that gives people the impression you spent the day before the interview shopping off the rack at your local used clothing outlet or low-end consignment shop. Regardless, hotels generally have irons, so by all means do take advantage of it. If your room is not equipped, ask at the front desk if one can be delivered to your room.

Smart, fashionable clothing is fine. Business attire is better. And do dress for the weather. Investigate the local forecast prior to packing. Arriving with warm weather clothing for an interview in a cold climate state (or vice versa) could send a red flag warning to your future employers that you don't do your homework and are not organized or prepared.

Finally, footwear. Don't wear six-inch heels without some backup. While those heels may make you look sharp, it will take weeks to recover from all the walking you might be doing. Wear those heels during your presentation, and when meeting the search committee or other important people. Bring a pair of comfortable shoes to walk between meetings, buildings, or other circumstances that you might encounter. Men—wear comfortable shoes as well. Your Stacy Adams shoes may look fantastic, but limping into a meeting because of sore feet demonstrates a lack of foresight and proper planning. Regardless of gender, wear good shoes. And it's okay to take a bathroom break to change them rather than in front of the search committee.

INTERVIEW DON'TS

For the many do's that go along with preparing and surviving the interview, there are an equal number of don'ts. The "don'ts" can and will be a death knell to your chances of success at the interview. Pay close attention now so you don't wonder later why you didn't get the dream job you are interviewing for.

Don't be late. You may be chuckling as you read this, but nothing says "don't hire me" more than tardiness. Regardless if it's for dinner, your ride from your hotel, getting to or from the airport, or moving from meeting to meeting—*do not be late!*

Perhaps you've traveled through one or more time zones to the job interview. No excuse. If you're staying at a hotel which offers a wake-up service, use it! If there is no wake-up service, set the hotel clock alarm *and* your cell phone alarm. Have a family member or friend call you one and a half hours before you are scheduled to depart from the hotel to the interview location. Do whatever you need to do to ensure that you will be ready to go.

Don't be lazy in your speech. If you have lazy speech patterns such as always using "you know," "like," "umm," and "ahh," lose them. These pauses make you look disorganized, disoriented, nervous, or outright unprepared. You need to impress the family with your ability to communicate—thoughtfully, succinctly, and clearly. The job interview is a dialogue, not an interrogation. Make an effort to communicate well with everyone you meet.

Don't disregard your body language. Your body language says more about you than your speech. Don't send negative signals with your body language to those interviewing you. For example, it's great to make eye contact—but don't stare down the person asking the question. A stare-down is great if you're a sports official who has just been accosted by a coach or fan. But this look doesn't go over well in an interview.

Don't tap your fingers, shuffle your feet, twirl your hair, chew, pop, or crack gum, or click your pen. And don't do any of these while avoiding eye contact. Also avoid shaky or swinging leg movements. It may be a habit, but it's an annoying one. Interviewers will assume you are nervous, unprepared, avoiding the question, lying, or ready to leave. These are not signs that say "I want this job."

Don't slouch in your chair. Yes, you've heard this a million times from your mom—don't slouch, stand up straight, and eat your vegetables. All is sound advice. Slouching, slumping, folding yourself into a chair, and sitting on your feet are signs of discontent, boredom, and laziness. These actions are very unprofessional and are not representative of the positive signs you want to send to your interviewers.

Don't cross your arms, jam your hands into your pockets, or use any other signs to tell your interviewers that you don't want them to get to know you. These are all signs that you are unwelcoming, defensive, threatened, or you don't wish to be bothered. Sometimes it's not what you say that counts, but how you appear.

Don't drink alcohol during the interview, regardless of where you might be. It's only marginally okay for those from the family taking you to lunch or dinner to have a cocktail, but it is definitely not acceptable for you to partake. Should you decide to have a drink after everyone has left you for the evening, don't show up the next morning hung-over or smelling like a brewery.

Don't overdo the perfume or aftershave. It's okay to smell nice, but you don't need to marinate in it. Leaving a lingering smell months after you've left is not the way to win the hearts and minds of the family.

Don't overdo the jewelry. Regardless of gender, this isn't the time to show off your Mr. T starter kit. For women, a simple necklace and earrings are great. For men, simplify if you have a pierced ear(s). Regardless of gender, take out nose and lip rings, and any other visible ornamental jewelry adorning your body. Consider covering up tattoos that might be less than, shall we say, professional. You want the family to remember you for who you are rather than your body art.

Don't be nervous. Easier said than done, true, but at the very least, try not to show how nervous you are by giggling every time you are spoken to, constantly apologizing for being so nervous, or not making eye contact. Being nervous is natural and expected. Reassure yourself that you are going to get a job, perhaps even this one. That way when you interview, you'll be okay.

Don't ramble on about yourself or your personal life. You will certainly be asked questions regarding yourself—what you like to do in your spare time, your hobbies or interests, and other questions. Do answer their questions, but don't go so overboard that you forget why you're there—to get a job. You may think you've had an interesting and fascinating life to this point, and perhaps you have. But you are the only one that wants to hear about it.

Don't be a name dropper. You may not realize this, being a newcomer to the profession, but dropping names doesn't impress us. This type of behavior gives us additional "references" and we can, and just might, contact those people to find out what you are like. Many in the family regularly attend professional meetings and are active on professional committees. While it's okay to acknowledge that you have worked with "so-and-so" on a project, dropping names serves no useful purpose.

Don't dress like Dennis Rodman or Lady Gaga. Use some common sense in your sartorial splendor. Wear clothes that fit well and are neutral in color (black, navy, brown). Wear business-appropriate attire and avoid wearing clothing that leaves nothing to the imagination. As mentioned earlier, don't wear heels or other shoes that will leave you hurting by the end of the day.

Don't smoke. If you smoke, either quit or figure out a way to go the entire day without a cigarette. Most folks don't like to be around smokers. Even if you smoke in a wind tunnel, there will be those who can still smell it on your breath, in your hair, and on your clothes. Besides, quitting now will allow you to spend that extra money on some nicer clothes.

Don't speak in negative terms about current or former employers, employees, library school faculty, or colleagues. The library world is relatively small, and you can never be sure who knows whom and what that relationship is like. Be polite and acknowledge that you know someone if you're asked. There's no need for further explanation. And remember what your mother said: if you can't say something nice about someone, then say nothing at all.

Don't be the class clown. This isn't an interview for the *Gong Show*. Everyone appreciates a sense of humor, and it's okay to let that come through during the interview. However, you are not there to do a 45-minute stand-up Ron White-esque routine.

Don't use foul language. If you have a potty mouth, clean it up before you speak. If you can't or don't choose to, then you might wish to explore career opportunities in libraries where this type of behavior is acceptable, though I'm not sure what kind of library that would be.

Don't tell insensitive jokes. In fact, it's probably best to not tell any jokes. What may seem harmless to you might be deemed offensive by another.

Don't bring politics or religion into the conversation. And if you must engage in conversation on these topics, be as value-neutral as possible.

Don't be contrary or argumentative.

Don't be poorly prepared.

INTERVIEW DO'S

Having read the list above, you might be wondering at this point if there is anything that you *should* do during the on-site interview. Of course there are a number of "do's," the biggest of which is to *be yourself*. Sounds easy, of course, but you may need to step outside of your comfort zone in order to make a positive impact. For example, if you're a naturally quiet person, you will need to speak up and make an effort to be more engaging than you might normally be around strangers. If you are a vivacious person, you may need to turn the volume down a few decibels. Throughout the course of the interview, you do need to be engaging, smiling, happy, and to some degree, entertaining. The spotlight will be on you the entire time you interview, so it's important to be "on" during that time.

WHAT TO KNOW BEFORE YOU ARRIVE AT THE INTERVIEW

This is incredibly important. Do your homework prior to your arrival. In fact, do your homework prior to your phone interview. A lack of knowledge about your prospective employer, potential colleagues, and job environment will ensure failure. Follow the six Ps and you can't go wrong—Prior Proper Planning Prevents Poor Performance.

Researching your topic for the presentation is one area that you must focus on. (See chapter 8 for a detailed discussion of the presentation.) It is important to know as much as you can about your potential employer, and those you will be meeting during the interview. As much as possible, know the institution, the administrative hierarchy, and the academic environment.

Who Is the Administration?

Regardless of the size of the institution, you will most likely be meeting with the library director or dean. A smaller institution might provide you an opportunity to meet with the provost, president, and other administrative officials. It's important to know something about these individuals besides their names and current positions. Information that may provide you with some insight includes their published research and other scholarly output, their leadership philosophy, the vision for the future of the library or institution, and how the library fits into the institution's strategic plans.

Know the Search Committee

At this point you have had, at a minimum, a phone interview with this committee, and it is likely that each member introduced themselves during that interview and perhaps asked you a question or two, giving you a sense of their personalities by the time you arrive for the on-site interview. Members of the search committee are, for the duration of the interview, your friends. They are responsible for bringing you to campus for the interview, and thus, they want you to succeed. They are also responsible for making a recommendation to the dean, director, or university officer who makes the final hiring decision. These are not the folks you want to alienate or leave with a bad impression.

Most typically, your interview will consist of a series of meetings with the search committee, a presentation before the entire library organization, and more meetings with other interested or pertinent committees or individuals. You will meet with a human resources (HR) person, staff who work in the area for which you are interviewing, and others within the organization. Depending on the size of the library staff and the length of the interview, you might very well meet everyone.

You will likely meet faculty outside the library. These individuals may work closely with library personnel, serve on a university committee oriented to library operations, or be faculty in an academic department for which you may have outreach and collection development responsibilities. They may attend your presentation, be an active part of the search committee, or simply have sufficient interest in library operations to attend your interview.

If this position is a tenure-track appointment, you will meet with a promotion/tenure committee comprised of library faculty who have successfully worked their way through the process. Listen carefully to the requirements for tenure and note especially what scholarly endeavors are needed to achieve tenure or promotion. Although this position may be a "stepping-stone" to your next position, you will be expected to participate in the tenure or promotion process. Regardless of your intended length of stay, this process will have an impact on your career. Don't disregard this.

Who Is Important in the Organization?

Everyone in the organization is important, but some are just a bit more important than others. For example, the chair of the search committee and the library dean or director are important people. Depending on how the organization operates, one of these people has your fate in his hands. Pay close attention to the questions they ask as well as their body language as you answer. These are keys to a successful interview. Others of importance include members of the search committee, administrative personnel (HR, administrative assistants), outside faculty, university administrators, and those attending any part of your interview day.

Everyone attending a part of your interview day will critique you. Feedback from library and university personnel is critical in the evaluation and selection processes. Therefore everyone you meet during your interview is important.

WHERE TO GATHER INFORMATION PRIOR TO YOUR INTERVIEW

The first place you may wish to start is the institution's and library's web pages. From there you can locate organization charts, committee minutes, brief biographies of the leadership, budgets, library functions, and other important and pertinent information you will need for the interview.

Reviewing the past few budgets for the university and library, if available, will provide you with many clues regarding those operations. Reviewing the minutes of library committees, if available, can reveal much about the internal operations of the library and its staff. Do all library personnel have a say in the library operations? Are the library committees merely pro forma, or do they actually contribute to library functions, operations, and directions?

It is equally important to review university policies, procedures, and functions. Reviewing the university web page as well as key administrative and academic department web pages will reveal other information about the university. For example, if you are interviewing for a tenure-track position, you need to completely and fully understand the requirements for tenure, regardless of how long you think you may stay at this position.

Read the local papers, community newsletters, and alternative press publications. All of these will reveal important information about the community to which you might be relocating.

It's also important to review county, city, and private enterprise websites. Information contained on these pages will run the gamut from obtaining a new driver's license to enrolling children into public or private schools. Many communities have move-in packages available which will offer savings on a number of services that you might need should you be successful in obtaining the job.

PREPARING THOUGHTFUL QUESTIONS FOR THE INTERVIEW

As you will be meeting with a number of groups and individuals, it's vitally important that you have questions prepared for them. Again, the interview is a two-way street, and if you are serious about the job, university, and local community, you need to have questions that reflect that attitude.

Ask questions about your subject or functional area of interest. Regardless of where or what your field of study might be, ask questions of those interviewing you about that area. For example, if you are interviewing for a public service position, inquire as to how the service desk is staffed, who does the desk schedule, and the number of hours per shift. If you are interviewing for a technical position, ask how others work in that area, if it's permissible to work from home, and what other expectations there might be.

It's perfectly acceptable to ask questions regarding the library and university budgets. If you have prepared well you are already aware of the economic situation of the institution as well as its funding from federal, state, and private sources. You need to know how the budget is appropriated and allocated. You need to know if funding levels are being maintained or will be changing due to economic conditions. While you may want this job, you may not want to get into a situation where the first week you arrive you're expected to cut your budget by half.

There will be multiple opportunities to ask questions about the local community. Early in the interview process, be mindful of what different individuals say about their personal lives. It's amazing what is revealed during breaks or lunch or dinner engagements. Ask everyone what they like most about living in this area and you will gather sufficient information to help you determine if you wish to live there.

For example, if you are an outdoor enthusiast, find out who hikes, bikes, or camps and ask them how they enjoy those activities. If you have an interest in sports, find out who among your interviewers attends local sporting events and ask questions of them. If you have family, you will want to ask questions about the school system, community events, and other resources for your family. Remember that many of the library family you will meet have lived in that community for some time, and they know where the best schools, restaurants, community centers, and other activities are located. The decision to relocate is huge; more so if you have other family members to consider. The more questions you ask, the more information you will obtain to help you decide if this is the right opportunity for you and your family.

Finally, always clarify any responses or feedback you've received during the day so you're sure you understand the job duties and expectations, working hours (e.g., nights and weekends may be expected), and, if pertinent, tenure requirements. Clarify your role in the library and department as well as reporting lines, supervisory role and expectations, and budget responsibilities.

While you may feel overwhelmed during the course of the interview, focus on who and what is being said. Ask questions and be prepared to answer the same question a number of times.

Most importantly—have fun, be yourself, and be ready to accept an offer.

ADDITIONAL RESOURCES

"Avoid These Job Interview Blunders," *USA Today Magazine* 138, no. 2771
    (2009), 11.
Charles Cotton, "Should I Bring Up Pay and Conditions Issues during the Job
    Interview?" *Community Care* no. 1765 (2009): 58.
Meredith Kopulos, "Common Sense Please," *Women in Business* 61, no. 1 (2009): 29.
Tamekia Reece, "How to Wow!" *Career World* 35, no. 3 (2006): 16–18.

CHAPTER 8

YOUR PRESENTATION
It Should Not Be Ridiculous

Bruce Neville and Sarah L. Stohr

AT VIRTUALLY EVERY academic job for which you interview, you will be asked to prepare a presentation on a designated topic. The presentation is a critical part of the interview process. It allows you to showcase your knowledge or expertise regarding a specific topic and gives audience members an opportunity to assess you not only as a candidate but as a public speaker or potential instructor. For many organizations, the presentation component is the only portion of the interview process that is open to all library employees rather than just the search committee, or other individuals and groups scheduled to meet with the candidate during the interview. You need to be able to impress them all with your presentation skills, your knowledge of the subject matter, and your ability to think quickly during the question-and-answer portion of the presentation.

When you are invited to an interview in an academic library, potential employers will often ask you to prepare a talk to give at some point during your time on campus. In many cases, you will be given a specific topic to address during your presentation. The topics usually relate to the position for which you are interviewing or to a wider issue or problem within your field of interest. For instance, if you are applying for a position in the instruction department of an academic library, you might be asked to offer your thoughts on the latest trends in assessment or to demonstrate how you would conduct an instruction session for students using a specific electronic resource. Search committees typically give considerable thought to the presentation topics they assign. Assigned presentation topics are usually quite open-ended. This allows the search committee and others viewing your presentation to see how you interpret the question or examine the topic at hand. The committee isn't trying to trick you; rather, the presentation is designed to offer you a chance to distinguish yourself from other candidates. It is important that you seize the opportunity.

HOW TO PREPARE FOR THE PRESENTATION

Not all search committees will assign you a presentation topic; some will leave the choice of topic up to you. If you are allowed to choose your own topic for a presentation, make sure that you select a topic that is of relevance to the organization and that will be interesting for your audience. Adapting your presentation topic to the organization will let the audience members know that you've done your research as a candidate. If you must come up with your own presentation topic and you're unsure of where to start, search the library literature and blogs related to the position for which you are interviewing. Are there current trends, hot topics, or controversies that might be explored during your presentation? Don't forget that your friends, professors, and colleagues can be a great source of help and inspiration when it comes to choosing a topic or figuring out how to tackle a presentation topic you were assigned. Bouncing ideas off of them is an excellent way to figure out how you want to proceed with your topic.

As you put your presentation together, pay attention to the directions given to you by the institution regarding the session. If you are given 30 minutes for a presentation, with a 15-minute question-and-answer session to follow, do not give a 15- or 45-minute presentation. We've witnessed countless candidates stand up and give presentations that were much too short or much too long. It's always embarrassing to watch as they are asked "Is that all you have?" or told "We have to cut you off because we're out of time." Practice giving your presentation so that you know without a doubt that you have the appropriate amount of material to cover within the given time frame. The search committee will certainly notice whether you went significantly under or over time. Don't let a situation that's so easy to avoid work against you, and please, if you are told that you're out of time, don't keep presenting!

Sometimes it will be necessary for you to use a resource that the library subscribes to as part of your presentation. You may need to demonstrate a particular database or software application. If that is the case, make sure you know exactly how the resource works and how to connect to it from the computer you will be using during your presentation. Audience members will be unimpressed with a candidate who doesn't know how to effectively use a tool that she has been asked to demonstrate. If you're asked to demonstrate a resource that you don't have ready access to, don't immediately panic. Search for nearby libraries that have a subscription to the resource and practice there. Be sure you're basing your presentation on the same *platform* that you'll be demonstrating. Each vendor packages databases differently, and you will need to know how to present for the appropriate platform. If you can't find a nearby library with the specified database on the specified platform, make sure you practice with and know the features of *both* the database and the platform, even if you can't practice them together beforehand. If you aren't able to arrange access to the tool locally, explain that to your contact at the institution and ask about remote access so that you can practice. Many libraries customize their databases to suit their users' needs, which may result in interfaces being dramatically different from library to library. Familiarize yourself with the tool you'll be using as much as you can beforehand so that any fumbling you might do during the demonstration will be kept to an absolute minimum.

DEVELOPING A PRESENTATION

So how do you give a presentation that will land you your coveted job? Ideally, your presentation will be both informative and engaging and will leave the audience interested and wanting to know even more about the topic and what you have to say about it.

You may have as much as a month to prepare your presentation, but you may also have as little as a week. In any case, you will need to work quickly.

Choose a facet of the topic that is of personal interest. If you are interested in the topic, it is more likely that you can interest the audience as well. If you're already interested in the subject, it's likely that you will have some background knowledge and a familiarity with the literature. It will make it that much easier to prepare a presentation under pressure. Presumably, you have some knowledge of the area of librarianship, or you would not be interested in or applying for this job. You may have personal experiences that you can work into the presentation. A personal investment in the subject goes a long way toward minimizing "stage fright" during the actual presentation.

Your audience will represent a cross-section of the library staff and all of its operations. Do not be too dependent upon acronyms in your presentation or expect your audience to be familiar with all of them. This is especially true if you are applying for a technical position. Many of the library staff will be unfamiliar with the inner workings of the technology. You should be prepared to explain any of your concepts in layman's terms, as well as know enough "jargon" to impress those in the information technology department. At the same time, avoid casual language.

Well-chosen graphics can be an excellent addition to any presentation. Charts or graphs can be made quickly and give the audience relief from slides full of text. A few *carefully chosen* and appropriate graphics can add a touch of humor to the presentation, but don't overdo it! Too many graphics on a slide can make your presentation look busy and confusing.

Be sure to stay on topic! Within the assigned topic, there will be room to explore tangents, but don't stray too far. As you develop your presentation, go back to the information you've been given. Make sure you are answering the question you have been asked to address. The audience will definitely notice if you wander too far from the topic you were assigned.

Perhaps the single most important thing to remember about giving a good presentation is that you must engage your audience. They may have already heard three other candidates discussing the same presentation topic, and you want to make sure that you stand out as exceptional. To keep your audience caring about *you* during your presentation, you need to work hard to engage them with the material. Try to incorporate active learning techniques into your session if appropriate. If you don't know much about active learning, there is a huge amount of literature published on the subject that can point you to ideas to use. Consider asking the audience to brainstorm ideas, or having them work with partners to discuss a question you pose to them—anything to get them participating so that they don't feel like they're merely being lectured at.

THINGS TO AVOID IN YOUR PRESENTATION

Before we leave the subject of preparing your presentation, perhaps it's fruitful to examine what doesn't work during a presentation. In this regard, try to avoid the following during your presentation.

Avoid Reading Your Presentation

The best presentations come across as conversations, and it's difficult to have a conversation with someone who is reading all their lines. During the presentation, don't simply read from your slides. Even worse, don't read from a paper script! This doesn't mean that you can't have what you are going to say written down in case you panic and can't form words. If you forget what you want to say, dig down deep and use your best acting skills to pretend that you're just glancing at your notes occasionally and not reading from them verbatim.

Avoid Having Text-Heavy PowerPoint Slides

Making the audience read slides full of dense information is cruel and takes their focus away from you. Do you like reading slides full of information when you're watching a presentation? If you do use slides, focus on one or two main points per slide, keeping text to a minimum. Bulleted lists are okay, but use them in moderation. "Build" the list as you make your points, rather than having a single, static slide. Make sure the font size you choose will be easy for someone in the back of the room to read. Make sure the color choices for your text and background will be suitable to either a poorly lit or a brightly lit room. Whether speaking from note cards or PowerPoint slides, a good presenter generally uses brief phrases and fills in the text during the presentation. With PowerPoint, you can add notes to each slide that print out on your own notes, but don't show to the audience. Don't be afraid to mark up your own notes with pauses, emphases, or factoids, either. Only you will see them. If you want to see examples of great slide-based presentations, check out Internet sites like Presentation Zen (www.presentationzen.com) for inspiration.

Avoid Making Assertions You Aren't Prepared to Fully Defend or Explain

You never know what questions audience members are going to ask at the conclusion of your presentation. Don't allow them the opportunity to ask anything that you won't be prepared to answer! If you make an assertion during your presentation, you can bet that someone in the audience is going to stand up at the end and ask you to defend, explain, or expand upon what you said. If you've done your research, you'll be prepared to handle that situation without a problem; if you know little about a topic, though, keep your discussion of it to a minimum so that you don't have to worry about getting hammered with questions relating to it. Familiarize yourself with the literature on your topic and you should be able to handle most questions that come your way.

Avoid Using a Software Program or Tool with Which You Aren't Comfortable

We've witnessed candidates begin their presentation by saying they've never used PowerPoint and asking the audience to "bear with them" as they "figure it out." This is a mistake on multiple levels. First and foremost, if you don't have experience using a piece of software that most in our profession would consider a basic tool, do not admit to it unless you are specifically asked about your experience with it. Second, if you decide to use a piece of software or a database during your presentation, make sure that you practice using it beforehand so that you project yourself as polished and capable. You don't have to use all of the bells and whistles, but you should be able to put together a basic presentation and move smoothly between it and your other screens.

Murphy's Law applies with deadly force to presentations. A live demonstration of the resource is great, but be prepared for the worst to happen. Always "can" your demonstration using screen captures so that if something goes terribly wrong with the Internet connection during your presentation, you can proceed without missing a beat. While screen captures are not as good as the real thing, they sure beat making your audience wait while the computer technician tries to reestablish the connection. Even worse is the embarrassment of not having a demonstration at all. Using screen captures shows your potential employer that you are prepared for these possibilities. Make sure you get *all* the necessary screen captures to demonstrate the entire process of what you are showing your audience. Even if you only stop on a screen for an instant, the audience will need a capture of each click you make.

Don't forget to make double or even triple backups of your presentation. Save a copy to a flash drive or on compact disc—even better, save a copy on one of each. Carry these with you on the plane to avoid the possibility of their being lost should there be a mishap with your checked baggage. When you're finished tweaking the slides, send a copy of your presentation files to yourself by e-mail. If all else fails, you should be able to download the e-mail version to the computer you'll be using for your presentation. Of course, be sure that you can get to your e-mail remotely on the Internet if you are going to rely on this method. If you don't already have one, now might be a good time to set up an e-mail account on one of the free e-mail servers available on the Web.

In the end, there may be just one thing to keep in mind when it comes to putting a great presentation together: "Present unto others as you would have them present unto you." You don't want to sit through a boring, uninspired presentation—neither does anyone at the institution interviewing you. If you've prepared in advance, you should have no problem giving an insightful and thoughtful presentation that your audience will remember.

ENSURING YOU HAVE WHAT
YOU NEED TO PRESENT

Before you head off to the interview, check with your contact at the institution to be sure that you'll have what you need upon your arrival. A computer and projector are standard equipment for interview presentations, but it never hurts to double-check that they will be available. Will you need other equipment? Will you need speakers? Make sure you let your contact know of any special needs in advance of presentation day. A remote "clicker" to advance the slides is useful and gives you freedom to move about during the presentation. You should ask if one is available, or check to see whether your school or current employer has one you can borrow. Will you want a podium? Some speakers prefer to use a podium, while others prefer to work without one.

Will you be using a microphone? Is one available? If your voice doesn't project well, you should request one. If you're not used to using a microphone, try to get your hands on one beforehand so that you can get some practice. Are you accustomed to your "microphone voice"? If you've never heard yourself broadcast over a public address system before, you may not recognize your own voice! Everyone's voice sounds different over a set of speakers from what they hear inside their own head.

Make sure you will have the correct version of your presentation software and any other software you will need. Remember, some newer software releases are not backwards-compatible. If you've used the latest version of a program to prepare your presentation, some of the newest features may not "translate" to the version you have available on presentation day. If you are using PowerPoint, there is a free viewer available from Microsoft that will let you project and print your presentation, but not edit it (Google "PowerPoint viewer" to be taken to the Microsoft download page). The viewer is small enough to fit on your flash drive with your presentation.

Make sure you ask your contact about Mac vs. PC. The morning of the presentation is not the time to worry about incompatible hardware! For better or worse, PCs are becoming the industry standard, so Mac users are more likely to need to arrange for appropriate equipment. Many libraries prefer Macs, however, so PC users should not necessarily assume that a PC will be available. You can always avoid the issue entirely by taking your own laptop with you. If you are going to rely on your own computer, however, make sure you know how to connect it to projection equipment and which keystrokes you must hit in order to get your presentation to actually project.

Are you planning a live demonstration? Will you need a live Internet connection? Be sure to ask about these things well beforehand. Make sure your examples work and that they demonstrate what you want them to show. When you get to the presentation location, run through your examples again quickly before the audience arrives in order to be sure they work on the local library's version of the resource, especially if the search platform is different. Many databases are available on multiple host platforms, so be sure you know what is being used at the interviewing library and how to use it.

WHAT TO EXPECT BEFORE, DURING, AND AFTER THE PRESENTATION

You should receive a schedule for the day of the interview before you arrive on campus. Generally, search committees try to schedule the presentation around mid-morning. Sometimes, though, the only time to schedule it is right after lunch or even toward the end of the day. Make sure you plan your own energy level to be at a personal best at presentation time.

You will typically be given some time right before your presentation to set up and get yourself ready. Make sure you have water handy. Use the bathroom! Even if you don't think you need to, go. At least use the time to make sure your appearance is in order and there are no remnants of lunch in your teeth. (Audiences generally don't worry as much about a candidate's appearance as the candidate does, but a check to reassure yourself doesn't hurt.) Now, take a couple of deep breaths. You can do this!

You've developed an excellent presentation and you've practiced on your friends, so there's nothing to worry about, right? Stage fright, or performance anxiety, happens to everyone—even to the most experienced speakers—from time to time. A survey reported by Peter Watson in the *Sunday Times* on October 7, 1973, listed fear of "speaking before a group" as the *number one* fear among those surveyed (41 percent), higher even than fear of flying or of death itself! "Speaking in public" tops another list of phobias published in *Health* magazine.[1] There's a lot riding on this presentation, so it's natural to be anxious. It's probably little consolation to the novice speaker to say that it generally gets easier with practice, but it does. Usually.

There is a large amount of literature published on stage fright and many theories about its causes. Regardless of the theory, there is general agreement that it includes psychological, physiological, and behavioral components and all are present to varying degrees. There is disagreement as to how much learning and innate biology respectively contribute to stage fright. There are things you can do to reduce your stage fright, but you're probably not going to eliminate it completely.

On The Day, you'll be given a little time before the audience arrives to familiarize yourself with the equipment you'll be using. Use it to your advantage. Stage fright comes from a feeling of being out of control, so control those things that you can. Bring up your presentation and run through a couple of slides to be sure all of the features work. If you have animations or embedded material in the slides, make sure they work on the new system. Make sure the Internet is working, both at the local institution and at the websites you plan to visit. Make sure you know how to move through the slides, either with the keyboard or the remote clicker.

One of the best ways to avoid stage fright is to know your material. This means *practice!* Run through your presentation *at least* once in its entirety before you leave for the interview. This will give you a sense of the time your presentation will take, so that you can be more or less within the allotted time frame. It also reassures you that you can make it all the way through. If you can, practice with a small group of friends who can give you experience speaking in front of a friendly audience and provide constructive feedback on your presentation. If they're very familiar with the topic, ask them to try to listen with "fresh" ears for jargon or faulty logic on your part. Ask them to be brutally honest. "It was great" doesn't really help you. Ask someone to count the number of times you say "um" and note any other nervous habits you might unconsciously display.

Don't tweak the presentation the night before. You've done all you can, so relax. It's easier said than done, but a good night's rest goes a lot further toward warding off stage fright than staying up late obsessing over it. Take a warm bath, watch a movie in the hotel room, or read something totally off topic to take your mind off of tomorrow.

Just before the presentation is also an excellent time to give yourself some positive self-reinforcement. If you go in with a confident attitude—I can *do* this!—you stand a much better chance of having a successful presentation. Your confidence will also make a good impression on your host as you get your presentation set up, which may help in the search committee's deliberations.

Your opening is the most important part of your presentation. It is your only chance to make a first impression on your audience. Stage fright usually peaks, however, in the moments just before and just after you start speaking. Anticipate this and be prepared. Use this initial period of stage fright to energize yourself for your presentation. A tasteful joke or a relevant personal anecdote is a good way to get the audience on your side.

There are a number of traditional tricks to reduce stage fright. The article by Auerbach gives excellent, concrete advice for handling stage fright both before and after the presentation.[2] Some tricks work and some don't. Do *not* imagine the audience in their underwear—librarians are generally not former underwear models! Instead, imagine that you're speaking to those friends on whom you practiced earlier. If you find your hands shaking, stand behind the podium and hold onto it. If you shake so much that the podium rattles, take a few more deep breaths! Taking a sip of water is another way to buy yourself a little time and help yourself relax.

During the presentation, movement is often a good thing, but make your movements natural. Once you've gotten over any initial panic, relax your vise-like grip on the podium and move around the area. Point to something on the screen if it seems appropriate. This has the added benefit of directing attention toward what you are trying to say and away from you.

Eye contact is important in any presentation. It helps put the audience on your side. Try not to stare at the wall behind the audience or blankly into space. Attempt to make eye contact with everyone in the audience at least once during your presentation. You should hold eye contact with a person for about 3–5 seconds, then move on. If you are feeling anxious, once you've found a "friendly" face, return to it occasionally throughout the presentation but don't look at them to the exclusion of everyone else in your audience. You will feel more like you're talking to one person than to a group, and a friend, at that.

Vary your voice's pitch, speed, and tone. Use pauses to punctuate your thoughts. A soft voice highlights your points. The most important parts of your presentation are the beginning and the end. Be energetic in the introduction. Use a strong voice. At the conclusion, a soft voice will make the audience "hang on your every word." Try to end softly, but without trailing off. Practice speaking slowly. Most people talk more quickly when they are nervous as they frantically try to get through their presentation and sit down. Taking a few breaths along the way not only calms you but may help slow you down as well.

It's hard to say how many people will be attending your presentation, even based on the size of the institution. They are taking valuable time away from their duties, so thank them for coming. Busy schedules make it difficult for folks to stay at your presentation the entire time. They may have to leave during the presentation to attend another meeting or sit on the desk, so don't be offended—or thrown off—if they come and go during the presentation.

You are being graded by each of the audience members, which can only add to your level of anxiety. This is your one chance to make a good impression on the entire organization. They will all have been provided with a copy of your resume or vita. They will know enough about you to be dangerous! They will likely have evaluation sheets that they will turn in to the search committee after your presentation, so you need to impress them all, not just the search committee.

Remember, though, that the audience *wants* you to succeed, or you wouldn't have been asked to the on-site interview. They know you're nervous, so most will give you the benefit of the doubt. They are looking to see how you stay on topic and if you can make it through the presentation without making a fatal faux pas. If instruction is part of the job description, they may be looking to see how you would perform in front of a class. *How* you present is at least as important as *what* you present.

You probably don't know these people or the local culture, so avoid topics, illustrations, or humor that might be offensive to someone in the audience. Taking your clothes off during a presentation (hey, it happens—we've seen it!) is not generally considered good form.

After the presentation, there will be time for questions. *Lots and lots* of questions. Some examples of questions that have come up in real interview presentations are given in figure 8.1.

There are things that can't be asked for legal reasons. You can't legally be asked any question that would indicate any of those equal opportunity protections, such as age, religion, marital status, or sexual orientation (among other things). Nor should you volunteer such information, besides what's in your resume or vita. The questions should relate to the activities of the job.

Lots of questions are a good sign; a lack of questions could be a bad sign. You will probably be asked to expand on some of the things you said in your presentation, which is why you don't want to bring anything up during the presentation that you cannot fully explain later. If the moderator doesn't ask the questioners to introduce themselves and their function in the organization, ask them yourself. Unless you're a real people person you won't remember everyone, but it will give you a context for your answer. If you can remember a few names and use them, it leaves an extremely positive impression on everyone present.

Don't ramble, and don't blurt answers. If you're having trouble with a question, don't be afraid to take a moment to think. A legitimate comment like "That's an excellent question. Let me think about it for a moment" will not be frowned upon (unless you tell the audience you need to think about every single question posed to you). You will be seen as someone who takes the time to work through a difficult question. If you're having real trouble with a question, try saying "I'm going to have to think about that and get back to you" to buy yourself some time, with the added benefit that there probably *won't* be time to get back to it! Think about an answer, anyway, in case you run into the speaker in another context later on.

Try to avoid a simple "yes or no" answer, even to questions that seem to require one. These are often "trap" questions. Always try to give a balanced

FIGURE **8.1**

Sample questions from the audience

Candidates should be prepared to answer a large variety of questions from the audience during the presentation portion of their interview. We've included a list of some of the most common questions we've heard during our own experiences here.

What part of this job appeals to you most? Least?

Can you describe your training or experience in bibliographic instruction/collection development/reference/electronic resources?

How do you keep current in your field?

How do you handle competing priorities?

Please describe a situation where you demonstrated leadership/initiative/creativity.

What can you bring to this position that other candidates may not?

Please describe your experience working with patrons from diverse backgrounds.

What would be your top priority if you were hired for this position?

(For tenure-track positions) What areas of research would you like to pursue?

How do you deal with frustrated patrons?

When working on a team for a project, what role do you generally play?

What are your professional goals for one year? Five years? Ten years?

Describe yourself in three adjectives.

What would you feel is your weakest area with respect to this job? [Caution: trap!!! Also worded as: In what part of the job do you think you would need the most training?]

In twenty-five words or less, please describe how you would effectively address the issues of race, class, and gender in issues of library accessibility.

What experience do you have with government documents? How do you see them fitting into your work environment? [Even if you aren't applying for a gov docs job, the gov docs librarian will ask this one!]

Please tell us about your professional affiliations or involvement with professional organizations.

answer, especially to a question that seems like a "trap" or one that might portray you in a negative light. If possible, give a brief example from personal experience.

Be sure to ask if your response answered the question and satisfied the questioner. Keep track of multipart questions. If you can do this mentally, fine. If not, don't be afraid to take notes. Saying truthfully, "I'm writing this down to make sure that I answer all parts of your question," gives a positive impression.

You will probably be asked if you have questions for the audience. Again, it's a bad sign if you don't. Have a few questions prepared in advance that you can ask the audience members. You should already have reviewed the library's website and that of the greater institution. These should provide you with enough fodder for plenty of questions. Be sure you don't ask questions on topics that are readily apparent on the institutional website—it *will* be noted! Some additional question suggestions are also provided in figure 8.2.

After the presentation, thank the audience for their time. You'll probably be mentally exhausted and won't want to talk to anyone for a week, but people will come up to greet you or introduce themselves. Be polite, even if you've temporarily turned your mind off. If you are offered the position, and they mention it later, you can always say (truthfully) that "I'm sorry, there were so many people that day, it's hard to remember everyone." You're probably ready for a nap, but there's more interview left. Part of the interview process is proving that you can be delightful, intelligent, witty, and lively even when you're totally exhausted.

It all sounds a little daunting, right? It doesn't have to be. If you know your material and know your audience, your presentation should be a successful one. It may not go perfectly (and you shouldn't expect it to), but if you've done your homework, you should survive relatively happy and unscathed. And don't forget that the reason you were invited to interview in the first place is because the search committee saw potential in you—they are interested in what you have to say. If you have any doubts at all after preparing for this part of the interview experience, keep it in mind that the search committee wants you to succeed, too.

ADDITIONAL RESOURCES

Rob Abernathy and Mark Reardon, *Hot Tips for Speakers: 25 Surefire Ways to Engage and Captivate Any Group or Audience* (Tucson, AZ: Zephyr, 2002).

Jeremiah J. Sullivan, "Six Hundred Interviews Later," *ABCA Bulletin* 43, no. 1 (1980): 2–5.

FIGURE **8.2**

Sample questions for the audience

Candidates should be prepared with a list of questions for the audience after the presentation portion of their interview. We've included some sample questions here.

What's the biggest challenge currently being faced by this library system?

Why do you like working here?

What do you think are this library system's best qualities?

Where do you see this organization in five years?

Does the library provide a formal or informal mentoring program for new librarians? (This is valuable for both tenure-track and non–tenure-track positions.)

What kind of support does the library provide for professional development, such as conference travel?

Could you describe the relationship between the library and the departmental faculty in the university?

For those of you who have been here at least ten years, what keeps you here?

I noticed a really interesting [some prominent object in the library or on the website] . . . Could someone tell me the story behind it?

Notes

1. Cassandra Wrightson, "America's Greatest Fears," *Health* 12, no. 1 (1998): 45.
2. Alan Auerbach, "Self-Administered Treatments of Public Speaking Anxiety," *Personnel and Guidance Journal* 60, no. 2 (1981): 106–9.

CHAPTER 9

JOB OFFERS, NEGOTIATIONS, AND ALL THE WONDERFUL THINGS YOU CAN ASK FOR!

Evangela Q. Oates and Teresa Y. Neely

TIME TO NEGOTIATE

Once you've prepared your packet and applied for the job, survived the telephone interview, and landed and aced the on-site job interview, the next step is the job offer, or, possibly, notification that you were not selected. Hopefully, it will be the former, and if so, it is officially time for negotiations! You have arrived at one of the most important, if not *the* most important, parts of the interview process. During this process, you should be careful not to shortchange yourself by selling yourself and your skills short. However, it is also important to find balance and to not exaggerate your worth for a particular position.

This chapter is not intended to discuss the fine art of negotiating; rather, its purpose is to share information about the types of things you can and should negotiate for. Most individuals think of salary as the biggest negotiation point, and in many professions, it may very well be. In higher education, however, there are other items you can negotiate for that can prove to be as valuable as salary for you and your work life at your new job.

At its simplest, negotiation can be defined as a discussion or dialogue between at least two parties to resolve an issue or to come to an agreement on issues. In terms of academic library jobs and for the purpose of this chapter, we define negotiating as the conversation you have with the hiring officer, dean or director, or possibly the provost, *after* you are offered the position. Even if a salary or salary range is included in the job description and comes up in conversation, it is not appropriate to begin negotiating at that time. Wait until you have actually received an offer before you begin negotiating any particular point.[1] As was indicated in chapter 2, some job ads do not include a minimum salary or salary range. Although it is inappropriate to attempt salary *negotiations* prior to a job offer, it is entirely appropriate to *inquire* about the salary or salary range, preferably to the appropriate university or library official. It is important for job seekers to have some idea about the salary for a particular position, and if the entire interview is conducted without mentioning it, then by all means, ask.

When an offer has been made, this is the opportunity for the candidate to tell the organization what she believes she is worth in terms of financial compensation and the resources she will need in order to be successful. Who you negotiate with is highly dependent upon the institution and position you have just been offered. At the University of New Mexico University Libraries, if offered a position, your negotiations would be with the dean.

Once you have received a job offer, it's a good idea to take some time to think things through.[2] Although you may be mere weeks away from graduating and being ready to move on, you want to make sure this position is a good match for you and that you really do want to pick up and move, say, 1,633 miles (and two time zones) away from your friends and family for your first job, as author Neely did for her first professional position in librarianship.

Any position worth accepting is one that will give you some time to make the decision. If you are expected to make the decision on the spot or in a couple of days, consider this as an example of how things are done at that institution and determine if that is the kind of work environment you want to voluntarily sign up for. I (Neely) was once offered a position where one of the three candidates they had invited to campus dropped out of the search the day I was interviewing on-site. In fact, we found this out during lunch. In any case, I was offered the position on a Friday, and although they told me I was their first choice, they added that they needed my response by Monday because their second choice (the remaining candidate) had a competing job offer and they didn't want to lose her. Needless to say, this wasn't a very difficult decision for me to make, and I was ready on Monday morning to decline the offer so they could have what appeared to me to be their "real" first choice. As an aside, it is absolutely legal and okay to turn down a job offer. You may learn things during the on-site interview that may change your mind, so if things don't feel right or you know this is not going to be a good fit, by all means, just say no.

Being creative in negotiating can also be beneficial. The previously mentioned access services librarian search resulted in the hiring of a candidate who, in the process of salary negotiations, offered to skip a scheduled interview at another institution in exchange for an increase in salary. She was the top candidate, her negotiations were successful, and she began work on February 15, 2010!

Many individuals decide not to negotiate because of fear. "People are afraid the job offer will be rescinded if they try to negotiate. They don't understand that some negotiating is expected to take place."[3] Dick Gaither, the president of Job Search Training Systems Inc., says that "job seekers need to understand a few realities about the hiring and negotiation process. First, if you don't ask for more, you will never get more. Even if you don't get everything you want, getting a little bit of something is better than getting a whole lot of nothing. If you end up with nothing, you've lost nothing." He continues and notes that "if they can't give you any more money, negotiate for things that you'd spend money for, things that make you a more valuable employee, things that enhance your quality of life or things that can be turned into money later. Examples of things you would spend money for are job-related tools, including computers and software, allowances for clothing, parking, gas, and day care."[4] Clearly academic libraries, unless unusually generous, will not provide allowances for clothing, gas, or day care. However, as an employee, you may be eligible to use a campus-sponsored day care center, or perhaps the institution's parking and transportation service has a commitment to sustainability and offers a ride-sharing program or loans bicycles or electric cars.[5] The benefits in the form of discounted services that are available to employees at the University of New Mexico include discounts for on-campus services (occupational health services, health education classes, recreational services); discounts for off-campus opportunities, such as tickets to a local amusement park and to Sea World; discounts on memberships at local gyms and the AAA; discounts for airport parking, therapeutic services, cell phone services for major providers (Verizon, Sprint, and T-Mobile); discounts for child care services; discounts on cars from Ford and services from Jiffy Lube; and rebates on the purchase of a new home.[6] Parking on college campuses can be very competitive and expensive, and negotiating for a parking lot close to your new job location may be an option.

Some of the negotiable items that Gaither lists are "things that make you more valuable as an employee." These things might "include an educational allowance, or ongoing and on-the-job-training (preferably in Hawaii)." One of the great things about working in an academic institution are the fringe benefits which, in addition to medical contributions, might include the opportunity to take courses or pursue a degree. On-the-job training is one of those things that you shouldn't have to negotiate for, because such training may be necessary for you to do your job. However, highly specialized training or workshops are absolutely negotiable. "Quality-of-life items include reduced travel, a day of telecommuting, or a work schedule that fits around family needs."[7] These items are absolutely negotiable as well. There is no guarantee you will be successful in your negotiations, but you need to take your home life into consideration as you move into this new work life. If your previous position allowed you to use flex time or work around your child care or other family issues, there is no reason to believe your new job won't do so as well, and there is no reason not to ask about this.

A CIO.com survey found the following when it asked its readers, chief information officers, and other IT leaders, "What do you ask for during job negotiations?"

- Salary—asked for by 83 percent
- Bonuses—asked for by 56 percent
- Vacation/time off (paid or unpaid)—asked for by 48 percent
- Relocation expenses—asked for by 28 percent
- Flex time—asked for by 27 percent
- Education and training—asked for by 24 percent
- Stock options—asked for by 24 percent
- Health care (medical, dental, vision)—asked for by 20 percent
- Perks (free parking, company car)—asked for by 18 percent
- Severance package—asked for by 12 percent[8]

With the exception of bonuses, stock options, and perhaps a severance package, particularly for beginning librarians, this is a pretty good list of negotiable items to keep in mind. Other items that could be on your list but are not addressed here in detail include:

- accommodations for a disability or health condition
- ergonomic keyboard, chair, and footrest
- tuition remission benefits extended to partner or spouse and/or children
- same sex partner/domestic partner benefits

These first four items may be required or denied under law, particularly the last ones, depending on the laws of the state where you are applying, but that doesn't mean they can't be on your list of things to inquire about. Other items that could be on your list include:

- life insurance
- mentoring programs

- annual leave, sick leave, professional leave, research leave
- gym membership, health support programs and classes

While you're off thinking about accepting the position and what that entails, your thoughts should also turn to your needs, the foremost of which will probably be salary. Salary is important because you've likely been a struggling (poor) graduate student for a while, and you're ready to upgrade from that graduate student assistant's salary to a position with benefits and a retirement package! However, research on job satisfaction among librarians reveals that salary is not the most important issue.[9] In fact, a 2007 *Library Journal* survey found that although library workers were dissatisfied with salaries and library funding, 93 percent of respondents reported they were "satisfied" or "very satisfied" with their current positions.[10] But keeping things in perspective, the folks participating in these surveys probably were already gainfully employed!

SHOW ME THE MONEY (SALARY)

It is natural that one would want to be compensated well for one's work. In turn, most credible organizations try to ensure that their employees have good salaries, including a benefits package, that are comparable to the industry and the experience of those in the same position. Salary books or the university budget with positions listed with salaries are generally available in libraries at state institutions. These can certainly be a resource when you're trying to negotiate a salary. However, there is research which suggests that "gender differences in pay outcomes reflect subtle differences in the ways that men and women think about pay and behave during the recruitment and hiring period when pay is open to negotiation."[11] So giving some thought to your expectations for salary, and your negotiation strategies, would be good things to keep in mind prior to negotiations. Additionally, keep in mind that experience and knowledge, along with whether the position is tenure or non-tenure track, whether the rank is an assistant or associate professor, lecturer or instructor, contract or temporary, and full-time versus part-time, are all considerations in determining salaries.

Here are a few things to consider when navigating the unknown of salary negotiation. First, one should consider the location of the position. Sure, you've worked in Los Angeles for the last five years, but it is very unlikely that you will be able to get the same salary in Mobile, Alabama. You may find dramatic differences in salaries based on the region of the country. There are multiple issues to take into consideration and a variety of sources you should consult before giving a figure to the person with whom you are negotiating. Organizations such as the ALA have resources that list salary information in reference to location/geographic region, type of library, position, and years of experience.[12] These could be very helpful in determining how much others are being paid in comparable positions with similar years of experience. Comparing job ads with similar requirements is also a helpful exercise.

Additionally, there are numerous cost-of-living calculators via the Internet that will give you the difference in the cost of living in different U.S. cities, states, and other countries. Many of these calculators will estimate the difference you may pay in housing, energy, food, health, and transportation. These calculators are essential tools to use prior to negotiation. It is important that you include this type of information in your research to make a stronger case for your desired salary. If you attempt to negotiate a salary that is not based on research, you could actually get less than you deserve. Researching the market empowers you as a new employee.

Failing to negotiate can end up being more costly than you realized, and conversely, negotiating a seemingly small increase in base salary can pay off over the long term. "Miranda, a recent Ph.D. in the social sciences, negotiated a 6-percent increase in salary over what her new department initially offered her, from $49,000 a year to $52,000. If we assume she enjoys a 30-year career and receives annual raises of 3 percent, the extra salary that she negotiated would translate into an additional $143,000 over what she would have earned without negotiating."[13]

READY, SET, GO!

When will you start? Be realistic! Will you really be able to move all of your belongings across the country within a week? You should be reasonable yet honest about the length of the transition between your current life and your new life as an employed librarian. Remember, you don't have to start when they say they want you to. The hiring institution understands that there are planned vacations and purchased plane tickets and such. Make sure you are honest about when you can actually begin. They will probably be more understanding than you think. They would rather you come prepared and refreshed than unprepared and frazzled. Once you decide on a date, if circumstances arise that force you to change the date, be sure to notify them immediately. They should be informed of any deviations in your plans, since they will be making preparations of their own. If you are possibly holding out for another position, then you should let them know right away, during negotiations and *before* you sign a contract. If you are as good as they think you are, they will understand if you have another interview and need more time to make your decision. Just don't make them wait forever. The library world is small and you would not want to jeopardize your reputation or future employment by trying to play one organization off against another.

WELL, WE'RE MOVING ON UP, TO THE EAST SIDE

Moving can be a stressful time, so it is best to nail down the details about who will be paying for your move during negotiation. You should ask about the type of assistance they offer for moving. Don't be deterred if they tell you they've never done this before. At a previous position, one of the authors of this chapter asked about moving expenses and was told by her potential boss (the library director) that even he had not received moving expenses when he went to work there. Luckily times had changed, because when asked, the provost agreed to pay moving expenses.

There are different ways in which organizations handle providing moving assistance to newly hired persons. Most will quote you a certain amount for the move, although the criteria for allotment will differ from organization to organization and for positions at different levels. For the most part, this means that you will have to pay out of pocket all expenses to move you and your possessions, and you will be reimbursed for your expenses once you have provided receipts of expenses incurred. It will be your responsibility to present these receipts within the time frame stipulated. Many colleges and universities may have a moving company they already work with, which makes it fairly easy for you to work directly with the company and avoid the need for up-front out-of-pocket expenses; nevertheless, you will need to stay within the amount quoted and agreed upon for the move. If your move exceeds the amount quoted, you will be responsible for any overages. And at the other end of the move, deposits for housing are not normally covered under moving expenses. This expense will rest entirely upon you. And as with any business agreement, you should get it all in writing. A final thought on support: if the organization does not, or can not, offer any help toward the move, it could be an indication of the amount of support they will be able to give you once you are there.

A JOB FOR YOUR PARTNER OR SIGNIFICANT OTHER OR HELP FINDING ONE

Although your partner or significant other may be your biggest supporter, he or she should not be mentioned in your cover letter, as noted in chapter 4 by

Sarah L. Stohr. On the other hand, your partner may be a part of your negotiation, especially if there is a vacancy for which he or she is qualified. However, depending on the type of position you are applying for, it may not be realistic to think you can negotiate a position for your partner. Regardless, it couldn't hurt to do your homework and find out what other positions the college or university is searching for, in the library or elsewhere in the organization. It can't hurt to ask your potential employer for suggestions, let them know you come as part of a team or family, and tell them about the skills your partner has, just in case they know of something that you haven't already found out in your investigation.

COMPUTERS AND SOFTWARE

In the past, asking for a laptop versus a desktop may have caused an eyebrow or two to rise at the audacity of such. Today, they are so common that your new employer may ask which you prefer. If you are not asked, it is still acceptable to let your employer know your preferences. As you morph from a struggling graduate student, you may or may not have a computer of your own at home. A benefit you may use in your request for, say, a laptop is the ability to work from home and to stay connected while attending conferences and workshops. Efficiency is key when making a case for the kind of machine you will be using.

The second part of this is the software and hardware you may need. If you will need any specialized software or hardware in addition to the computer itself to carry out your duties, you must make it known during negotiations. This will give the hiring institution time to acquire the machine and outfit it so that it will be available to you on your first day of work. You must remember that your performance evaluation will be based on your librarianship, which is generally defined as how well you do your job. You must ask for the tools that will enable you to be successful in completing those duties. For example, let's say that you will be responsible for creating online tutorials. In order to do this, you will need the appropriate software to complete the task; and as the expert, you are the best person to know what software you will need to do this successfully. Additionally, you might also ask if there are any other software products that they already have licenses for that may be helpful to you. And by all means, ask what comes standard on all employee computers. Depending on the nature of your position, you may be able to negotiate for items such as high-speed Internet access and a web cam, as well as any external hard drives or other peripherals you may need, such as color printing and having a printer in your office, rather than using a common printer/copier.

And finally, do not make assumptions about what your new workplace "should" have. Upon arriving for her first day at work, one of the authors of this chapter complained that the computer she had been assigned was the slowest ever. Unfortunately, one of the library technology folks was nearby, overheard this remark, and became upset, almost as if it was his personal computer she was bad-mouthing. He said, "This is one of the best computers in the library." She knew then she was "not in Kansas anymore"!

Outside of negotiating for a laptop versus a desktop, there are some things that may be due to you as an employee. These are not negotiable items, but are included here as a reminder to you to ask so you know the lay of the land. Make sure you

- have up-to-date, current software versions and document readers
- know what you can and cannot do to the computer on your desk. Can I download iTunes and Kodak applications myself?
- know what security measures are in place. If it's a laptop, is there a security lock? Can I take it home with me or does it have to stay here all the time? If I can take it home, is there a form I need to fill out first? Is there a chip or some other type of tracking device in case it is stolen?
- Do they have any Mac computers, or does everyone use a PC?
- Is there remote access? Will I be able to access my files remotely if I'm working from home or at the reference desk down the hall from my office?

Knowing the answers to these questions is essential to the way many of us work today.

PROFESSIONAL DEVELOPMENT: WORKSHOPS AND CONFERENCES

Support for professional development is crucial to your development as a librarian and a professional; whether you are an instructor or lecturer or are all the way up there as an administrator, the opportunity for additional training is essential. Although most organizations do not pay for membership in professional organizations, depending on the budget, they may pay some expenses toward attending conferences and workshops. This will vary largely by organization. You should ask about the amount of support you will receive for professional development. Some organizations assign professional development funding based on status (tenured vs. nontenured), or by the participant's level of involvement in the organization or at the conference (committee work, presentation, etc.). Meals, transportation, lodging, and registration fees are sometimes covered as well; however, you may have to pay some or most of the expenses yourself. In fact, it is not uncommon for librarians to pay for conferences entirely out of pocket.

Professional development expenses can occur in the form of specialized conferences or workshops that are critical to your job duties. Sometimes there is additional funding, outside of the general professional development budget, available for attending specialized conferences, specifically those where you will be representing your institution. It is appropriate to negotiate for support for events such as these.

DAILY WORK SCHEDULE

For most of the items in this chapter, you will need to negotiate directly with the hiring officer; however, your daily work schedule is something that should be negotiated with input from your direct supervisor. The last thing you want is for your supervisor to find out from you that the deal you cut with the dean or provost allows you to work from home one day a week, or that you won't be working nights or weekend reference shifts during your first six months!

Negotiating a daily work schedule can and should take into consideration your home life needs as well as your work needs and priorities as mentioned previously in this chapter. Applying for a position that requires you to be on-site five days a week during business hours, and then asking to work from home one day a week, might not be the best negotiating strategy.

PARKING

Negotiating parking can be tricky and iffy. Either you can or you can't. Parking on campuses these days is at a premium and it may be a non-issue, but it can't hurt to ask. You may be dealing with someone who can actually pull those strings and get you that parking pass for the premium spot, or at least a spot on campus where you don't have to be bused in!

RESEARCH LEAVE

Time away for research is not a luxury vacation, as those who are not required to publish might think, but an additional responsibility, especially for those who are expected to publish as part of their appointment. For many professionals, time is as important as money and research leave is right up there at the top. Having uninterrupted time away from day-to-day duties to conduct research and write is a valuable commodity, and too few professionals take advantage of this opportunity. Depending on the position you are applying for, it should absolutely be discussed during negotiations. Tenured and tenure-track faculty are generally granted research leave; thus, if this is not a given for the position you have applied for, ask for it, and make the case why you need this time away. Do you have a strong publication record, or are you looking to become published? Are you completing a degree and need time away to finish writing the dissertation or thesis, but you took a job because you have a fondness for food, clothing, and shelter? All these things come into play at negotiation time. Remember, if you don't ask, then you don't get. Even if it's only an extra few days tacked on to spring break, it's time you otherwise would have been obliged to give to the office and job duties.

Tenured and tenure-track positions are not the only reason one may need to take time away for research. Are you writing a grant? Or working with colleagues from other institutions on a proposal? These are legitimate grounds for requesting research leave. Something else to think about is how else the organization can support your research. How much is it going to cost to copy, print, and overnight your book manuscript? You may not have a dollar amount, but it is still important to come to an agreement about the level of support they can and will offer.

In addition to research leave, you might also consider negotiating time to work from home. Will you be sharing an office with someone or working in a cubicle with no ceiling and no door? Perhaps your home office is better equipped than the one your new employer will provide. If this is the case, it might be ideal for you to ask about the possibilities of working from home, or working four ten-hour days per week, particularly if your home office includes high-speed Internet, scanning, faxing, printing, copying, and e-mailing capabilities, a web cam, and chat software to ensure you are well connected with your colleagues at the office.

SABBATICALS

Hand in hand with research leave are sabbaticals for tenured faculty. At most institutions, tenured faculty are eligible to apply for a sabbatical every six years. For example, at the University of New Mexico, six-month sabbaticals are taken with full salary, and one-year sabbaticals with half salary. These guidelines, however, will vary according to institution and local practices. Generally, you apply for a sabbatical by submitting an application which spells out what you will be doing while you are away, and also, who will be doing what you do while you're away. It is doubtful that you will be granted a sabbatical to spend time with your friends like the television show *Friends'* character Ross Geller, who spent his sabbatical hanging out with his friends. Instead, you will have to produce a viable scholarly-based proposal and, upon your return, evidence of the implementation of the proposal and the resulting research or whatever you said you would do in the proposal.

In general, sabbaticals are not automatic and not a right, but a privilege. Unfortunately, in 2008 sabbaticals were suspended at the University of Georgia due to budget restraints, triggering concerns about faculty morale and the ability of the university to attract new faculty.[14] There can also be backlash to one's sabbatical. In her article "Sabbatical Planning: Lessons Learned the Hard Way," published in the *Chronicle of Higher Education,* Meg Robbins told the rather traumatic story of her husband's sabbatical, in which they ended up taking a trip around the world after multiple mishaps and selling both of their cars. After reading Robbins's article on her sabbatical, library director Philip J. Tramdack wrote a letter to the editor pointing out the "ill-timed, in-very-bad-taste-article" and the ill effects of the economy on the people and the town of New Castle, Pennsylvania. He became outraged "thinking about the problems of everyday people . . . who have no job, no education, no health care, no prospects, and no hope."[15] Depending on the state of the economy in your proposed new city and new workplace, I would heed the advice of Tramdack: "My advice to Ms. Robbins, who suggests that you not tell your friends about your planned junket abroad because they will be 'unkindly envious,' is: Don't write articles in national academic newspapers about your travails, either."[16]

Given the tough economic times these days, there is not enough money to grant paid leaves which may require the hiring of temporary employees to cover the work while faculty are on leave. If you are in a position to negotiate sabbaticals, meaning they really want you or you have proven yourself at previous institutions and have a significant record of scholarship, you might be able to negotiate applying for sabbatical a year or so earlier than the local practice. Try to be practical and realistic in your requests, given any local issues. If in doubt of how things are, ask.

KNOW THE DIFFERENCE BETWEEN THINGS THAT ARE NEGOTIABLE AND THINGS YOU ARE DUE AS A HIRE

One of the smartest things you can do is have an understanding of what you are worth and what makes you unique, and also, what you are due by virtue of being employed by a particular organization. For example, you should expect a computer in your work as a librarian, but, as noted above, you can negotiate what kind of computer you get. In terms of office space, depending on work expectations, you are due some kind of space with a desk and a modicum of privacy, but this will vary widely from institution to institution. Some universities actually have guidelines on what type of space employees are due based on their position type and title. For example, the University of New Mexico's policy 5200, "Allocation and assignment of space," addresses unallocated university space, space for classrooms and departments, and quantities of space, which provides a guideline on the size of office space.[17]

You can certainly negotiate for office space with no office mate or some other amenities, but be aware that your negotiations might backfire, particularly if everyone has an office mate except you. We recently completed on-site interviews for the access services librarian position at UNM, where the office for the lucky candidate was spruced up and pointed out in the tour of the facility, so if that individual decides she doesn't want to live next door to her new boss, she will at least have that information about where we were going to put her to take into her negotiations with us. Absolutely ask to see the space they intend to house you in if you are interviewing on-site. Overall, you want to make sure you have a space that allows you to do your work. If that space is a tight fit for one person and you're the outreach librarian or liaison to an academic department that's very active in the library, you will probably need an office with a door and enough space to include more than one chair for consultative purposes.

Business cards are essential and something you are due, particularly if you do outreach, instruction, and public service work. However, if business cards aren't mentioned, please do ask. Given these tough economic times, also recognize that the hiring organization may have resorted to cutting expenses, such as supplies, and perhaps business cards. In any event, it's nice to know what the state of operations is at this potential place of employment.

E-mail is a critical thing to have in most professional jobs these days, and you should have your e-mail account set up, if at all possible, prior to your arrival. Likewise, a telephone with a long distance code and voice mail. All these things cost money, and you need to make sure you ask in advance about them. You will probably have a working phone on your desk and be issued a long distance code because all library users are not local, and at some point you will have to contact them, or a vendor. Voice mail and long distance codes may be on the chopping block during tough times, so it pays to put these on your list of things to ask about.

Benefits packages often come with health care, dental, and vision, and optionally, flexible spending accounts, though it is worth visiting the institution's human resources site to know what your options will be. Retirement plans can be researched the same way.

And finally, last but certainly not least, Get It All in Writing. The most appropriate place for this is the actual offer letter, and not the contract for employment itself. When the letter arrives, make sure all of the things that you negotiated and agreed to with the hiring agent are in that letter. If not, then contact them immediately. Also, make sure someone else at your new job knows what you have negotiated. One of the authors of this chapter negotiated a laptop and support for an upcoming conference. Unfortunately, none of this was in writing, and upon her arrival at the new job, there was that slow computer, the hiring officer was on vacation, and no one knew about the promised support for the conference scheduled for the following month.

There are lots of other things you can negotiate for in higher education that are not addressed here. Bryant and Marks remind us of things to remember when we're thinking about how to negotiate:

- Consider the offer you have in hand, and others you may have anticipated. Rank them. Realize that you can ask for more time.
- Ask for more than you expect to receive. Be willing to consider a compromise in response to your counteroffer.
- If you must, forgo one-time expenses to net greater salary increases.
- Determine your deal breakers. Be prepared to reject the offer if the terms are unacceptable to you.
- Don't fixate on one aspect of the offer. We know of a humanities Ph.D. who needed $5,000 more in salary and was willing to forgo a relocation allotment; however, the university would only increase her starting salary by $2,000. Instead, she sought additional start-up money for her office. Understand your priorities, but be flexible and open to compromise.
- Request the newly accepted terms in writing. If they are not in writing, they're not yours.

- Above all, remain calm, professional, and honest. Whether or not you join the faculty, you are likely to interact with the people you've met at future events, conferences, or even job interviews.[18]

It's a small world after all!

Notes

1. Rebecca A. Bryant and Amber Marks, "Go Ahead, Haggle," *Chronicle of Higher Education* 52, no. 12 (2005): C2–C3.
2. Ibid.
3. Corinne A. Marasco, "Negotiating an Academic Job Offer," *Chemical and Engineering News* 86, no. 3 (2008): 63–65. See also Bryant and Marks, "Go Ahead, Haggle"; and Jamie Eckle, "Career Watch," *Computerworld* 43, no. 7 (2009): 32.
4. Eckle, "Career Watch," 32.
5. University of New Mexico Parking and Transportation Services, "Alternative Transportation," http://pats.unm.edu/alternativecommute.cfm (accessed December 13, 2009).
6. University of New Mexico, Division of Human Resources, "Discounted Services," http://hr.unm.edu/benefits/discounts.php#lobocard (accessed March 14, 2010).
7. Eckle, "Career Watch," 32.
8. CIO Research, "What You Want," *CIO* 22, no. 1 (2008): 16.
9. Carolyn A. Sheehy, "Who Says It's Always Greener on the Other Side?" *American Libraries* 31, no. 8 (2000): 52–54; John N. Berry III, "Great Work, Genuine Problems," *Library Journal* 132, no. 16 (2007): 26–29. See also Teresa Y. Neely and Lorna Peterson, "Achieving Racial and Ethnic Diversity among Academic and Research Librarians: The Recruitment, Retention, and Advancement of Librarians of Color: A White Paper," Association of College and Research Libraries, 2007, www.ala.org/ala/mgrps/divs/acrl/publications/whitepapers/ACRL_AchievingRacial.pdf (accessed December 9, 2009); and Kaetrena D. Davis-Kendrick, "The African American Male Librarian: Motivational Factors in Choosing a Career in Library and Information Science," *Behavioral and Social Sciences Librarian* 28, nos. 1 and 2 (2009): 23–52, for a review of job satisfaction studies in library and information science.
10. Berry, "Great Work, Genuine Problems," 26.
11. Vickie S. Kaman and Charmine E. J. Hartel, "Gender Differences in Anticipated Pay Negotiation Strategies and Outcomes," *Journal of Business and Psychology* 9, no. 2 (1994): 183–97.
12. American Library Association, "Library Salaries Information," http://ala.org/ala/educationcareers/employment/salaries/ (accessed December 30, 2009).
13. Bryant and Marks, "Go Ahead, Haggle."

14. Robin Wilson and June Audrey Williams, "Facing State Cuts, U. of Georgia Abruptly Blocks Some Research Leaves," *Chronicle of Higher Education* 55, no. 2 (2008): A15. For similar decisions in Great Britain, see Zoë Corbyn, "Time-Off Scheme Faces the Axe as Costs Rise and Deadlines Are Missed," *Times Higher Education* no. 1856 (2008): 11.

15. Meg Robbins, "Sabbatical Planning: Lessons Learned the Hard Way," *Chronicle of Higher Education* 56, no. 3 (2009): B13.

16. Philip J. Tramdack, "Professors on Sabbatical: A Mandarin Class?" *Chronicle of Higher Education* 56, no. 6 (2009): B29.

17. University of New Mexico, University Business Policies and Procedures Manual, "Policy 5200—Allocation and Assignment of Space," www.unm.edu/~ubppm/ ubppmanual/5200.htm (accessed December 30, 2009).

18. Bryant and Marks, "Go Ahead, Haggle."

CHAPTER 10

THE EIGHT-MONTH MARATHON

From Library School to New Librarian

Silvia Lu

THE PREVIOUS CHAPTERS have accurately captured the search process at academic libraries, while offering amazing access to all of the search committee's secret deliberations and quiet frustrations. You should, at this point, be familiar with this normally mysterious process, and have a good idea as to how to best present yourself, and avoid the common mistakes made by many applicants. Each chapter represents another step toward a position in an academic library, and you are prepared for each of them. Feeling confident?

Well, I have some bad news.

Your job search timeline will look nothing like the table of contents for this book. If, and only if you are the successful candidate, will you have the opportunity to join the search committee for each step as outlined. Unless you are uniquely and universally perfect for every job for which you apply, your process will probably require you to repeat some chapters tens, if not hundreds of times, and others, just once.

Based on numbers collected by the U.S. Bureau of Labor Statistics, the average period of unemployment has increased from five months in February 2009 to seven and a half months in February 2010.[1] Add an additional month to account for your disadvantage as a new graduate without professional experience, and you will have a good idea as to how far before your graduation date your job search should begin. I read my first job posting in July 2009, completed my MLIS in December 2009, received an offer in the same month, and started my job in February 2010. There are innumerable ways to arrive at your dream job, but the following is how I applied the advice from the previous chapters and ended up as a new librarian, right out of graduate school.

Your job search begins the day you decide to start reading job postings. Start to do this as soon as possible, preferably before you have registered for your last semester of classes. This will allow you to adjust your course load if you discover that you are missing a skill that appears in the minimum qualifications of all the jobs in which you are interested. For me, this was collection development. Thanks to my early start, I was able to add a course in collection development, and find a practicum opportunity that allowed me to gain practical experience in assessing and purchasing for a subject area. My job postings were drawn from the following locations:

- ALA's JobLIST: http://joblist.ala.org
- HigherEdJobs, with a search limited to librarian positions: www.higher edjobs.com
- LISjobs: www.lisjobs.com/jobseekers
- LibGig: http://publicboard.libgig.com

If you are exclusively interested in academic positions, these sources should provide good coverage of what is available. You can also look for listings posted by your LIS program, or programs at other institutions, and check for listings devoted to a specific geographic location, such as the Pacific Northwest Library Association's "Jobs" page (www.pnla.org/jobs/index.htm). I used Google Reader (google.com/reader) to organize the RSS feeds for these sources. Google Reader collects all of the postings, so you will never miss anything, even if you forget to check back for a week. Using an RSS feed reader made it easy to skim through hundreds of postings at a time, and to search through postings from all sources.

In general, I spent a few hours a week reading through job postings, each time skimming for two key pieces of information:

- Do I meet all of the minimum qualifications, and some of the preferred qualifications?
- When is the close or review date for the position?

I entered every job for which I was qualified in my calendar, along with the persistent link to the posting. Now was not the time to decide whether the job was appealing, or if I would be comfortable moving to that location. If no deadline was provided, I put the position on my calendar no further than two weeks from the date it was posted. By doing this, I knew what to expect in terms of the time I needed to spend each week on applications, and saved myself the trouble of searching for job postings once I was ready to apply.

At the beginning of each week, I set aside time to consider the job postings in earnest. For some weeks, especially in June and July for fall semester hires, and September and October for spring semester hires, there may be seven to ten deadlines in one week. It is imperative that you choose only two or three on which to focus, lest you end up turning in rushed, half-hearted application packets. This is the time to consider all of the elements discussed in chapter 3, and to apply the advice in chapter 4. Be sure to research the surrounding area, as well as the position and the institution. For me, this meant checking for the availability of direct flights to my home in California from the local airport, and making sure there were Trader Joe's and J. Crew locations within a reasonable distance.

I was contacted for the next step in the search process between three days and eight weeks after submitting my application packet. As reiterated through-out the other chapters, be prepared for inconsistent timelines, and to wait, wait, wait. More importantly, however, I was not contacted for my first phone interview until three months after submitting my first application packet, and all four of my phone interviews came from application packets compiled in the latter half of my job search. Though most of you will consider yourselves to have strong written communication skills, the cover letter requires a very different tone and style from the analytical or argumentative writing that has been required from you thus far. It will take some time before you find the right voice for your cover letters, so don't worry if your first application packets don't yield immediate results.

Once you start submitting application packets, you will also start getting rejections. It will hurt. Badly. My most heart-wrenching rejection came at the hands of an institution I revered, perhaps too much. Shortly after what I thought had been a promising phone interview (it lasted more than an hour! Everyone laughed at my stories!), I received a call from the institution's human resources department. The administrative assistant verified my identity, and extended an invitation to visit the campus. My heart leapt! I responded enthusiastically in the affirmative, and then, she paused. And put me on hold. Nothing seemed amiss at this point, and as I cheerfully waited for her return, I started to share the good news with my friends via chat. After a few minutes, the administrative assistant returned, only to say that she would need just a bit more time. I started to feel a little uneasy. This proved to be the right response, as she returned to explain that she had read the e-mail list incorrectly. While the institution appreciated my interest, they would *not* be inviting me to campus, after all. She apologized profusely, and we said our goodbyes. I ended the call and sat there, stunned, by what had just happened. I am not ashamed to admit that I subsequently crawled into bed, curled into a ball, and felt very sorry for myself.

I hope you will be spared this kind of emotional devastation, but there will almost certainly be similarly painful episodes in your job search. It is an inevitable result of the process, but there are ways to temper the sting of rejection.

Do not get too attached to any one position. Had I not been so attached to the position in question, the above rejection would not have been nearly as traumatizing. As it was, I had decided that this position was the only position in which I could truly be satisfied. Not only was this incorrect, it was foolish. I found various housing options, researched the local government, and plotted farmer's markets as I built an increasingly elaborate fantasy life around my job at this institution. This was ridiculous. Don't do it! Be pragmatic, rational, and treat each opportunity equally.

Apply for as many positions as time allows. While it is important to apply only for positions in which you are sincerely interested, it is equally important to give yourself as many opportunities for success as possible. By the time I received my job offer, I had ten application packets out in the world. My peers and other librarians reported sending out between ten and thirty applications before accepting a job offer.

Continue applying as searches move forward. It is tempting to pour all of your energy into preparing for an upcoming phone interview, or the presentation for your campus visit, rather than write yet another cover letter. Until you are made an offer, and sign a contract, however, nothing is secure. Things can go wrong at every step of the process!

At times, rejection feels imminent. Perhaps you applied for a job without meeting all of the minimum qualifications. Or, in the case of my first phone interview, you choked, got flustered, and never recovered. Other times, you send in a flawless application packet, perform articulately through a phone interview, charm everyone during a campus visit, and still do not receive an offer. This is the reality in a highly competitive job market, as evidenced by the hundreds of applications received for the entry-level positions described in chapter 2. Post-rejection, you may be tempted to write and ask the reason for your rejection. If you do so, be prepared to hear the worst about yourself. More likely than not, your rejection can be attributed to any of the following three reasons.

The other candidates were better qualified. This should not surprise you, nor should you worry about it too much. Instead, focus on what makes you uniquely qualified for other positions.

You were not a good fit for the institution. What constitutes fit? This varies from institution to institution, though in most cases it refers to a combination of experience and personality. Are you detail-oriented while your potential colleagues are big-picture types? Do you have the grant-writing experience they need to start an informatics program? At the University of New Mexico, for instance, fit means the successful candidate will be able to fulfill the expectations of the position, but it also means that he or she should be able to bring something remarkably delicious to all holiday potlucks.

The institution was unable to complete the search. Occasionally, a search will be canceled due to a disappointing applicant pool, or when the top candidates drop out of the search. These days, it is much more likely that the search will be canceled due to hiring freezes, hiring pauses, or other budgetary issues.

Rejection is demoralizing, but you must stay confident. Do not despair, keep applying, and you will certainly be successful. You will find the perfect job at the perfect institution, and all of this trouble will seem entirely worthwhile. Even if it does not, remember that this first job is unlikely to be your last, and the experience you accrue will make you all the more competitive when you next enter the academic job market.

Still, as you begin your new position, the next job search will probably be the last thing on your mind. As it should be! It will take considerable energy to learn your job responsibilities, accustom yourself to the projects in progress at your institution, and meet everyone in your new library family. Do not, however, grow complacent. Maintain the ambition that served you so well during the job search, and use it to create the career you want. Challenge yourself on the job, and externally, by taking advantage of networking opportunities, professional development opportunities, and getting involved with national service in your area of interest. Do more than what is required. Strive to become a contributing and productive member of the profession. Stay curious.

Good luck!

Note

1. U.S. Department of Labor, Bureau of Labor Statistics, "Table A-12: Unemployed Persons by Duration of Unemployment," in Employment Situation, www.bls .gov/news.release/empsit.t12.htm (accessed March 20, 2010).

CONTRIBUTORS

DR. CAMILA ALIRE is dean emerita at the University of New Mexico and Colorado State University in Fort Collins, Colorado. She has additionally served as dean/director of libraries at the University of Colorado in Denver. She currently serves as professor of practice (adjunct) for Simmons College's Ph.D. program in Managerial Leadership in the Information Professions, and adjunct professor at San Jose University's executive MLIS program. She has co-authored books on academic librarianship, emotional intelligent leadership, and library services to Latino communities, and has edited a book on library disaster recovery. Camila received her doctorate in higher education administration from the University of Northern Colorado and an MLS from the University of Denver.

PROFESSOR DANIEL C. BARKLEY is currently the data librarian for government information and political science at the University of New Mexico University Libraries. Dan's background in librarianship has centered on government information. Dan has worked at the University of Kentucky, the University of Kansas, and Wake Forest University. Dan received his BS in political science from Miami University (OH) and an MLIS from the University of Kentucky. He has written extensively on issues relating to government information and has served on numerous local, state, and national committees (GODORT, DLC). Dan would like to dedicate his chapter to his mom Lois and his dog Nikki.

SEVER BORDEIANU is professor and a serials cataloger at the University of New Mexico University Libraries with extensive technical services experience. He has also worked in public services and collection development. Sever holds a MLIS degree from the University of Texas at Austin, as well as an MA in French with minors in both German and philosophy from the University of Mississippi. Sever has written articles about cataloger productivity, and has co-authored a book on outsourcing cataloging in academic libraries.

CHRISTINA M. DESAI is associate professor and a reference/instruction librarian at the University of New Mexico University Libraries. Her research interests focus on virtual reference assessment and on ethnicity and war/peace issues in children's literature. In 2007, with Stephanie Graves, she received the Emerald Literati Network Award for Excellence for Outstanding Paper in Information and Knowledge Management, as well as the ALA Library Instruction Round Table's Top 20 Award for 20 Best Articles on Library Instruction and Information Literacy, for articles on instruction via chat and IM. She received her MLIS from the University of Illinois and her MA in English from the University of Pittsburgh.

MONICA ETSITTY DORAME is a library specialist of 22 years in access services, reference, and government information at the University of New Mexico University Libraries. Monica received her master's degree in public administration and a BA in American studies from the University of New Mexico. She has served on many search committees and is knowledgeable of the hiring process of library staff and faculty.

KATHLEEN B. GARCIA is a library information specialist in access services at the University of New Mexico University Libraries. She received her BA in sociology with a minor in psychology from the University of New Mexico. Kathleen has over 11 years of experience in both public and academic libraries.

SILVIA LU began her professional career as an access services librarian at the University of New Mexico in early 2010. She received her MLIS from the University of Illinois at Urbana-Champaign and her BA in literature and government from Claremont McKenna College.

BRUCE NEVILLE has been a professional librarian since 1992 and is currently a science & engineering librarian at Sterling Evans Library at Texas A&M University. Prior to joining Texas A&M, he was interim director of the Centennial Science and Engineering Library at the University of New Mexico, and also served as science librarian at the University of Texas at El Paso. Bruce is active in the Engineering Libraries Division of the American Society for Engineering Education. He has recently participated in the hiring process from both sides. He received his MLS from Florida State and a BS in biology and chemistry from the University of Miami. Bruce is a co-author of *Science and Technology Research: Writing Strategies for Students* (2002).

EVANGELA OATES has been a librarian for five years and is currently the coordinator of instruction and reference at Mount Saint Mary College in Newburgh, NY. She was the UNM UL resident from 2005 to 2007 and has served on search committees for hiring residents, library staff, and librarians in her role as a supervisor. Evangela was a 2007 ALA Emerging Leader and a 2008 participant in the ACRL Information Literacy Immersion Program. She received her MLS from North Carolina Central University and holds a BA in music from the University of North Carolina at Greensboro.

SARAH STOHR is a distance services librarian at the University of New Mexico and a 2008 ALA Emerging Leader. She completed an academic librarian residency at the University of New Mexico and received her MSLS from the University of Kentucky. She received her BA in English from Lewis & Clark College. Sarah has participated in the hiring of academic library residents and new employees, and has written a chapter in a forthcoming book about academic residency programs.

INDEX

You may also be interested in

MARKETING ACADEMIC LIBRARIES ECOURSE/EBOOK BUNDLE
Brian Mathews

In this eCourse, Matthews, an experienced academic librarian who has used technology for a variety of library outreach initiatives, will help you make sure your library is more popular than ever. Quizzes at the end of each lesson test your knowledge, while Further Reading suggestions point you in the direction of additional information. The companion eBook, *Marketing Today's Academic Library*, is also included.

ITEM #: 7800-0773
Self-paced eCourse estimated to be 4.5 hours of instruction
9 Lessons included

INFORMATION LITERACY ASSESSMENT
TERESA Y. NEELY
ISBN: 978-0-8389-0914-0

REFLECTIVE TEACHING, EFFECTIVE LEARNING
CHAR BOOTH
ISBN: 978-0-8389-1052-8

WEB-BASED INSTRUCTION, 3E
SUSAN SHARPLESS SMITH
ISBN: 978-0-8389-1056-6

TEACHING INFORMATION LITERACY
JOANNA M. BURKHARDT AND MARY C. MACDONALD WITH ANDRÉE J. RATHEMACHER
ISBN: 978-0-8389-1053-5

CREATING THE CUSTOMER-DRIVEN ACADEMIC LIBRARY
JEANNETTE WOODWARD
ISBN: 978-0-8389-0976-8

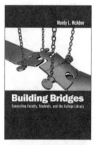

BUILDING BRIDGES
MONTY L. McADOO
ISBN: 978-0-8389-1019-1

Order today at **alastore.ala.org** or **866-746-7252!**
ALA Store purchases fund advocacy, awareness, and accreditation programs for library professionals worldwide.

Best Ideas
FOR READING
From America's
Blue Ribbon Schools

What Award-Winning
Elementary and Middle School
Principals Do

National Association of
Elementary School Principals

NAESP

CORWIN PRESS, INC.
A Sage Publications Company
Thousand Oaks, California

For information:

Corwin Press, Inc.
A Sage Publications Company
2455 Teller Road
Thousand Oaks, California 91320
E-mail: order@corwinpress.com

SAGE Publications Ltd.
6 Bonhill Street
London EC2A 4PU
United Kingdom

SAGE Publications India Pvt. Ltd.
M-32 Market
Greater Kailash I
New Delhi 110 048 India

Printed in the United States of America

Library of Congress Cataloging-in-Publication Data

Best ideas for reading from America's Blue Ribbon Schools: What award-winning elementary and middle school principals do / National Association of Elementary School Principals.

    p. cm.
  ISBN 0-8039-6772-1 (cloth: acid-free paper)
  ISBN 0-8039-6773-X (pbk.: acid-free paper)
  1. Reading—United States. 2. Elementary school principals—United States—Attitudes. 3. Middle school principals—United States—Attitudes. 4. Blue Ribbon Schools Program (U.S.) I. National Association of Elementary School Principals (U.S.)
  LB1573 .B439 1998
  373.12′012—ddc21

                                         98-40125

This book is printed on acid-free paper.

98 99 00 01 02 03 10 9 8 7 6 5 4 3 2 1

Production Editor: S. Marlene Head
Editorial Assistant: Kristen L. Gibson
Cover Designer: Tracy Miller
Typesetter: Rebecca Evans

Contents

 # Foreword

In his State of the Union Address on February 4, 1997, President Clinton issued a Call to Action for American Education. This call provides a clear set of challenges for educators and all Americans concerned about fundamentally improving our schools.

The Department of Education responded to the President's message with seven priorities that frame our action agenda:

1. All students will read independently and well by the end of third grade.
2. All students will master challenging mathematics, including the foundations of algebra and geometry, by the end of eighth grade.
3. By 18 years of age, all students will be prepared for and able to afford college.
4. All states and schools will have challenging and clear standards of achievement and accountability for all children and effective strategies for reaching those standards.
5. There will be a talented, dedicated, and well-prepared teacher in every classroom.
6. Every classroom will be connected to the Internet by the Year 2000, and all students will be technologically literate.
7. Every school will be strong, safe, drug-free, and disciplined.

Legislation and funding to support reading and school improvement, like the America Reads Challenge, reducing class size, modernizing school buildings, raising standards with Goals 20 funds, the college work-study program, and funding to bring computers to the classroom can help us move forward toward achieving these priorities.

Of equal importance, however, are the lessons we can learn from schools that are already providing the kinds of educational experiences that prepare all our students for success in the complex and competitive world of the 21st century. The Blue Ribbon Schools are an excellent resource for improving education for all our children. These award-winning schools provide disciplined places for learning where dedicated, well-prepared teachers employ strategies that help all students achieve. Achievement is based upon challenging curricula, and clear standards and accountability measures accurately reflect what students know and can do. Students are reading independently and well and mastering the important mathematics skills that prepare them for college. The school environments are safe and drug-free. Parents and communities are partners in the life of the school. Most important, many of the schools achieve these goals under the most challenging circumstances. Their knowledge and experience can benefit all schools.

I hope that you will call upon the programs and resources of the U.S. Department of Education to enhance your own initiatives in providing the best education for all students.

Richard W. Riley
U.S. Secretary of Education

Introduction

"We ought to commit ourselves as a country to say by the Year 2000, 8-year-olds in America will be able to pick up an appropriate book and say, 'I read this all by myself.'"

President William Jefferson Clinton,
Sept. 12, 1996

President Clinton's challenge to Americans to ensure that all children can read well and independently by the end of third grade weighed heavily in our thinking as we approached the publication of this third volume of *Best Ideas From America's Blue Ribbon Schools.*

The leadership of elementary and middle school principals as they work with teachers and communities to respond to the President's Call to Action and especially to meet the *America Reads* challenge by the Year 2000 is crucial, and nowhere is that better demonstrated than in the Blue Ribbon Schools. Enabling these schools to share their successful reading strategies and programs with others is a way to further the work of all schools in attaining this important goal. It is not surprising, then, that we have designed this volume as a mechanism for doing just that.

We asked the principals of the 1996-1997 Blue Ribbon Schools to share with us their best ideas for improving students' reading abilities and were richly rewarded by their responses. Their contributions provide ideas for working with individual students, small groups, whole classes, and the total school. Some strategies are classroom based and implemented by the teacher, others can be effectively reinforced by volunteers and families, and there are ideas for involving the entire school and community in making reading a priority.

Consistently evident throughout the collection of ideas is the direct involvement of the principal in motivating, monitoring, and acknowledging student progress in reading.

As indicated in the President's challenge, there's important work for everyone to do, and this book brings both time-tested and innovative ways to approach that work. We thank the Blue Ribbon Schools for making this a useful resource for educators, with whom NAESP shares a common commitment to ensure that America's children become effective and enthusiastic readers.

Samuel G. Sava
Executive Director
National Association of Elementary School Principals

The love of reading.

Working With Individual Students

Engaging Literacy

Best for: Individual students who are having problems applying reading and writing strategies

Implemented by: Trained teachers, Reading Recovery teachers, and parents

Description

In a population of students where literacy is neither important nor modeled in the home, many students were not successful in using or applying literacy skills.

We met as a school to decide how to assess, plan for instruction, and follow up on these students. We used the Reading Recovery programs, the classroom teacher, and parents to achieve our goal of bringing these children to grade level. Our approach was whole-part-whole teaching in addition to a Reading Recovery approach.

The classroom teacher's responsibility is to assess children using running records, integrate the curriculum, model effective reading and writing strategies, and provide many opportunities to practice the taught strategies. The Reading Recovery teacher worked 40 minutes a day per student in areas of phonemic segmentation, cut-apart sentences (to reinforce writing and sight word recognition), and comprehension of text read. Parents were required to observe the classroom teacher and the Reading Recovery teacher to understand how to better work with their child. Books previously read and new books were sent home each night for practice. The classroom teacher and Reading Recovery teacher met daily to discuss progress and the plan for instruction. The result has been that 80% of the students receiving this program were reading at grade level at the end of 20 weeks.

Benefits

When everyone works together to structure success for a child, many needs are met. Students in this program begin as nonreaders who do not understand the importance of reading and writing. They complete instruction as students who research interest topics in the library; write clear, concise stories; and choose literacy activities during free time. Parents and teachers report these children read environmental print anywhere they go. Most important, you may very well see this new student helping another student with reading and writing. Reading and writing are life skills!

Mary Castleberry
Carver Elementary G.T. Magnet School
Wendell, North Carolina

Centennial Reading Clinic

Best for: *Individual students in intermediate grades*

Implemented by: *Trained coordinator and volunteers*

Description

Learning to read proficiently is critical to future success. We found that a portion of our students were not functioning at grade level and that remediation was necessary. We established a Reading Clinic using an aide as coordinator and trained volunteers as tutors.

Each teacher is then asked to submit a list of students for the Reading Clinic. They use a variety of assessments to determine who would most benefit from the program.

When students first come to the Reading Clinic we determine at what level the student is functioning in reading. This is done through the use of the High Utility 1,020 Words by Rebecca Sitton (in *The Quickword Handbook for Everyday Writers*, Curriculum Associates, 1994), the student's Curriculum-Based Measurement (CBM) testing scores, and results from recent CAT testing results.

We improve deficiencies on a one-to-one basis of student-to-volunteer. Most students come in twice a week for 25-minute sessions. Each session is divided into four steps. The first is called Familiar Reading. The student demonstrates the enjoyment of reading familiar texts. This empowers the student to gain automaticity and in turn to become a more proficient reader. The second is the Sight Word activity. The volunteer uses words from the Sitton Word List, words from a familiar book, or words the student would like to add. These words are kept and reviewed each time the student attends. The third is Making Words. Using a magnetic white board, magnetic letters, erasable markers, or other materials, the volunteer guides the student through a multilevel, hands-on Spelling and Phonics activity. In this activity, students access decoding skills as well as meaning and pronunciation. Fourth is Introducing a New Book. The student and tutor take a picture walk through the book, which assists with comprehension.

Benefits

Through teacher observation and quarterly CBM testing, we have validated the effectiveness of the program.

Kevin Silberberg
Centennial Elementary School
Bakersfield, California

Parents Assisting Learning for Success (P.A.L.S.) Volunteer Program

Best for: *Students in all grade levels*

Implemented by: *Trained parent volunteers through principal and teacher inservice*

Description

My 1991-1993 doctoral dissertation study, titled "The Perceptions of Parents and Teachers Regarding a Home-School Partnership in an Elementary School Setting," focused on the recruitment and direct involvement of parents in the classroom. This study went beyond the typical volunteer who works in and around the school setting. I took the research of Dr. Joyce Epstein of Johns Hopkins University and applied it to a pilot project. This project recruited and trained parents to work directly in the classroom with the teacher, highlighting work with small-group or one-on-one tutoring in reading and math. Parents read to students, listen to students read, review vocabulary and spelling words, and ask comprehension and higher-level questions to check for understanding of the content. Parents may choose to work with their child or other children. All parents are given an indepth workshop on volunteering in the classroom while maintaining confidentiality and professional behavior.

Benefits

The results were highly successful, and today we have more than 250 parents who represent all classes in the building of 34 classrooms. This project took major staff inservicing and plenty of leadership to convince people to take a risk by starting out slowly and inviting parents to take part in the teaching-learning process. The benefits have indicated a steady increase in overall student achievement scores schoolwide. It also supports the research of Dr. Epstein, which indicated that students are more highly motivated about learning and feel better about their school environment when their parents are directly involved.

Roger A. Stock
Chesterfield Elementary School
Chesterfield, Missouri

Homestart Reading Program

Best for: Individual students in kindergarten, an entire class

Implemented by: Library/media specialist, volunteer parents, and classroom teachers

Description

Although one of the goals of kindergarten is to encourage students to want to learn to read, too often kindergartners are not given access to quality books on a regular basis.

After the winter holiday vacation, a letter is sent home to parents explaining the benefits of reading aloud to kindergartners. Parents are asked to help their child by reading aloud a book that is sent home from the library each night (5 nights a week). The PTA purchased a large collection of quality children's books (ones that the teacher and principal deemed important to have introduced to every child) to be sent home in book bags each evening. Volunteers as well as the media specialist collect the bags daily and change the books in them so that each child has a new book to read. Prizes are given along the way in this Homestart Reading Program for 5, 10, 15, 20, and 25 books read. At the end of the reading program, a party is given in the media center. Students are presented with certificates, given refreshments, and read to by the principal. After the party, the students are allowed to begin checking out books from the school library on a daily basis. The habits established while participating in this program carry over through the remainder of the year—and for years to come.

Benefits

First, parents who have never read aloud to their children have gotten into the habit of reading by the time the program concludes. It strengthens family relationships, especially with siblings. Students experience increased interest in reading and in going to libraries. They learn to talk about what they have read and share with other students about the good books in the collection. By participating in the Early Start/Homestart Reading Program, parents become partners in the future reading success of their children. They learn the importance of reading aloud and become responsible for following through with a school program.

Nancy Krodel
Coronado Heights Elementary School
Oklahoma City, Oklahoma

Searching on-line.

Reading Strategies Matched to Level

Best for: *Individual middle school students and/or total class*

Implemented by: *Teachers and individual students*

Description

Entering middle school with reading deficits impairs student success in all areas. Because the State of Minnesota requires Grade 8 students to take a basic standards reading (and math) test and pass it before graduating, students at risk were selected based on scores on the ITBS from the previous year. Students selected were given the Gates McGinitie Reading (Riverside Publishing Company, Itasca, IL) pretest and were then presented with many reading strategies over a period of one semester followed by a posttest.

Students used on-line weekly modified newspaper articles and questions from the Minneapolis *Star Tribune*

```
http://idea.startribune.com/
```

aligned with the Degrees of Reading Power level of reading so that articles could be matched to ability level. Also used was the Reading Attainment System (Educational Design, Inc., NY), oral and silent reading, magazine articles, plays, and novels. Modification of the Marie Carbo (an author and consultant on effective strategies for raising reading achievement) method of repeated reading was also integrated into the class. Integral skill development from a variety of sources included fact, opinion, inference, sequencing, comprehension, main and support ideas, context clues, and cause and effect. Students were encouraged to do home reading and credited for it. Students in class gained up to a 30% increase on the posttest.

Benefits

When placed in materials matched to their individual reading level, students were highly motivated by their success and could see their gains through charting themselves. Having the fluidity to increase or decrease the reading level based on success allowed self-confidence to build. Unison reading and reading aloud plays of interest involved students. Crediting home reading for class invited family support and encouragement. Skill development was based on student need, and "learning the tricks" for building success enticed student involvement. A side benefit? Several of the at-risk students passed the state reading test!

David D. Thompson
Farmington Middle School
Farmington, Minnesota

Reading Songs

Best for: All students with decoding difficulties, individual or group

Implemented by: Teachers

Description

Teacher types up a song that a student knows by heart. Teacher manipulates size and spacing of type to fit student needs. Student is told to practice song on his or her own, matching words in head to words on the page. When students feel ready, they read the song to teacher, pointing to words as they read. Then, words that follow frequent patterns are selected and rhyming lists are developed for each selected word. Students read story and word lists in subsequent lessons.

For a group, the activity can be adapted. A song is selected that is familiar to many students. The song is played for students prior to introduction. The song is given to the group. Students read chorally and individually, as teacher points to each word. Words are selected and lists of rhyming words are developed, as a group.

Obviously, this approach does not work for students who cannot remember the words to any songs. Also, it is a supplemental reading activity, not a total program.

Benefits

Many students with decoding difficulties are unable to profit from the language experience approach, either because they lack sufficient language or cannot remember what they have just dictated. Reading songs is superior for these students because they already have the words to the songs in their heads. Therefore, they are able to make the decoding discoveries, matching letters to sounds and sounds to words, without being hampered by memory or language problems.

This is a very motivating activity for students because they want to be able to read the songs they listen to. Also, many students who have limited success with other approaches can be quite successful with this approach.

Sally L. Smith
The Lab School of Washington
Washington, DC

Reading Intervention
in the Primary Grades

Best for: *Individual students in primary-grade classrooms*

Implemented by: *Trained teachers and reading specialist*

Description

To meet the needs of an increasingly diverse population of students, we have developed the Reading Intervention Program. Now in its 9th year, Reading Intervention has become integral to our primary grade curriculum.

Designed as a push-in program, the reading interventionist meets with the individual child or small group of children within the classroom during the specified "language arts block." Experienced as a classroom teacher herself, she works closely with the classroom teacher to follow each student's progress by addressing special needs these professionals have collaboratively identified. The students receive individual instruction in the areas of reading strategies, phonics, writing, and semantics, through literature-based activities.

The selected children are not classified as learning disabled but rather they are developmentally young or are simply showing early signs of a reading difficulty. They are chosen collectively by the classroom teacher, the parent, and the reading interventionist. Our goal is to help them master the skills necessary for them to reach their true educational potential.

Our pride in our Reading Intervention Program extends to the specialists providing this service; to the classroom teachers who have willingly integrated it into their classrooms; and most important, to our students, whose achievements are examples of its success.

Benefits

Initially begun in the kindergarten and first grade, Reading Intervention is in its 9th successful year and has expanded to include the second grade. Presently, one interventionist serves each primary grade and all three work closely with the teacher providing for a low teacher-student ratio within the classrooms. The children benefit from the push-in program by working on the same activities within the classroom setting. This assures a buildup of confidence for the children as they can work at their own pace with very little catch-up necessary when one misses the regular classroom activities. They also work both individually and cooperatively with the skill-intensive assistance of the interventionist.

Patricia Coldrick
Lakeview Elementary School
Mahopac, New York

Lion's Loft Reading Program

Best for: *Individual students in Grades 1-6*
Implemented by: *Librarian*

Description

The Lion's Loft Club is our reading incentive program, designed to encourage students to increase their pleasure reading. Students in first through fifth grade may pick up Lion's Loft slips in the library each month that state they "have read, been read to, or have read to" at least 6 hours the previous month. Signed by parents, membership runs from month to month and must be renewed each month. Lion's Loft members receive a bookmark monthly with their name on it and are entitled to read during quiet reading time in the for-members-only Lion's Loft, equipped with a great view, bean bags, and soft chairs.

A second library program features a Word of the Week (WOW). The librarian selects a word that is appropriate to the week's activities or special events. Each morning on our in-house television network, the word is introduced, defined, and used in a sentence. During the day students who define the word and/or use it correctly in a sentence are permitted to check out an overnight book from a special shelf near the librarian's desk.

Also available on overnight checkout from the library are Science Kits that contain simple experiments that students and parents can do at home.

Benefits

Since the introduction of the Lion's Loft Club and WOW, library usage has doubled and so has circulation. Currently, 285 of the 380 eligible students have been Lion's Loft members for at least 1 month since September.

Pauline Schara
Linda Vista Elementary School
Yorba Linda, California

AmeriCorps Tutoring

Best for: *Students in Grades 1-3 reading one to two levels below grade level*

Implemented by: *AmeriCorps tutors, parents, and community volunteers*

Description

Reading scores are a problem in urban districts, and Springfield and Pleasant Hill are no exceptions. This year, we had the opportunity to have a Capital Reading Corps tutor in our school 4 days a week. The Capital Reading Corps is an AmeriCorps project.

In the first phase of this project, the tutor spends 30 minutes a day with each of the students he or she tutors. During that time, the tutor will read a book with the student and do the writing activities. The tutor will meet with the student 4 days per week, so a student will read four books a week in a one-on-one session. Students tested at midyear show an average of a one-level gain. By the end of the year, 86% of the students tutored should have gained up to two reading levels.

In the second phase, AmeriCorps runs four training sessions for any parents who want to learn to read a book with their child. It is hoped this will help support reading during the summer.

Benefits

Obviously, having a tutor read a book with a student 4 days a week is a positive benefit for that student. It should be noted that the increase in reading skills not only has an immediate benefit to the students but also has implications for their future learning.

Deborah Hapli
Pleasant Hill Elementary School
Springfield, Illinois

Reading Workshop Setting

Best for: *Individual elementary students, small and large groups*

Implemented by: *Trained teachers*

Description

Pond Springs Elementary wrote a campus goal adhering to the Texas State and local district goal that states: "All students will read at or above grade level by the end of third grade."

Teachers help students reach the goal by providing reading instruction in a Reading Workshop Setting (RWS). A typical RWS includes a mini-lesson, silent reading time from self-selected books, students reading aloud, and response time.

In RWS, as soon as a student completes a book he or she selects and begins another. In this way, groups are flexible and students read more books. While students read silently, the teacher works with individuals, compiling an anecdotal reading record on each student during the year. One of the most important parts of RWS is response time. Students begin by answering a given question in small groups.

Then, they either meet in large groups or compose a written response to a question. A typical RWS question is: "Who is the main character of your book? How do you know? Support your answer from text."

Benefits

Students who read self-selected books feel an ownership in their reading development. Listening to students read individually provides teachers with the means to closely monitor student progress and needs. As the routine becomes comfortable, students develop critical thinking skills through discussions and written responses. The oral component of RWS encourages reluctant readers to participate in small-group discussions in a nonthreatening, supportive atmosphere. Large groups allow students the opportunity to find general themes in literature. Students respond favorably to the RWS experience. Teachers report student growth in reading and in self-esteem.

Cheryl Smith
Pond Springs Elementary School
Austin, Texas

Undivided attention.

OASIS (Older Adult Service
and Information System)

Best for: *Individual students in primary grades*

Implemented by: *Classroom teachers, reading specialists, administration, and trained volunteers*

Description

Our reading/language arts program includes many strands that encompass the teaching of basal reading skills and formal grammar instruction, including mini-lessons within the context of and extended to familiar and related readings. Teachers provide the students with lessons and activities that necessitate the application of reading proficiencies, comprehension strategies, and evaluate skills in the context of whole-literature selections.

Although the instructional strategies foster an appreciation for reading, several young students lack the motivation to read independently. For many of these Grade 1-3 students, the home environment is not supportive of a young and enthusiastic new reader. Consequently, we work with primary-age students who do not have a family member with whom to share their newfound skill and love of reading. As a result, the burning desire to read too soon cools to indifference.

Ross School provides opportunities to build relationships with senior citizens in the community. OASIS (Older Adult Service and Information System) volunteers read with students in Grades 1-3 on a weekly basis, share in student achievements and struggles, and form a bond that is fostered and continues through the grades.

Benefits

Young children have the privilege of an interested audience, a friend, and a surrogate grandparent. OASIS volunteers are paired with students with whom they develop 3-year-long partnerships. Relationships built on trust and a common interest in educational success are formed as a result of this program. Children develop valuable skills to enhance their self-image and assume greater responsibility for their own reading success. OASIS is a program embraced by Ross School. It emphasizes the value of reading and its importance in acquiring knowledge in all future learning. Teachers measure significant student growth and success in reading and in social and emotional development.

Linda Williams
Ross Elementary School
St. Louis, Missouri

Recorded Books

Best for: *Below-grade-level readers*

Implemented by: *Trained teachers and instructional assistants*

Description

Most teachers face the problem of having some students who are not reading at grade level each year. Many students experience difficulty when participating in whole-class activities derived from the basal reader.

After researching several programs, the Stemley teachers decided to become trained in Reading Styles. Dr. Marie Carbo founded the National Reading Styles Institute and pioneered her own style of recorded books.

Teachers follow certain guidelines in recording books and teach students to use these books in a special way. This portion of reading instruction is on an individualized basis. Teachers give students a choice of several books on their level. The students are trained to track the words with their fingers as they listen. Books are recorded in small portions with much expression but slow enough for the students to track.

Benefits

When students listen and point to the words simultaneously, they remember the words more easily than when using traditional methods. Recorded books is only one of the reading-style strategies that have given our students a more "comfortable" way to learn. This method is easy to use in primary grades because their books have relatively few pages. The method can be used successfully in upper grades using magazine articles of high interest to the students.

Vicki S. Oliver
Stemley Road Elementary School
Talladega, Alabama

Roving Readers

Best for: *Students in elementary grades who need a boost to their self-esteem*

Implemented by: *Classroom teachers and roving reader coordinator*

Description

Often students need a boost to their self-esteem and confidence level. The Roving Reader program is a vehicle for helping students improve these attributes.

The teacher chooses one student each day to go to another class and read a book aloud to the class. The student chooses a book that he or she can read fluently. When the student is finished, the class usually gives a round of applause, and the teacher tells that student what a great job he or she did. The teacher uses a hole punch to indicate on the student's roving reader bookmark that the student has successfully read the book to the teacher's class. At the end of the year, students who have been roving readers at least five times during the year receive a certificate on awards day.

The coordinator of this program prepares a schedule for the teachers to follow. Each teacher is assigned a different class to which to send roving readers during a given grading period. Usually, students are assigned to read to the same or a lower grade level to minimize any frustration they might feel about reading in front of others.

Benefits

Over the past few years, we have seen an increase in the number of students who wish to participate in this program. Students are encouraged but not forced to read to another class. Teachers report lower achievers "beaming with pride" as they return from a successful roving reader experience.

Vicki S. Oliver
Stemley Road Elementary School
Talladega, Alabama

The Reading Teacher's Role in Early Intervention for At-Risk Students

Best for: At-risk students in primary grades

Implemented by: Consulting teachers of reading

Description

Often children are identified as having difficulty with reading once they reach Grade 3. Studies show that a child's performance in Grade 3 is often an indicator of future school success. Our objective was to identify the at-risk students at a much younger age and provide the proper intervention necessary to prevent that child from "failing."

We work with all kindergarten students, focusing lessons on phonology, letters/sound recognition, letter formation, rhyming words, and patterns. We are continually evaluating and assessing students to identify children at risk. Children are screened in the spring of their kindergarten year using an emergent literacy survey with a strong focus on phonemic awareness.

All children are screened again in September of first grade. Children who are still lacking prereading skills are identified and qualify for small-group instruction. Lessons are multisensory, and a variety of approaches are used to assist these students in literacy acquisition. Children are continually assessed and receive support as long as necessary.

Benefits

All too often, children at risk are headed for failure. By providing early intervention, children gain the skills they need to have successful experiences with reading. We focus on their personal successes to build self-esteem and foster a lifelong love of reading. We promote a strong connection between home and school. Parents are involved in daily reading with their child as well as participating in schoolwide reading events. Our joint efforts have proven successful in providing the support these at-risk students need.

Maureen Dwan
Steward School
Topsfield, Massachusetts

Early School Preparation (ESP) Program

Best for: *Individual preschool students and parents*
Implemented by: *Trained teachers and volunteers*

Description

Counselors, teachers, and parents recognized a need for special assistance for approximately 50% of the preschool children who are not ready for school each year. Primary teachers at Taylors Elementary believe that "learning to read and write in school will be easier for the child with rich preschool literacy experiences than it is for the child with almost no literacy experiences," as stated by Marie Clay (a noted New Zealand educator). In an effort to reach those children with such limited experiences, teachers at Taylors developed the Early School Preparation (ESP) program. The ESP program, implemented by faculty and PTA volunteers, includes meetings with parents of preschoolers and kindergartners and a unique packet with clear, concise suggestions for helping their children at home. The packet explains how parents can help children with fine motor skills, counting, recognizing letters of the alphabet, and many other emerging literacy skills.

Books, developed and compiled by parent volunteers and teachers, are provided to show letters, numbers, colors, and shapes. A trade book, with suggestions for developing early concepts about print, is included. ESP, the first program of its kind in the local school district and a model in the state, symbolizes the extent to which needs data are analyzed and used productively to enrich student learning.

Benefits

The ESP program and packet provide for a smooth and successful transition into kindergarten and first grade. One parent said, "He thought it was really neat to go see his new school and also to get a gift!" By receiving the "gift," children are motivated to "play" school and exercise their early literacy experiences as well. Test scores on the Cognitive Skills Assessment Battery, given at the beginning of first grade, showed 88% of first graders were ready to begin first grade.

Mary D. Woods
Taylors Elementary School
Taylors, South Carolina

Paired Reading Program

Best for: Individual students in primary grades

Implemented by: Trained volunteers and reading coordinator

Description

In addition to regular reading classes, students in our kindergarten through third grades benefit from a unique Paired Reading Program. Paired Reading volunteers are trained by our reading coordinator using a short video and live demonstrations. The unique aspect of this program is that both reading partners read the words out loud together at the same time. The student chooses a book through interest more than by readability, and the volunteer (adult or older student) helps the less able reader enjoy his or her chosen book. A good analogy to this support in reading is teaching a beginning swimmer to float. The helper's arm under the swimmer is like the voice of the helping reader, ready to assist if needed, always there to keep things going successfully. Each adult volunteer comes in once a week to read for 20 minutes with each of his or her four students, keeping the same partners for the whole school year.

Benefits

Benefits of the Paired Reading Program have been both academic and social. Our less able readers in four grades have gained skills through these extra practice sessions. They find enthusiastic coaches in their adult partners (who are mostly senior citizens), coaches who celebrate their progress and boost their confidence. The adult partners often bring in other books or related items to support their students' interests (shark teeth, bee honey, etc.) Phone calls, notes, cards, and visits are exchanged, attesting to the deepening personal relationship between the children and their grandparent-like friends. The community has become more involved with the school by coming into the building on a regular basis. They recognize students out of school, too, and are delighted to be greeted on the street or at the post office.

At the end of each year, as we celebrate our Paired Reading Program, it is evident that its value on a human level is equal to if not greater than its academic importance.

Alan Campbell
The Tisbury School
Vineyard Haven, Massachusetts

Comparing book baskets.

(Photo courtesy of Center School, Litchfield, Connecticut.)

Facilitating Reading in Small Groups

Using Book Baskets to Enhance Reading

Best for: *Small groups of primary grade students*

Implemented by: *K-1 classroom teachers*

Description

Reading and sharing real books with young children on a daily basis has been shown to have a direct impact on their reading success. However, finding the time to provide engaging, leveled reading material as a supplement to regular reading instruction can be difficult.

Our K-1 teachers have implemented a successful learning environment with a built-in classroom management plan to provide this daily supplemental reading. Each classroom has four baskets with about 15 books in each basket for designated small groups. The books are supplemental readers and trade books including fiction, nonfiction, alphabet books, and so on. Within each basket a range of about two levels is provided for the student to choose from.

During basket reading time (about 25 minutes), the children work in small groups, or individually with a self-selected book practicing the problem-solving reading strategies taught by the teacher during regular reading instruction. As the students read, the teacher moves around the room and monitors the students' reading and often makes a running record or anecdotal notes. The titles in the basket are updated about every 3 to 4 weeks.

Benefits

The book baskets have provided a framework for students to self-select books and practice independent reading strategies in an informal setting. It also demonstrates the value for leisure reading. The students can participate in making a good choice for time spent reading.

The teachers have observed the students using good reading strategies. The students are also being exposed to a wide variety of reading materials in a short amount of time. We hope each student will become a lifelong reader.

Richard D. Waldrop
Beaverdam Elementary School
Beaverdam, Virginia

Chat 'n' Chew and Lunch 'n' Listen

Best for: *Small groups of students, Grades 1-6*

Implemented by: *Parent volunteers*

Description

Developing a love for reading that carries on outside the classroom is key to enhancing students' skills. The Lunch 'n' Listen and Chat 'n' Chew reading programs provide an opportunity for small groups of students to share favorite stories in an informal setting at lunch. There are three levels: Lunch 'n' Listen (Grades 1 and 2), Chat 'n' Chew (Grades 3 and 4), and Chat 'n' Chew Challenge (Grades 5 and 6).

The PTA coordinators for each level meet with the teachers prior to the start of school to select the books. Primary teachers often choose award-winning books that extend units of study in social studies and science. Books at the intermediate level are chosen based on their readability and interest level.

Students are divided into small groups of six to eight for their monthly book chats. During Lunch 'n' Listen, the book is read by the parent volunteer and a hands-on activity is planned to add excitement to the story. During Chat 'n' Chew, students read the book selection prior to the meeting. Parent volunteers are trained to lead the small-group discussions. Treats are often provided. Chat 'n' Chew Challenge adds a knowledge bowl quiz as a motivator. Teams of students read a variety of book selections each month. Then a team tournament is held to check students' comprehension. The winning teams are recognized on the daily announcements.

Benefits

Students are reading more independently as a result of these recreational reading programs. Parent volunteers report they have increased their own skills as parent educators and find they have a renewed enthusiasm for reading as adults. The program is easy to organize and there is minimal financial investment. Parents, teachers, and students working together—it's a winning combination.

Betsy Degen
Broken Arrow Elementary School
Shawnee, Kansas

Scrabble Games for Vocabulary Development

Best for: Small groups of students in upper elementary classrooms

Implemented by: Trained teachers

Description

Vocabulary development is a critical component of reading and writing success in upper elementary classrooms. However, we found that although our fifth-grade students were being exposed to challenging vocabulary through various units of study, the words were quickly forgotten after testing. Because we wanted a more advanced vocabulary to become an integral part of our students' reading, writing, and oral vocabularies, we decided to purchase multiple Scrabble games for use in the classroom.

After teaching students the rules, we divided them up into groups of four. Each group was given a dictionary and lists of previously introduced vocabulary words. They were instructed to use these aids during the game. In addition to regular scoring, bonus

points were given for using words with more than five letters and
vocabulary words.

After the first game, subsequent board teams were chosen based
on scores to keep players more evenly matched and thus maintain
interest. The challenge was further intensified when we invited dads
to class to play Scrabble in teams with their children.

Benefits

Using Scrabble games in the classroom provided multiple benefits to our fifth-grade students. Teachers noticed greater word recognition and understanding in daily reading. They also observed that
students were more experimental with vocabulary words in their
writing because they felt more comfortable with these words after
using them in Scrabble games. Use of the games also developed dictionary skills and increased problem-solving skills as students tried
to use words to fit patterns and increase point counts. The greatest
benefit, however, was that students discovered another way that
learning can be fun!

Raymond E. Johnson
Grace School
Houston, Texas

Early Reading Intervention

Best for: *Small groups of students in Grades 1-2*

Implemented by: *Trained university graduate students*

Description

When our district lost all federal and state Title I funding at the
conclusion of the 1995-1996 school year, an administrative decision
was made to commit the remaining district monies designated for
remedial programs to an early reading intervention program for our
youngest students. As the 1996-1997 school year began, our school
district implemented a balanced literacy language arts program that
includes a supplemental reading support program for students in
Grades 1 and 2. This program provides 1 half hour of instruction

daily in addition to the 2 hours of classroom language arts instruction. Each day, in groups of three to five, the children read for fluency; practice encoding, decoding, and reading comprehension strategies; and write in response to the book they are reading.

Two graduate interns from a local university deliver the program. In exchange for their university tuition, these interns work full time at our school. They receive intensive training, supervision, and support in the administration of this program and have proved to be an extremely valuable asset to our educational program at Highland School.

Benefits

During our first year, we were able to provide intensive reading intervention to 75 children in Grades 1 and 2. At the conclusion of the 1996-1997 school year, 97% of these first-grade children were proficient in letter recognition, 72% in sentence writing, and 94% in word recognition, based on May screening results. In Grade 2, 88% of the children entered the program in October reading at a 1.1 level. In May, 37% read at a 2.1 level, 18% read at a 2.2 level, and 45% had advanced to a 3.1 level. Although these statistics are impressive, the real success of the program is reflected in the smiling, confident faces of our young readers.

Diane Hartman Chesley
Highland Elementary School
Cheshire, Connecticut

Inclusion With Drama

Best for: *Students in primary grades*

Implemented by: *Students, faculty, parents, and volunteers*

Description

Hood Street School, a school on a military base with a mobility rate of 43%, houses students in pre-K, second, and third grades. Because of their mobile lifestyles, many students have a difficult time adjusting to new situations. Our role is to find these students, identify their needs, and meet those needs as quickly and successfully as we can, knowing these children will be with us only a short time.

Our Inclusion With Drama program was originated several years ago in hopes of better reaching those children with special needs, whether they be academic, social, physical, or emotional. Our secondary motive was to find additional ways to get the parents of those students more involved in the school and have them assume a more visible role in their child's education by assigning them a role, a duty, or a reason to be more interested. What better way than to make their child a star!

Once each semester, teachers identify two students from each class to be members of the Drama Club. The only prerequisite is that the children selected must have some apparent need that is not being fulfilled. These students meet after school with the principal and parent volunteers to stage a production in which each has a part. Much work and preparation go into these practices, but students in the Drama Club receive recognition and status from all of their peers, something they sorely need. Their positions in their class and throughout the school are elevated through their selection, and their confidence and self-esteem soar.

The greatest reward is production night when all are dressed in their costumes, their proud parents are beaming in the audience, and the students are finally able to feel successful and good about themselves. Although the production is presented to the student body during the day, the real test comes during the evening performance when the parents, brothers, sisters, neighbors, and friends come to see the performance. What a profound effect this has on a child who has never before been able to receive recognition or to feel confident or capable in the regular classroom setting!

Benefits

Inclusion With Drama has had results that we never dreamed possible! Because teachers carefully select children who are desperately in need of recognition, our cast is usually made up of students who feel defeated or insecure at the start. To see the transformation that Inclusion With Drama makes on these children is phenomenal. Self-esteem soars, confidence grows, and the child, often treated with disdain by the parents because of learning or behavior problems, suddenly becomes a source of pride and satisfaction. Parents who previously had never set foot in the school have a positive reason for being there and an opportunity to see their child in an entirely different light.

Teachers report positive changes that carry over long after the production has ended. Although much work (and patience, with some of the selected casts) is required from the principal and parent volunteers who rehearse daily and direct the affair, all agree the rewards far outweigh the consequences. To see a star born, although for only a short time, and the changes that occur as a result, makes the experience tremendously gratifying for all those involved.

Carol J. George
Hood Street Elementary School
Columbia, South Carolina

Literacy Groups Incorporating Reading Recovery Strategies

Best for: *First graders on the Reading Recovery waiting list, second graders who are previous Reading Recovery students, and kindergarten students who have difficulty with readiness skills*

Implemented by: *Trained Reading Recovery teachers*

Description

Reading Recovery is an early intervention program for first graders who are at risk of reading failure. It is designed to target the lowest 20% of first graders. We have seven first-grade classes and only one trained Reading Recovery teacher. We needed to develop a way to use the Reading Recovery strategies and meet the needs of as many students as possible. Developing a format for Literacy Groups has done just that. Our Reading Recovery teacher has four traditional Reading Recovery lessons each day and the rest of her time is spent facilitating small groups. For the first 9 weeks of school, the Reading Recovery teacher had Literacy Groups composed of second graders who had been successfully discontinued from Reading Recovery as first graders. She also had Literacy Groups composed of first graders who were in the lowest 20% but were on the waiting list for individualized instruction. After the first nine weeks, all of the

Literacy Groups were first-grade students who were on the waiting list or who recently had been discontinued from Reading Recovery but required some maintenance for their continued success. The last 6 weeks of school, Literacy Groups will be composed of kindergarten students who are exhibiting difficulty in learning reading readiness skills. These students are identified by their teachers and recommended for service through our school's Student Support Team.

Benefits

The Literacy Groups program has achieved what it was designed to accomplish. Many more students have been supported by this one trained Reading Recovery teacher than would have been if only individualized Reading Recovery lessons were available. The second graders who participated in the Literacy Groups continued to read at or above grade-level material. The second-grade teachers spoke highly of the results they witnessed in their classroom instruction. Some of the first graders in the Literacy Groups who were on the waiting list for Reading Recovery progressed out of Literacy Groups without ever needing individualized lessons. We are excited about the possibilities the Literacy Groups program holds for kindergarten students. As a result of the Literacy Groups, many students who may have become further confused about reading were supported, thus becoming average or above-average readers.

Teresa Tice
Inverness Elementary School
Birmingham, Alabama

Extend the Day and Increase Time on Task

Best for: Individual students and small groups in elementary grades

Implemented by: Trained teachers and aides

Description

In an effort to increase the effectiveness of our remedial and enrichment reading programs, our school council decided to look at the length of the typical school day in a different way. Our school day typically starts for most children at 8:40 a.m., but several of our staff have revised their schedules to start 40 minutes earlier, at 8:00 a.m. Although we have not increased the length of the day for our professional staff, we have been able to increase the length of our academic day for those children who can benefit from it.

Now, to provide remedial reading, instead of pulling children from the classroom during a subject such as science or social studies, we ask that they come to school early. This instruction is now in addition to those disciplines as opposed to being in place of them.

By seeing children in small groups on a regular basis, our staff is able to provide a developmentally appropriate, supportive reading program that is in addition to and complementary of that being offered in the regular classroom setting. Each teacher sees two groups of between one and three children each morning.

Our enrichment program runs some mornings and/or meets as a "Lunch Bunch." Our reading specialist will eat her lunch a little earlier and then facilitate a discussion concerning a book that the group has been reading. This enrichment program is open to all students who wish to participate. Typically, students meet in small groups of four to six for a period of 6 to 7 weeks.

Benefits

When a child is identified as an at-risk reader, we now have the ability to give him or her not only one-on-one or small-group instruction with trained professionals but also more time on task and less time out of the regular classroom. The same holds true for our enrichment program.

We have been running this program for a couple of years now and have been thrilled with the academic growth of our children and the consistency it is providing within the classroom with regard to decreased pullouts and increased inclusionary practice. Parental support has been tremendous. Parents have really expressed positive support and appreciation for this program. An added bonus has been the effect on our staff members. Some have middle school children and prefer to be home when their children get home; these new hours help them accomplish this. Primarily, our Title I teachers, reading specialist, and aides have been involved in the earlier starting time.

Kevin Crowley
Johnson Elementary School
Natick, Massachusetts

Hands-on learning.

(Photo courtesy of Jan Miller, Walker Elementary School, Springdale, Arkansas.)

Kid City Lab

Best for: Students in elementary grades

Implemented by: Trained teachers and community partners

Description

Meeting the needs of diverse readers is a challenging task in the traditional classroom. The current paradigm in education is shifting toward a student-centered approach in teaching. With the need of all our students to improve their reading and logical thinking skills, and in an effort to afford them real-life experiences in which to apply these skills, we have developed our Kid City lab.

The Kid City lab is a hands-on, interactive lab designed to resemble six of our neighboring Austin businesses. A classroom was divided into these six businesses and room dividers depicting each business were constructed. The room is awesome and affords small areas that simulate a real-life business in which each corresponding lab activity is conducted. Lessons using reading and higher-level thinking skills are structured around the theme of each business. The ambiance of the lab and its manipulatives provide a unique opportunity to tap into as many styles of learning as possible within each lesson.

The Kid City lab is coordinated and staffed by one teacher who works directly with each grade-level team of teachers to develop and conduct the weekly lessons. The curriculum and student-centered reading activities provide a fun yet productive way to meaningfully connect reading with everyday life skills.

Benefits

The use of reading in a connected, real-life environment has helped all our students to develop and appreciate this valuable skill. Our goal is to enable our students to be lifelong learners. Reading is a key factor in achieving this goal. Happy students and increased reading scores on our state-mandated assessment of minimum skills have been the evidence we need to continue this approach to teaching and using reading at our school.

Mamie Robinson
L. L. Campbell Elementary School
Austin, Texas

Literacy Club

Best for: *Students in intermediate grades*

Implemented by: *Classroom teachers*

Description

All children in the third grade who have a desire to share their love of books and writing have the opportunity to join the Literacy Club. The objective of the club is to sharpen reading and writing skills of students before they move on to the intermediate level. The club meets once a month for 1 hour. Each month, a different book with a different pattern is used to encourage creativity and provide motivation. After a book(s) with a specific pattern is read to the students, the whole group collaboratively writes a club story using the same pattern. Following the group activity, individuals write or coauthor their own inventive stories following the same pattern. If the students publish (edited story with a cover) their book, it will be placed on a special shelf in the school library. Through this club, students increase their repertoire of ideas for creative writing and further develop a broader appreciation for a variety of the children's books available to them.

Benefits

The benefits of this program can be seen in the increased number of third-grade students who choose to write stories during "free" time. Students frequently request books by the authors they have heard during club meetings. This process removes some of the intimidation of writing a composition and builds confidence through success.

Joy O'Dell
Lucy Franklin Elementary School
Blue Springs, Missouri

The Hive

Best for: *Small groups of students in Grades 1-5*
Implemented by: *Teachers and administrators*

Description

Although Nelson Elementary boasts strong standardized test scores well above the 50th percentile in reading and especially in math, our reading scores typically decline as students move into higher grades. In addition, transient students and new students who enter the school in fourth and fifth grades experience difficulties in reading in the content areas. Tutoring is offered to some of these students through an academic assistance teacher during the school day, parent and senior citizen readers, and Saturday school; but there are others who still need attention.

Seeking to address students' needs and to make reading our first priority at Nelson, The Hive, an afterschool tutoring program, was created through support from a district school improvement grant. The Hive is held 2 days per week from 3:15 to 4:30 p.m., with bus transportation provided home at the end of each session. Ten students at each grade level (first through fifth), who have been recommended by teachers and parents, participate in The Hive. Each group of students is tutored by a regular grade-level teacher and participates in activities that focus on reading. In addition, students are taught organizational skills, which include use of an assignment book and student reading notebook to strengthen study-skill habits. Parents and core classroom teachers are informed of weekly progress through the use of computer-generated reports and e-mail.

Benefits

The Hive has become our first line of defense above and beyond our traditional schoolday interventions in our efforts to help each and every student become a competent and avid reader. The use of core classroom teachers who already have an understanding of reading instruction at each grade level has improved student reading skills as well as the completion of homework assignments. Students have become more self-confident in reading through organization, repetition, and attention to learning styles in an extended school-day environment. We feel our students have benefited from The Hive and that we will see improved test scores as well as a school where all students value reading for learning and enjoyment.

Charlene N. Herring
Lonnie B. Nelson Elementary School
Columbia, South Carolina

The BRIDGE Program

Best for: *Students in Grades K-1*

Implemented by: *Reading specialist and trained aides*

Description

The BRIDGE (Beginning Reading Instruction During Guided Experiences) program began as a means of reducing early reading failure among students whose language and conceptual background were deficient for the learning-to-read process. The program accomplishes its objectives by

- Improving children's literacy strategies so they can better profit from ongoing classroom instruction within a short period of time
- Helping these children develop a self-improvement system for continued growth in reading

In kindergarten, a preassessment is administered to identify the neediest students and an aide is trained to deliver the program in two small groups of six students 30 minutes per day, 4 days per week. Students engage in multisensory activities, language experience, and oral language activities. Parents are partners with a monthly calendar and log to verify daily silent reading.

The first-grade program includes identification of 10 of the weakest students, who are instructed individually 30 minutes per day, 4 times per week, by a trained aide. Their program is literature based with heavy emphasis on writing, word rings, multisensory activities, and phonics.

The reading specialist conducts periodic assessments of all these students and confers regularly with the aide and classroom teacher. Parent meetings are held at least twice yearly and conferences are scheduled regularly.

Benefits

A recent review of students enrolled in the district who were BRIDGE participants from 1993 to 1997 revealed that among BRIDGE participants in first grade, 40% were reading at or above grade level and at Grades 2 and 3, almost 70% were reading at or above grade level.

First-grade percentages were especially impressive: 65% of students who were in the BRIDGE program scored at or above grade level in Grades 2, 3, and 4.

In addition to classroom reading success, students acquire individual literacy strategies that allow independent reading to occur. They feel more confident among their peers and, with consistent parental support, are very well prepared for the reading demands of the Grades 5-8 middle school after leaving New Eagle.

Beth Anne V. Kob
New Eagle Elementary School
Wayne, Pennsylvania

Extra help in an in-class setting.

What Is the C-Team?

Best for: *Small groups in primary and intermediate grades in the classroom*

Implemented by: *Classroom teachers and auxiliary credentialed teachers*

Description

The Orangethorpe reading assistance program has two major tenets: It is a non-pull-out program, and it is taught by credentialed teachers. The in-class policy was developed by a site-management team that believed the challenge was to make it possible for students with reading problems to learn in their classroom environment. The program is brought to the child rather than the child to the program. The teachers are called the C-Team—for collaboration, consultation, and cooperation. At least three credentialed teachers (funded through Title I) and the special education resource teacher make up the team. The speech and language specialist often participates. The teachers work 4 mornings a week (40%) in assigned classrooms for 30 to 60 minutes each. Arrangements include small-group instruction, working with the class while the teacher works with a small group, team teaching (especially during a written language assignment), and one-to-one conferencing or tutoring. The credentialed C-Team members plan lessons and prepare follow-up activities and homework, which reduces the teacher's workload. Lessons are based on the core curriculum and may include directed reading of fiction or nonfiction, a sequential phonics program, phonemic awareness, or preview-review of content-area materials.

Benefits

Working with the students in the classroom reduces stigmatization and segregation and increases self-esteem. Low achievers interact with good role models. Special education students work with regular education classmates. All students work with core-curriculum materials. (When alternative materials were used, skills did not transfer, students were not always motivated, they missed classwork, and they knew they were labeled.) More minutes of real reading occur.

Classroom teachers have a second person with whom to talk over strategies and share ideas for helping at-risk students. The lower student-teacher ratio results in more instructional time.

Patrick J. Backus
Orangethorpe Elementary School
Fullerton, California

Starlight Program

Best for: *Small groups of students in a primary classroom*
Implemented by: *Teachers, with the assistance of business partners*

Description

The primary objective of this program is to prevent learning discouragement in the area of reading in the primary grades. Our program, designed for at-risk students, increases vocabulary understanding, critical thinking, comprehension, and self-esteem while assisting students in reaching appropriate grade placement in the area of language arts.

Targeted students receive small-group (six students per group) instruction by a certified reading specialist on a daily basis where "I can read" and "I can write" activities are enhanced. Integrated reading and writing is encouraged, and students participate in buddy reading, group story writing, and sharings throughout the duration of the program.

A variety of multimedia materials, acquired through business partnership grants, are used, including "First Start" easy readers, "I Can Read" books, "Wings" critical thinking games, and Scholastic's "Wiggleworks" computer program. This variety allows for a multisensory approach whereby students see, feel, hear, and interact with the learning materials and the teacher.

Benefits

The greatest highlight of our program is the increase in self-esteem and motivation. Because students actually read a wide range of books with success, they look forward to reading. In addition, the writing and illustrating of stories and books make the processes of reading and writing natural and integrated. The students, motivated by their successes, show an increase in reading levels and writing ability. This motivation spills over into every area of school, thus affecting total school success.

Evelyn M. Kingston
Our Lady of Prompt Succor Parish School
Chalmette, Louisiana

Phonological Awareness Program

Best for: Students in Grade 1

Implemented by: Team composed of first-grade teachers, language arts consultants, and speech/language pathologist

Description

This year, the Peck Place School has implemented a collaborative program designed to support our emerging readers in first grade. The Phonological Awareness/Language (PAL) program has been prepared and implemented by the speech/language pathologist (SLP), the language arts consultant (LAC), and the first-grade teachers. It is a classroom-based intervention, designed to complement the Houghton-Mifflin literature-based reading program used in our school. The team works together to develop activities to heighten the children's awareness of sound, sound-symbol relationships, and sound manipulation within the structure of words. The children engage in activities of rhyming, segmentation, syllabication, and sound blending. Through multimodal presentations, children are exposed to, and instructed in, strategies to strengthen encoding and decoding skills. They are made aware of the structure of the spoken and written word. The team approach affords the opportunity for small-group instruction to meet a variety of appropriate instructional levels that fall under the phonological umbrella.

The team meets weekly to review lessons, assess student needs, and plan future activities. The LAC and SLP present 30-minute weekly lessons in each first-grade classroom, and these are supported by follow-up activities implemented by the first-grade teachers.

The PAL program is evolving, and as such, is consistently undergoing evaluation, modification, and revision to best meet the needs of the individual emerging reader.

Benefits

We are all very enthusiastic about this new venture. The children now have the foundation necessary for success in reading and writing. Phonological awareness skills that have been taught are being transferred into the daily reading and writing activities presented through our literature-based program. The children do not hesitate to use their new-found knowledge to unlock words and to use their strategies for spelling. The language arts curriculum has been greatly enhanced by the addition of the PAL program.

Nicholas Tirozzi
The Peck Place School
Orange, Connecticut

Reading Rescue: An Early-Intervention Program for First-Grade Students

Best for: *Students in Grade 1*

Implemented by: *Reading specialist*

Description

Reading Rescue, designed by Dr. Kerry Laster, is based on the research of Marie Clay. Participating first graders attend 30-minute supplemental sessions daily, which are taught by a reading specialist. Reading Rescue is an intensive early-intervention program designed to meet individual reading needs of students.

Participants are identified from norm-referenced tests given to all first-grade students in the fall of each year. Additional information to assist in student selection is provided by classroom teachers and parents. Participants on the bottom quartile are identified as being at risk, therefore performing at an inappropriate developmental reading level.

Reading Rescue provides individual and small-group sessions so that a minimum of 22 students receive 30 minutes of supplemental

reading instruction daily. Once strengths and weaknesses are assessed, an individually designed program guides each child's daily
instruction.

Reading Rescue is a holistic, literature-based early-intervention
program that meets the individual needs of first graders considered
at risk of not becoming successful readers. Materials used daily include patterned and repetitive literature, stories on tape, the children's own writings, student-made recordings, and manipulatives.
Components of each lesson include reading familiar books, shared
reading of new books, creative writing, word study, and reading at
home.

Benefits

Many students enter first grade with the anticipation of learning
to read, only to become discouraged and frustrated when that task
becomes overwhelming. Reading Rescue provides individualized
support for struggling first-grade students.

Approximately 36% of all first-grade students at Shreve Island
fall in the bottom quartile when pretested. Reading Rescue (1988-
1998) has dramatically reduced the retention rate at Shreve Island
Elementary and produced fluent first-grade readers.

The program has served as a training site for other districts and
states.

Kerry Laster
Shreve Island Elementary School
Shreveport, Louisiana

First-Grade Reading Support Program

Best for: Small groups of elementary students in regular classrooms

Implemented by: Certified reading teachers and assistants

Description

The demographic characteristics and portfolios of approximately
25% of the children entering first grade identified them as children
with a high risk of failure to complete the first-grade program successfully. The literature-based curriculum is particularly successful

when all critical aspects are implemented. The final critical elements for this high-risk group of children and their families were found to include a need for a structured program that included additional classroom support, increased home-school communication, and training for parents.

The classroom part of the program involves reading teachers and assistants working in the regular classroom with individuals and small groups of children three to four times per week for 30-minute sessions to review, reteach, practice, and extend developmental reading and writing skills and strategies. All parents of program children are required to participate in an evening training program with the reading teachers to learn the program, the materials, and the role of the parent in the program. Family packets are sent home each Friday and are due back the following Wednesday. Packets contain a journal of student writing and notes between parents and teachers. It also includes home reading and writing activities to be completed. Additional communication during the program includes regular parent conferences, telephone conferences, book lists for parents, and strategies for working with specific skills and comprehension.

Benefits

The classroom element provides additional intensive instruction that is coordinated with classroom curriculum using a team approach while allowing the student to remain in the classroom. The home-school element involves parents in a constructive and confident manner in their children's education. The ongoing communication brings all of the key individuals together in the beginning and ensures that everybody understand the importance of their role. The major benefit is to the children, 95% of whom successfully complete the first-grade program with the skills needed to move to a second-grade program. The sense of competence demonstrated by the children is a key factor in their continued success. Historically, 100% of children pass the state reading competency exams given at the end of third grade.

Barbara Hildreth
Waterford-Halfmoon Elementary School
Waterford, New York

A classroom of smiles.

(Photo courtesy of Liz Agee, Lonnie B. Nelson Elementary School, Columbia, South Carolina.)

Engaging Entire Classrooms and Grade Levels

Exploring Reading Genres

Best for: *All students in Grades 2-5*

Implemented by: *Grade-level teachers*

Description

A three-point reading program, Exploring Reading Genres, was created for the third-grade students by their teachers. Already pleased with the literature that their students were reading, the teachers decided that enriching the program with integrated language arts study guides, restructuring the reading schedule, and offering motivational reading games would be beneficial. During the school year, the students are immersed in seven genres: humorous fiction, mysteries, poetry, fables, biographies, tall tales, and historical fiction. A study guide for each book within each genre emphasizes vocabulary, English, phonics, and comprehension questions based on Bloom's taxonomy.

By restructuring the reading schedule, students receive an hour of uninterrupted reading time and are grouped to achieve maximum learning. All the remedial reading students are taught by a third-grade teacher and the remedial reading teacher. This classroom teacher's remedial reading students stay, but the remainder of her students are distributed to the other teachers for the reading hour. Continuous collaboration by the teaching team assures coordination and communication. Only the pace and number of books read separate the remedial reading students from the other students. All have high standards to achieve while completing their study guides.

Benefits

The creation of the study units unified our language arts instruction into an effective and efficient program. Our standards were also unified by the creation of a rubric that was used as an evaluation tool after each study guide. Parents are especially appreciative of this program because they receive the study units, are aware of our standards through the rubric, and see their children motivated to read through the incentive reading game. Students eagerly read other books within each genre and share them with other classmates!

Robert Meyer
Austin Road Elementary School
Mahopac, New York

Power Hour

Best for: Students in Grades K-2

Implemented by: Teachers and specialists

Description

We noted through our school improvement process that we had many students with attendance and tardiness problems, particularly in kindergarten. There were also many students academically at risk in the early grades due to below-grade-level reading achievement. We decided to implement a "Power Hour" emphasizing the importance of being at school on time and focused on instruction.

Power Hour is an uninterrupted, intensive instructional hour at the beginning of the school day concentrating on reading instruction at kindergarten through second grade. Our teachers enthusiastically embraced the idea of having an uninterrupted teaching hour. Our specialists (including Title I reading specialists, learning disabilities specialist, and speech/language pathologist) rearranged their service delivery models to serve students in the classroom during this period. Support staff (music, PE, media specialist, computer teacher) also refrained from scheduling classes during this hour. With the inclusion of our specialist and support teachers, small-group instruction is made even more intense.

Our Title I schoolwide project and Kansas Accelerated Literacy Learning (KALL) programs are highlighted during Power Hour. These programs use research-based instructional practices to develop and accelerate early reading. Follow-up to our Power Hour instruction in reading is provided by trained volunteers.

Benefits

Power Hour appears to be helping us achieve our goals of accelerating achievement and reducing absences and tardies. Our preliminary data suggest that this program is at least contributing to our positive growth. Our attendance problems have decreased by more than 50%. We have met the state standard of excellence in reading. Although our successes cannot be attributed only to this program, we feel that the Power Hour provides an excellent format for our early intervention.

Catherine McDonald
Central Elementary School
Olathe, Kansas

Reading Beyond

Best for: Students in Grades 1-6

Implemented by: Students and parents

Description

At Colegio Catolico Notre Dame Elementary School, we are always pursuing new alternatives to help students improve their reading performance and become active readers.

One of our local newspapers, the *San Juan Star* (Spanish edition), recently began publishing "The Mini Page" dedicated to young readers. Our third-grade teacher motivated her students to bring in the section to be read in the classroom. Now, our third graders anxiously await every Tuesday for Mini Page Day.

They are thrilled to read about different topics that cover all academic subjects and other activities such as puzzles, crafts, ideas, and even recipes for beginners. The outcome of this activity has been so effective that we are implementing it in their English class and in other grades as well.

Benefits

This activity helps students reach out beyond reading requirements. It has proven to give them a feeling of achievement and increased self-accomplishment. The Mini Page could be considered a resource for curriculum connections and it could easily be used by both self-contained and departmental teachers. It also offers an opportunity for parents and children to sit down and read together. If there is no Mini Page in your area, perhaps you could contact your local newspaper and provide the idea. It is really a worthwhile commitment.

Sister Bernardine Marie Fontanez-Cotto SSND
Colegio Catolico Notre Dame Elementary School
Caguas, Puerto Rico

Book Studies

Best for: *Students in primary grades*
Implemented by: *Classroom teachers*

Description

Cranbury School students enter first grade functioning at various reading levels. To address individual needs of the students, they are grouped within the classroom for reading instruction based on their reading ability. The first-grade reading level ranges from the primer to the second-grade level. The first-grade book studies enable the teacher to address each reading group's skill level while providing for whole-class instruction in reading.

The current reading program makes use of a basal and whole-language approach to the teaching of reading. The teachers incorporate phonics into the basal program, emphasizing the relationship of sounds to symbols during instruction. The basal series makes use of a controlled vocabulary and addresses comprehension and language arts skills in the process.

To provide our students with the opportunity to read real literature, the school instituted the use of book studies to provide opportunities for students to read an entire book, rather than the short basal stories typically associated with the teaching of reading in the primary grades. This enables the school to implement a whole-language approach in the teaching of reading.

Teachers make use of fictional and nonfictional books at the first- and second-grade levels. Such books as *Nate the Great, Cam Jansen, Henry and Mudge, Horrible Harry,* and *Amelia Bedelia* series, along with *The One in the Middle Is the Green Kangaroo, Freckle Juice, Chocolate Fever, Keep the Lights Burning Abbie, Frog and Toad Are Friends, Hop on Pop, Arthur's Eyes, Ira Sleeps Over, Corduroy,* and *Morris Has a Cold.*

In the course of the year, the whole class completes four book studies. As a result of the book studies, the students are able to learn new vocabulary associated with each story. Opportunity is provided for children to discuss their reading, compare characters, compare and contrast books, identify the parts of the story, engage in art projects related to the story, and write stories of their own based on what they have read.

Benefits

After completing an author study, the students were also motivated to read other books on their own written by the same author. They were exposed to chapter books at a younger age. Teachers noticed an increase in reading enjoyment and an improvement in students' reading comprehension and vocabulary.

The book studies can be used as a whole-class reading lesson or with small-group instruction. Book studies lead to enrichment activities in reading, writing, critical thinking, word analysis, and vocabulary development.

Robert Bartoletti
Cranbury School
Cranbury, New Jersey

Helping Students Make
Interdisciplinary Reading Connections

Best for: *All students taught in block or team format*

Implemented by: *Two seventh-grade and two eighth-grade blocks at an urban middle school*

Description

Although most of our native-born students were able to read at grade level, as a faculty we became concerned that many students were not using reading as a way to make the vital interdisciplinary connections that we were seeking. At the same time, as adults we wanted a way to reinforce the notion that reading does not occur only in their English class. Our full-time reading specialist came up with an innovative way to help.

Each teacher in seventh and eighth grade was given a chart with five pockets attached and labeled, one for each subject taught in the block. Each week, each teacher in the block wrote out one to five vocabulary cards, with a word on one side and its definition or a related activity on the reverse. Cards were distributed to other teachers in the block.

During class time, teachers used the cards to review, make connections between subjects, and help students find meaning through etymology. Students were encouraged to use the charts independently for test preparation, vocabulary review, and as an aid for homework. Words ranged from basic vocabulary to enrichment terms and were treated both in and out of context.

Benefits

The reinforcement of materials outside of the expected classroom setting helps to break into the "forgetting curve." Research indicates that students tend to forget a large portion of new material unless it is readdressed within a limited time period. This reinforcement allows the brain to encode the information deeper. Knowledge then goes from short-term into long-term memory. On a more conscious level, students see the transference of knowledge through reading modeled before them as teachers seek ways to incorporate the new vocabulary into the language of the classroom.

Michael D. O'Branski
East Middle School
Binghamton, New York

Developing Strategic Readers

Best for: *Students in Grades 1-2*

Implemented by: *Trained teachers*

Description

Recognizing that our first and second graders weren't reading as well as we wanted them to, we decided to employ the Cunningham 4-block model of instructional delivery. With the 4-block model, students are given daily opportunities to learn and employ reading and writing strategies, read independently on an appropriate level, and work intensively with words using several research-based approaches. Appropriate instruction and independent reading levels are determined using the John's Reading Inventory. Once these levels are determined, the teacher selects a variety of appropriate books from which the student may select one or more to read independently. Students are instructed using grade-level texts 3 days a week and easier texts 2 days a week. During this instructional time, students are taught reading skills and strategies that they apply immediately after the lesson. During the writing time, students are taught appropriate writing skills and strategies and watch while the teacher models those same skills and strategies. During the time provided for working with words, the teacher demonstrates phonetic decoding strategies and gives students an opportunity to manipulate words.

Benefits

All students benefit from daily practice in reading and writing. Research has shown that the more students read and write, the better they will be at it. Students feel more successful when they are given an opportunity to practice on an appropriate level. Teachers have reported that students are performing on a higher level than they were at this time last year. But all of the benefits are immediate. Continued use of the 4-block instructional delivery model will provide students with an appropriate foundation on which to build future content area studies.

Zandra Cook
Easterling Primary School
Marion, South Carolina

Second Helping

Best for: *Small classes of students in middle school setting*

Implemented by: *Teachers with reading specialist or LD certification*

Description

Our plan for assisting students whose reading skills are below grade level is called Second Helping. This is a 12-week course (due to become a 24-week course next year) that replaces an elective. Specific students are recommended by teachers or parents, and are based, in part, on standardized tests. The student-teacher ratio is approximately 10:1.

The class atmosphere is informal and encourages a feeling of readers and writers coming together. The curriculum focuses on two areas: increasing students' abilities with phonemic awareness and vocabulary and establishing the connection between reading and writing.

Phonics rules are applied to multisyllabic words, and vocabulary is developed using the Megawords series by Kristin Johnson and Polly Bayed. The reading-writing connection is fostered by reading high-interest novels, such as *Pigman* by Paul Zindel and Jeremy Thatcher and *Dragon Hatcher* by Bruce Coville, then writing about those novels using Diana Hanbury King's writing series, Writing Skills. It is reinforced using comprehension and written language activities from the Language Circle series Project Read by Victoria E. Greene and Mary Lee Enfield. This series focuses specifically on analysis of reading skills and application to writing processes.

Benefits

As teachers know, as class size diminishes, activity options are increased. This program provides a positive climate and low student-teacher ratio to motivate readers and writers. To further emphasize individual needs, students are required to sign a contract promising to work to the best of their abilities. Integration of reading and writing skills reinforces reading comprehension. This enhances learning across the curriculum, as students apply their new skills to learning.

Charles A. Davis
Grayslake Middle School
Grayslake, Illinois

Make-a-Book Literary Project

Best for: Total classes in primary and intermediate grades
Implemented by: Teachers and parent volunteers

Description

Make-a-Book is an arts-based literary project at Harrisville Elementary School. An adaptation of Image Making Within the Writing Process, developed by Beth Olshansky of the University of Rhode Island, it currently is being used by second- and fifth-grade students as a part of Reading Buddies (younger students paired with older students for reading activities.)

Make-a-Book integrates reading and writing with art. Focusing on books by Eric Carle and Leo Lionni, students listen to and read picture books with collage illustrations. Students create personal portfolios of hand-painted texture papers. Emphasis is placed on identifying the main idea, plot, setting, and details. Parts of a book are also learned including title, dedication, and "About the Author/Illustrator" pages. Once art portfolios are completed, students look for story ideas within their paintings. Stories are developed, using steps of the writing process. Students confer with peers, reading buddies, and teachers to revise and edit stories. During the writing process, illustrations are created using collages made from texture paintings. Parent volunteers assist in typing the books, then students complete their illustrations. Books are bound using spiral binding and plastic covers. The final project activity is an author/illustrator tea.

Benefits

The Make-a-Book project has been highly successful in enhancing learning in the language arts. It respects diverse abilities and learning styles of students. Each child can be successful in the reading, writing, and art aspects. Texture paintings require no particular artistic talents. They are a springboard for each student to tell or write a story. Teachers who have implemented this project report improved reading and writing skills, as well as enhanced self-esteem. Enthusiasm is continuous as students share their "real" books throughout our school!

Mr. Marion Roby
Harrisville Elementary School
Harrisville, West Virginia

Steps to Success in First Grade:
Motivate, Measure, and Monitor

Best for: Individual students in primary grades

Implemented by: Classroom teachers

Description

Motivation is the key to learning how to read. The teacher and the child must have a firm belief in the child's ability to learn. Positive affirmations such as "I believe in you!" and "I am a confident learner!" begin on the first day of school. Reading skills are evaluated and an individualized plan of action is created for each child. We start where the child is, using a variety of teaching strategies. Growth is measured monthly. New goals are set. Progress is shown on each child's individual graph called "Steps to Success." This graph monitors vocabulary words and oral reading levels. The steps lead to success and second grade. The children are highly motivated because they have a clear vision of what they want to achieve. They can see their own personal growth in reading as they climb the steps.

And they can imagine taking all the steps to achieve success. Monthly progress reports are given to parents and the principal. Because discouragement is a roadblock to learning, we encourage and celebrate every small step along the way. The children are willing to work according to the plan, knowing that it will bring them a step closer to their goal.

Benefits

Every child has made tremendous progress. During the current school year, every child has reached grade level in oral reading (Level 18) and in vocabulary. The first graders have been highly motivated: "Please test me! I think I can climb up another step on my graph." Parents report that their children are happy and proud of their great accomplishment: "I can read!" Getting everyone on grade level in oral reading and vocabulary by the end of December has given us lots of freedom to work harder on comprehension and enjoy more art, music, and drama. The students and the teachers joyfully report that "school is fun!"

Robert W. Hansen
Jefferson Elementary School
Clovis, California

Take-Home Readers

Best for: First- and second-grade readers

Implemented by: Teachers and librarian

Description

Our first- and second-grade students know that they are readers. Parents of young readers requested ways to read with their children in texts that were not frustrating for both the parent and child. Our take-home book program was fully implemented to provide emergent to fluent readers with many opportunities to practice their strategies at the appropriate instructional level. The children wanted the chance to choose from many types of books and topics.

With initial funding from the PTO, we purchased individual copies of books at emergent to early fluent levels, which became part of the library resources. We have made additions to this collection from community grants and the school budget a priority. Our collection has grown to more than 900 books. Library checkout frees the teachers to discuss books with students. The books are leveled according to the Reading Recovery levels used for classroom texts. They are stored in clear bags in ranges of levels so children can self-select books that meet their interests. The children have "Blue Ribbon" take-home bags as an incentive for reading and taking care of the books.

Special times are set up to allow circulation on a daily basis. Students may return books during their weekly library visit and during class time at their teacher's discretion. On two mornings each week, first and second graders have a "special time" when only they are allowed to arrive before school opens to return their book bags. Art and music teachers are on duty to assist children in selection and checkout. It is exciting to watch the interaction of students recommending books to others and discussing topics and types of reading.

Mary Hosking
Michael Kennedy Elementary School
Houston, Texas

Reading Intramurals

Best for: Students in Grades K-4

Implemented by: Teachers, paraprofessionals, and volunteers

Description

In 1994, we started serving breakfast at Lake Agassiz. We found we had some time between the time students finished eating and the time school started. We brainstormed what we could do and came up with the idea of Reading Intramurals.

Now, as soon as students finish eating they are escorted down to the Reading Intramural Room and are read to for 15 minutes. The students sign in as they come in and sit on the carpeted floor. Afternoon kindergarten students are read to in the media center 15 minutes before their session begins.

Every Friday names are drawn, and a book is given to the winner. Students who do not eat breakfast can come into the building and go to Reading Intramurals, too.

Our readers are parents, school staff, and community volunteers.

During our fall open house and any other events during the school year we ask parents to sign up to read.

Benefits

Students love to be read to, and we want to have them hear good literature. Supervision before school is always a concern, and this really solves that problem.

Parents feel great with being able to drop their children off and know they are having an additional academic experience. Parents like being able to volunteer to read to their children and their friends.

Teachers feel good knowing that their students get an extra boost by being read to before school starts.

Our business partnership likes to volunteer because it only takes 20 minutes of their time.

This program makes everyone a winner!

J. Sharon Gates
Lake Agassiz Elementary School
Grand Forks, North Dakota

Power Readers Prove Potent!

Best for: *Students in primary grades*

Implemented by: *Classroom teachers and library staff*

Description

Excited about their children's readiness to read independently but disappointed with the choices available for independent practice, our first-grade teachers went in search of appropriate, appealing reading material for these fledgling readers. Discussions with the librarian led to a look at the many "easy-to-read," "first-step," "on-your-own," and similar books that the library had and that publishers were rapidly producing. Teachers and librarian decided to pull all of these books, shelve them together in one area of the library, and let first graders use them as practice and/or take-home readers. The books were dubbed "Power Readers" and given a colorful label to help children identify them. As the children became proficient enough to participate in the program, they selected a book from this section, read it, documented this via the teacher or parent, and (usually the next day) returned the book and got another one.

Orientation on procedures and on the child's selection of books at his or her level were conducted as students became participants in the program. By February, all first graders were participating and coming to the library daily to get empowering Power Readers.

Benefits

Power Readers expose beginning independent readers to real stories by recognized authors. They allow students to self-select their own reading material while requiring that they exercise metacognitive skills as they discriminate in choosing books that are on their level. Because there is much sharing/recommending of books among classmates, even young readers are involved in authentic discussions about books. Because most participants come to the library each day, they perceive the library as an accessible place that has much to offer them. The daily flow of on-level, appealing books the program provides to young readers helps build reading proficiency, fluency, and confidence.

Elayne Kuehn
Memorial Drive Elementary School
Houston, Texas

Multisensory methods.

Story of the Week Reading Program

Best for: *Students in pre-K, kindergarten, and primary grades (1-3)*

Implemented by: *Teachers and individual students*

Description

The Story of the Week Reading Program uses whole-language, thematic, and multisensory methods to address curricular concepts in the areas of reading, language, science, social studies, social skills, and independent living. With this program, the teacher is able to meet the needs of different types of learners within the concept that is to be addressed; for example, a color, shape, or science concept. On Monday, the teacher reads the story to the class. Using a story chart, the children discuss the characters, setting, problems and solutions, and concept, including cooking, arts and crafts, drama, and games. Special-area teachers or therapists may also do related activities. Students frequently reread the story, find certain sight words within the story, find words that include identified letter sounds or combinations, and do writing activities that may include rebus stories, word lists, or original stories.

Benefits

Students are exposed to and practice a variety of objectives while experiencing fun and varied activities. They are able to make logical connections between reading and other curriculum areas. Students develop social skills by working together on projects and performances. Learners of different styles—auditory, visual, and kinesthetic—are all able to participate fully and benefit from the same group instruction. Reading skills, including vocabulary development, comprehension, phonetics, and sequencing, can all be addressed.

Sharon McMillan
The Midland School
North Branch, New Jersey

Reading Across the Curriculum

Best for: Students in Grades 1-6

Implemented by: Classroom teachers

Description

To make learning meaningful and authentic for students, reading is integrated throughout all content areas in interdisciplinary units of study that focus on connecting curricular knowledge to universal concepts, as well as character values.

Teachers select a content area, usually science or social studies, that is most grade appropriate for the universal concept (unity/ diversity, systems/interdependence, limitations/interactions, change/continuity, cause/effect) they are studying. For example, under the concept of systems/interdependence, first graders may be learning about community workers, third graders may be investigating various ecosystems, and sixth graders may be examining economic systems and global interdependence. As they study and make generalizations about systems and interdependence, students deepen their understanding and appreciation for the values of cooperation, sharing, responsibility, and respect.

Throughout the unit, students are engaged in personal inquiry, higher-level thinking skills, and language skills (reading, writing, speaking, and listening). Music, art, and other curriculum areas are integrated naturally. Students are given choices as to the various types of independent or group projects they will produce and share with the rest of the class.

Benefits

Reading is meaningful and highly motivating as students seek answers to their own questions. In the process, students are applying reading skills (predicting, validating, questioning, visualizing, retelling, identifying main ideas/themes, evaluating, drawing conclusions, and making applications to their lives), engaging in various type of reading (content area, literature, fiction, nonfiction), and accessing information from multiple sources—print and nonprint (video, CD-ROM, Internet). Students are also increasing their vocabulary, learning new concepts, expanding their base of knowledge, and broadening their interests.

Doreen Y. Higa
Momilani Elementary School
Pearl City, Hawaii

Reading 1, 2, 3

Best for: Individual students in Grades 4-5

Implemented by: Trained teachers

Description

For students to achieve reading at grade level and beyond requires a three-part program at our school. Because all students learn in their own unique way and at their own pace, our job is to teach every student using a variety of approaches.

The first and most basic approach is through intense questioning strategies to enable the students to engage in higher-level thinking. Each student is gently encouraged to reach beyond the obvious, to make validated inferences, to understand character motives, and to see connections to other literature and life.

The second part of our program remediates and accelerates readers at their own pace through the use of CCC computer software. Each student is gently encouraged to reach beyond the obvious, make validated inferences, understand character motives, and see connections to other literature and life.

Third, each student is required to read independently from an extensive list of Accelerated Reader books. They are assigned to read on or above their grade level any book of their choice on any topic. Time is allotted in class as well as on special reading days to create excitement for reading. When the book is completed, a short test is given to assess comprehension. Regular celebrations are held to recognize accomplishments in this program. Teachers also read dramatically to students from books on this list to tempt them to read.

Benefits

The three-part reading program builds better readers through interactive discussion in the classroom, remediation, acceleration through the computer programs, and independent exploration of available literature. As students participate in our program, teachers and parents report a greater interest in and excitement for reading quality literature. Those who have not been active, independent readers gain the skills and desire necessary to take a step toward becoming lifelong readers.

Jean Brassfield
Pershing Elementary School
Muskogee, Oklahoma

Reading Roundtable

Best for: Students in Grades 1-5

Implemented by: Students, parents, and teachers

Description

This great idea in reading is called Reading Roundtable, named to coordinate with our school theme of the Rossmoor Knights. It is most appropriate for primary and intermediate students, specifically students in Grades 1 through 5. The program, designed for pairs of students, is composed of an emerging reader and a more experienced one and is meant to occur in a "lab" setting under the supervision of a credentialed teacher. Implementation of this program involves students (about 60 at a time), classroom teachers, and parents of the participating students.

Reading Roundtable matches older and younger students in a tutorial setting designed specifically to strengthen and reinforce reading skills of primary children who are recommended for reading support by their classroom teachers. Upper-grade students are recruited to work in the program during their lunch free time each day for 7 weeks. Prior to meeting their tutees, older students receive approximately 8 hours of training from the school learning specialist on topics such as "ways to praise," "what to do if your student gets stuck," and "how to introduce a book." The training and format of the daily 30-minute session is adapted from the Reading Recovery model. Using a wide variety of trade books from preprimer through second-grade reading level, tutors are responsible for helping their students read at least two books a day during the 7-week period. They are also responsible for keeping records of their tutee's progress and for communicating frequently with the learning specialist, who gives approval before increasing the reading level of the tutee's books. Parents of older students must give permission for their child to participate as a tutor, and parents of younger students must agree to work with their child each night.

Benefits

Since September 1994, 230 primary and 270 upper-grade students (about 30 pairs each session) have participated in Reading Round-table. The program, combined with excellent classroom reading instruction, produces strong readers. An "average" primary student participant reads 135 books during the 7 weeks and gains three to five Reading Recovery book levels. In addition, 90% of participating students continue to read at or above grade level at the end of the fifth grade. Parent and teacher surveys completed after each session are always 100% positive. Other significant benefits are the gains made by the older students in responsibility and self-esteem and the "polishing" of their own reading skills.

Laurel Telfer
Rossmoor Elementary School
Los Alamitos, California

Preschool Library Program

Best for: 3- and 4-year-old preschoolers
Implemented by: Librarian

Description

Many of our entering kindergartners are lacking in basic skills. As an outreach to our community, we offer a weekly half-hour Preschool Library Program. Each program begins with a greeting followed by a story, finger play, action rhyme, matching activity, and occasional craft.

When the preschoolers arrive, they find their name strip on the table. (They have progressed to recognizing their name in print.) The librarian holds up one strip at a time and as the preschooler recognizes his or her name, responds with "Good morning." The preschooler then tells what letter his or her name begins with and its sound. The letter is then located in the alphabet. This is followed by the ABC song and a short alphabet matching game.

Various mini-lessons have included colors, shapes, opposites, counting, sequencing, left/right, classifying, and the senses.

For our Easter week story, we read *Max's Chocolate Chicken,* had a match-the-egg game, made bunny ears, and had an egg hunt. The preschoolers found the table that had a basket with their name on the handle. Then they put the paper eggs only in their basket that had a letter of their name. They also got to pick up the jelly beans and cookie treats for their basket.

Benefits

Each of the programs follows the same format. Through this continuity the preschoolers become comfortable in the library setting. Painfully shy preschoolers who wouldn't join in can now say their name to check out their own book. The primary goal is to instill a love of books, from which we hope will develop a love of reading. By working on skills such as listening, visual and auditory discrimination, fine motor coordination, and concept of print, we have a group of preschoolers with exposure to early literacy and with readiness skills essential for future reading success.

Betsy Palmer
G. L. Scarselli Elementary School
Gardnerville, Nevada

Book buddies.

Multigrade Book Buddies

Best for: *Students in all grades*

Implemented by: *Teachers and students*

Description

A large percentage of kindergarten students enter school with little or no literacy background. In an effort to provide these students with more opportunities to listen to stories and books, Book Buddies was initiated. Selected kindergarten students were paired with a fourth-grade book buddy. The fourth-grade students were instructed in reading aloud, encouraging participation, listening strategies, and tracking print.

Book Buddies met three times a week for 20 minutes. Appropriate emergent literature books were shared with their buddy, and fourth-grade students in turn shared a book with the kindergarten student. Following the "buddy reading" time, fourth graders reflected in a journal on the time spent with their buddy. As the kindergarten students reading improved, the fourth-grade buddies shared in the excitement, often asking the teacher to "listen to my buddy read! He can read it all by himself."

Benefits

Book Buddies provided the fourth-grade students with a purpose for reading and improved their self-esteem. The kindergarten students received additional exposure to literature while improving listening and thinking skills. All students involved benefited in the areas of reading and writing.

Kerry Laster
Shreve Island Elementary School
Shreveport, Louisiana

Teaching Literary Analysis to
Intermediate-Grade Students

Best for: *All students in intermediate-grade classrooms, particularly Grades 5-6*

Implemented by: *Teachers*

Description

Our school recognizes that movement beyond the levels of recall and comprehension is important for the formation and nurturing of higher-level critical and creative thinking skills. Additionally, a conscious effort to address multiple intelligence is crucial to stimulate all types of learners. Toward these goals, Patricia Sullivan, fifth-grade teacher and national certified trainer for Project Success Enrichment (PSE), employed PSE literary analysis strategies and techniques promoting multiple intelligence to introduce her students to the concepts of theme, moral, conflict, setting, plot, protagonist/antagonist, and character education.

In late October and early November, short but quality works of children's literature were read aloud (*The Widow's Broom* by Van Allsburg, *The Rag Coat* by Mills, and *Something From Nothing* by Gilman), each seemingly very different on the surface, but each with an emerging theme of thanksgiving. Using class discussions, cooperative learning, triple Venn diagrams, and personality trait matrices, Sullivan was able to elicit from pupils the similarities and differences in theme, moral, conflict, personality traits, and protagonistic and antagonistic characters and ideas. Students then used their notes, diagrams, and matrices to compose paragraphs detailing the aspects of the three books and to participate in small- and large-group discussions.

Benefits

This 2-week lesson proved to be a channel for ensuring success, especially for reluctant readers. It was exciting to see small children using and understanding "big kid" terminology; their self-esteem and pride in their learning were self-evident! It was rewarding to witness 10-year-olds venturing into the realm of abstract thought by discovering that the antagonist in Gilman's book was not a character, but rather the passage of time. Students have since demonstrated mastery of literary analysis as they discuss and write about novels they read. They have internalized concepts they will not soon forget!

Janet P. Murray
St. Ignatius Catholic School
Mobile, Alabama

Express yourself.

Reading and Technology

Best for: Individual or grouped students in Grades 2-8
Implemented by: Trained teachers and technology instructor

Description

To encourage a love of reading and to engage students in activities in which reading is fundamental, St. Peter's School staff initiated a program to integrate subject matter with technology. This program allows students to explore, express creativity, and communicate through a variety of technological means. Reading facilitates such a program and is an integral part of every step in the process.

The topics that formed the program were those covered in other subject areas and were suggested by classroom teachers for extended study in the computer lab. The use of Encarta, Internet, trade books, and biographies was the springboard for a variety of projects. Science students studied biomes and presented elaborate "HyperStudio" projects on biomes of the world based on the teacher's criteria. Music students used the "Multimedia Workshop" to explore a variety of musical styles and to make a presentation containing historical highlights, musical selections, and information about artists. Sixth graders also used the "Multimedia Workshop" to develop a multimedia promotional tool for a local outdoor school that fosters hands-on learning in a natural environment. On the topic of Alaska, second graders prepared personal journals and were able to weave research with creative writing through the use of "Kid's Works Deluxe."

Benefits

The integration of curricular topics, technology, and the reading/writing process produces an effective holistic learning experience. A high level of interest was observed in the students as they came to the computer lab eager to create their multimedia projects. Using this program, students are actively involved in reading as a natural part of the process of creating the entire project. Reading is experienced in relationship with other content areas rather than in isolation. Students realize the importance of reading to accomplish

74 BEST IDEAS FOR READING

their goals, and excitement is generated as students share what they
have learned with others.

James R. Smith
St. Peter's Elementary School
Mansfield, Ohio

Commitment to Early Literacy

Best for: Students in primary classrooms
Implemented by: Trained teachers

Description

How can we improve the effectiveness of reading instruction for
primary learners? Reading Recovery offers intensive intervention
for the most needy beginning readers, but other students also need
a jump-start to become competent, confident readers. Our solution
was to train K-2 classroom teachers to use the strategies of Reading
Recovery in the classroom setting.

Over the course of 2 years, all K-2 teachers participated in district
training and attended workshops to gain information about how
children learn to read and research-based instructional techniques.
The commitment to early literacy by all primary teachers created a
network for teachers and a literacy culture in the school. Although
the emphasis was on early literacy instruction, schoolwide goals focused on assessing and teaching at the appropriate level and increasing the availability of books at all levels.

Immediately, primary classes were structured to offer a balanced
day that included

- Daily reading, writing, and oral language instruction
- Phonemic awareness and explicit phonics
- Whole-group instruction, small-group instruction, and inde-
  pendent centers

- Assessment-driven instruction based on analysis of running records
- Daily guided reading at the appropriate level
- Language arts instruction interwoven throughout the day across all subjects

Specific instructional practices that develop independent problem-solving readers and writers are

- Word wall
- Making words
- Interactive writing
- Word analogies
- Development of concepts of print in kindergarten
- Daily practice with leveled book baskets or partner reading

Benefits

Training classroom teachers to use effective early literacy strategies benefited teachers and students. Teachers collaborated to develop and share ideas or materials that worked. All available resources were used to increase the abundance of books at all levels, especially for beginning readers. Students enjoyed consistent instructional language and procedures from grade to grade. Instruction focused on the learner and his or her needs rather than the material being used. Although specific data are not available, teachers note that for the past 2 years children are entering the next grade better prepared. They read at a higher level with more strategies, and they write with more detail, expressive language, and correct conventions and spelling than in years past.

Commitment to early literacy instruction, consistent effective practices, and continuous assessment have improved language arts skills among our primary students.

Marie Bairey
Sonoma Elementary School
Modesto, California

Puppet Phonics

Best for: *Primary grades in teaching phonics*

Implemented by: *Classroom teachers*

Description

Puppet Phonics (by Terrie Frantz, second-grade teacher at the Hebrew Academy of Huntington Beach) incorporates large animal puppets and large monsterlike marionettes to teach phonics. Using the puppets, the teacher creates new ways of presenting vowels, combinations of letters, blends, and so on.

Stories used to make the puppets "speak" are extremely ridiculous and humorous. These two characteristics create a lasting memory of the sounds.

Stories are repeated daily before reading, choosing a puppet whose vowel or blended sound will be necessary for the story of the day. Starting with the basic vowel sounds and proceeding through a normal sequence of single sounds to more complex blends of sounds, students build their skills.

Students become involved with the silly stories the puppets tell. For example: Goofy and Henry are twin puppets who help Izzy Lizzy (the vowel "I") get over her fear of the night by standing next to her and giving sight with a bright light at night, which gives her might not fright to be all right and not uptight.

Naturally, Goofy and Henry also enjoy being silent in words and sometimes provide an "f" sound—depending on the phonics lesson.

Puppets become such good friends that children are permitted to take them home to share the stories with their parents, reinforcing the lessons learned in school.

Benefits

Repetition of the sounds in memorable stories provides students with a new and different way of becoming familiar with the various blends of vowels and consonants. The puppets are particularly at home in the second-grade classroom where the basic sounds of single letters have presumably been mastered in first grade and students are now ready to tackle the more difficult combinations of letters.

Parents report real excitement when students have an opportunity to show them how much they and the puppets know about phonics when the puppets come home with students. The puppets in this case are a welcome public relations tool, too!

Cinda Russell
Hebrew Academy
Huntington Beach, California

Reading Mentors

Best for: *Individual students in primary classrooms*

Implemented by: *Reading and classroom teachers and faculty student council adviser*

Description

In January of this year, we began an intensive schedule of training and reflection meetings. During this time, fourth-, fifth-, and sixth-grade mentors were taught reading strategies and practical suggestions to use with their first-, second-, and third-grade students. The upper-level mentor was paired with a lower-grade-level student according to specific reading levels, interests, and personalities. With this careful planning, trusting and effective relationships developed. Once this rapport was established and the training was completed, the magic began: Struggling students became involved in fun and effective reading practice.

Benefits

The addition of this reading mentoring program has most definitely added to our school's success story. For example, during the 1997-1998 school year, 34 third-grade students received remedial reading services. On the May 1998 New York state reading prep, 94% earned a passing score. Also, several second-grade students have shown dramatic reading improvement. Specifically, Kiera was reading at 1.5 grade level in December 1997 and improved in May 1998 to a 3.0 reading level! Along the same lines, Dominique was reading on a 1.5 level in December 1997 and in May tested to a 3.2 reading level! (It is important to note that these second-grade students were paired with mentors in January.)

These reading mentors put forth an increased amount of effort and commitment in helping these younger students become better readers. (Some gave up lunch recess and special periods to meet with their young mentor buddies.)

It is clear that this reading mentoring program not only is effective in increasing reading levels but helps to form genuine student relationships and responsibilities that otherwise would not have developed.

Rachelle M. Salerno
Thomas O'Brien Academy of Science and Technology
Albany, New York

Visualization to Enhance Reading Comprehension

Best for: *Individual students in primary classrooms*

Implemented by: *Trained teachers and aides*

Description

Often, success in reading is measured by a student's ability to decode the text. However, a better measure of reading competence would be, "Do they understand the text?" Although fluency is important, comprehension is the most important reading goal.

Many studies conclude that comprehension must go hand-in-hand with associations to the text. Comprehension "is not a purely verbal process; for the written symbols to have meaning, they must be associated with the objects, actions, and qualities they represent." Some years ago, Joel R. Levin (coeditor, with V. L. Allen, of *Cognitive Learning in Children: Theories and Strategies,* Academic Press, 1976) conducted an experiment with students. "One group of these students was told to read a story and imagine a picture for each sentence that was read. The second group read the same story but without imagining pictures. The students who visualized images to go with the sentences scored forty percent higher on reading comprehension."

Because comprehension is paramount to success in reading, we look for ways to increase this skill in our students. One way to accomplish this is to have the students illustrate the stories they have just read. For the younger students, we create response journals where students respond to the classroom literature. Students first draw a picture of the story about their observations, experiences, and so forth. Older students illustrate the main idea of the story or the part they liked best.

Benefits

The use of visualization to enhance reading comprehension demonstrates an irresistible way to get students personally involved with this skill. When students involve themselves in reading, they open opportunities for us to use those "teachable" moments. In Bloom's taxonomy, personal experience is at the top with respect to "true" learning. The use of illustration for enhanced reading comprehension is but one way to foster personal experiences to literature. However, we find it to be one of the best ways. With new connections to reading comes an increased interest in linking up life experiences with school experiences. These connections make for not only a more well-rounded student but a more well-rounded human. After all, as the saying goes, "A picture is worth a thousand words."

Betty Ann Courtney and Sherry Steen
Valley View Elementary School
Austin, Texas

Pick a theme for your school.

(Photo courtesy of Katherine Barton, Oak Grove Middle School, Oak Grove, Missouri.)

Involving Everyone in the School

"Hand-in-Hand We Can Change the World!"

Best for: *Students in all elementary grades*

Implemented by: *The entire school is involved with the program's implementation. Planning for the program originates with our "Dream Team," who develops our schoolwide and grade-level themes for each school year.*

Description

"Hand-in-Hand We Can Change the World!" is Bethel's schoolwide theme. This theme serves as a focus for all that we plan for the school year. Each grade level has a theme and service project related to the schoolwide theme. This is in addition to our schoolwide projects.

The philosophy of working cooperatively as a school is integrated throughout our instructional program. Reading and writing are intertwined life skills that comprise the language arts area. You cannot teach one without the other.

Two of our instructional activities include our schoolwide Writing Day and Bethel Scramble. Our schoolwide Writing Day may focus on one of our grade-level themes or on other motivational topics. A story starter is presented to all of our students and teachers, and they write the rest of the story. At one time, the footprints of each grade level's "mascot" appeared in the hall of the school. After discovering the prints, the children were prompted to write, "What happened?" These stories were then read in class. Our Bethel Scramble involves all staff members, teaching and nonteaching, "scrambling" to other grade-level classes to share a book with the students.

Benefits

The life skills of reading and writing are integrated with our schoolwide and grade-level themes. Learning becomes relevant and meaningful. The children see the connection between reading and writing through the schoolwide Writing Day.

Bethel's Scramble provides positive role models and produces the biggest benefit. By working together as a school family, relationships are firmly established. A nurturing environment exists so that our children take risks with their learning. The enthusiasm we see daily reinforces the importance of a love of learning. We truly believe that "Hand-in-Hand We Can Change the World!"

Katherine H. Howard
Bethel Elementary School
Simpsonville, South Carolina

Schoolwide Reading Program

Best for: Individual students in preschool through eighth grades

Implemented by: Teachers and parents

Description

Our school has developed a yearlong (September-June), school-wide reading program that incorporates family involvement, comprehension questions, and friendly competition.

Each child in our school is assigned by the teacher to the blue, red, or yellow reading team. To certify the number of books read by each child, students submit verification forms signed by their parents. On the verification form, students list the names of five books read and the total number of pages. Students are encouraged to continuously bring in reading forms throughout the year. We translate the number of pages read into book equivalents: Kindergarten to Grade 2, 25 pages equals one book; Grades 3 to 5, 50 pages equals one book; Grades 6 to 8, 75 pages equals one book.

After each book is read, parents are required to ask two comprehension questions. The school provides each family with suggested comprehension questions, which can be applied to any book. Sample questions include: "What would be another possible title for your book?" "What are three things that happen in the book?" "What event came first, second, and then third?"

The progress of each reading team is monitored throughout the year. We cheer on each of the reading teams throughout the year to help maintain enthusiasm. The total number of books read by each team is regularly tabulated and posted for all to see on our colorful reading mural in the lunchroom.

At the end of the year, the number of books read by each child is placed on the student's report card, as well as the book equivalent average for the class. Parents can then monitor the number of books read by their child in relation to the norm by the class.

Benefits

We emphasize with parents that there is no better way to encourage student achievement than by reading. A great benefit of the program is parental involvement. Books read to children by parents in grades preschool through second count in the contest and are included on the verification form. Parents also are engaged with students because of the requirement of asking comprehensive questions. Our experience is that the reading program, especially for elementary students, has provided an incredible incentive for reading. Books that are read over the summer from the school's official reading list are eligible to count toward the next year's reading program. The reading program has fostered a positive climate of reading in our school. We make a big deal about the top reader in each class, regardless of which team they are on, and we publish their picture in the local newspaper. In 1996-1997, our 490 students read 36,494 book equivalents and 88% of our students were at or above grade level in total reading as measured by our spring 1997 Stanford Achievement Testing.

Robert H. Tennies
Boca Raton Christian School
Boca Raton, Florida

Reading Incentive Program

Best for: *Students in all elementary grades*

Implemented by: *All teachers*

Description

The Reading Incentive Program, in its ninth year, celebrates and reinforces reading for all students who participate in the 3-month-long program.

The Reading Incentive kick-off begins with a schoolwide reading rally. The assembly introduces the theme for the year. Themes have included, for example, Exploring New Worlds, Camp Read-a-Lot, and Blast Off With Books. The staff and students perform skits, sing songs, and do readings to excite the students about reading. The process of the program, including the game board, is explained.

Kindergarten through first-grade students are encouraged to read 15 extra minutes per night; second- and third-grade students are encouraged to read 20 minutes extra; and fifth- and sixth-grade (and staff) read 30 minutes extra per night. Parents or other caregivers sign each student's game board as the student completes each block of reading. Staff members post theirs to share as well. Students receive a new game board each month to record their nightly reading. They color in one space for each night. They are allowed to miss 8 days during the month and still qualify for a prize. Prizes may include free movies or swim center passes, McDonald's coupons, or other certificates donated by local businesses. Also, students receive other thematic prizes such as pencils, bookmarks, and erasers. The culminating prize for those students who turn in a completed game board for 3 months is a book of their choice.

The culminating event for students who participate for the 3 months is Friday Night Prime Time. Friday Night Prime Time varies for the different grade levels. Kindergarten through second-grade students and parents have an activity and reading evening. Students rotate through activities such as creative dramatics, T-shirt fish printing, stargazing, storytelling, beach ball volleyball, and other relays. Most important, between each activity, students disperse to various classrooms to listen to staff and parents read stories and to partake of a healthy snack. Third and fourth graders enjoy a sleep-over at school after an evening of energetic activities and stories. Fifth and sixth graders spend an evening at the swim center with staff members. Students learn to dive and hone swimming abilities through the various relays that earn them books.

Each year, the reading specialist and the staff gather to brainstorm new ways to enhance Meneley's literacy program. This year, a Family Reading Evening was added. Family Reading Evening includes various hands-on activities to assist parents in knowing ways to strengthen their child's love for reading. Teachers and community members share in literacy activities such as felt-board stories, puppet making, book projects, sing-alongs, storytelling, read-alouds, computer reading and writing activities, big books, and pattern books. Family Reading Evening was held in conjunction with our Book Fair. Teachers gave book talks and assisted parents in selecting books.

Pauline Moley
C. C. Meneley Elementary School
Gardnerville, Nevada

Reader's Workshop

Best for: *Students in Grades K-6*

Implemented by: *Individual students, teachers, administrators, parents, and volunteers*

Description

At Center School, we are especially proud of our language arts program. For the past few years, we have been researching and implementing Reader's Workshop. This approach, which was taught to us by Lucy Calkins and her staff at Teachers College of Columbia University, has at its core individualized reading for each student in the class each day. The goal of this approach is to encourage our children to become highly competent, lifelong readers who initiate reading and construct meaning. Because this is an individualized approach, each child reads at the child's own level and progresses at his or her own pace; however, it is the responsibility of the teacher to closely monitor and assess the child's progress. At the heart of this is independent reading. Partner reading, book shares, read alouds, children making appropriate book choices, reading each night at home, and quality assessment are additional components used to build the literate community.

Our language arts coordinator, who is integral to the success of this philosophy, initiated connections with Lucy Calkins of Columbia University. Lucy and her staff spent several days inservicing our staff during the summer and school year.

Benefits

We are extremely proud of our Reader's Workshop. The reactions from children in terms of their enjoyment of reading has skyrocketed. We have created lifelong readers in our school's literate community. Our Connecticut Mastery Test scores have risen greatly in the area of reading, and our D.R.P. scores in Grades 2 and 3 have risen accordingly. The parents have expressed a high level of support for the approach as they experience their children reading at levels the children had never before achieved. We are thrilled with the enthusiasm of the children for reading, which they consider fun and exciting.

Andrienne Longobucco
The Center School
Litchfield, Connecticut

International Week

Best for: *Students in Grades K-8*

Implemented by: *Entire school and parents*

Description

International Week is a series of both classroom and schoolwide activities that highlight specific countries. The initial steps involve scheduling, recruiting volunteers, getting teacher acceptance, and providing training. During International Week, we ask parents to assist with schoolwide decorations, help classroom teachers, or volunteer their expertise on a country. Our teachers have responded positively to this thematic event, with each grade level adopting a different country. International Week is designed to be multidisciplinary and culminate in a presentation for other classes. For example, in math the currency, demographics, climate, and measurement systems of the country selected could be highlighted. Excellent literature and AV support will be within the easy grasp of any librarian. Language arts might revolve around letter writing and creative writing projects. Our students have written their own plays and puppet shows. The students dress in native costumes, sing songs of the country, describe what they have learned, and often share food they have prepared.

Principal support would include payments for teacher resources (food, crafts, etc.), scheduling of presentations, schoolwide assemblies, and decorations. We often use flags of different countries for decorations. Large globes (16-foot diameter) are available and we even brought in a hot air balloon that was painted like the globe.

Benefits

Students and teachers are excited about the learning that occurs as a result of a schoolwide theme. Parents provide extra help and are very complimentary about the efforts. Students are more aware of the needs of people in other parts of our world. They also have a better understanding of geography, customs, religions, and cultural distinctives.

R. Mark Beadle
Cincinnati Hills Christian Academy
Cincinnati, Ohio

Effective Schoolwide
Reading Improvement

Best for: *Students in Grades K-5*

Implemented by: *Teachers, staff, and parents*

Description

Language arts instruction is the cornerstone of our curriculum. Teachers, staff, peers, and parents are all viewed as teachers of reading at Diplomat Elementary School. Special area teachers and other staff members teach reading during a block scheduling time. Students are empowered to select reading materials that suit their own interests, needs, and purposes. Decoding and comprehension skills are taught through the use of themes, basal texts, and literature. At the same time, effective skill instruction takes place in each classroom. Our schoolwide theme offers activities that foster reading and writing in the areas of social studies, science, health and mathematics. It includes a home-school reading program titled Parents as Reading Partners (PARP). In addition, a computerized reading management program supports and builds reading confidence through independent reading, fostering a love for literature. Students assess and monitor their growth and progress through computer-generated tests and individual reports. All of our students in Grades 1-5 participate in this program. During the 1997-1998 school year, Diplomat students read over 12,000 books and scored an average of 85% on comprehension. Our total reading program is highly motivation because it invites children to make reading choices, set and achieve personal goals, and become lifelong readers.

Benefits

As a result of implementing the computer-managed assessment, PARP, and theme activities that encourage reading, standardized test results have shown improvement. Student scores in reading comprehension rose significantly when compared with prior years. Teachers at all grade levels spent the first instructional hour of the day on language arts instruction. This time included direct instruction, sustained silent reading, and small-group work. Throughout the year, as students met their goals, they were rewarded and featured on the morning news. This keeps the motivation high. When we saw children choosing reading over recess activities, we knew that our reading program had turned our students into lifelong readers.

Linda L. Caruso
Diplomat Elementary School
Cape Coral, Florida

Reading at the Core

Best for: Students in all elementary grades

Implemented by: Faculty and staff

Description

The first goal of Eastside's School Improvement Plan places reading at the core of learning with a systematic, balanced approach using basal readers, phonics instruction, quality literature, and several innovative programs. Traditional strategies enhanced by technology-based methods provide the building blocks for a foundation in language arts. Science, social studies, and other subject area concepts and skills are introduced in reading thematic units and reinforced through hands-on activities. Discipline-based arts instruction enhances and supports the language arts curriculum, increases critical thinking skills, and adds enriching cultural experiences. Choral reading, reader's theater, dramatic play, and oral reports foster creative expression and increase pleasure in reading and oral communication. Flexible grouping and reduced class size provide for individual needs.

Accelerated Reader, a motivational program for comprehension and vocabulary improvement, allows students to accumulate highly prized points through computer assessment. Cross-grade-level pairing of students as book buddies and DEAR (Drop Everything and Read), a 20-minute schoolwide silent reading program, increase reading time and enjoyment.

Writing processes across the curriculum emphasize their connection to the real world. Journal writing and Wee Deliver, an in-school postal system, encourage writing with purpose.

Internet research for information and theme-related writing is integral to the program.

Benefits

Eastside's self-assessment, goal setting, desire for improved student reading, and affiliation with the League of Professional Schools during the past 3 years have been the impetus for a schoolwide transformation leading to student gains in reading and overall school improvement. Forty-seven percent of third- and fifth-grade students scored at or above the quality performance level on the state Curriculum Based Assessment (CBA). Writing results for Grade 5 reveal a continuous increase in the percentage of students scoring in the advanced writing stages on the CBA. Most students participate in the Accelerated Reader program and regularly check books out of the school media center. A recent Family Night in the Library brought more than 300 students and parents to the school for an evening of reading and literature-based programs. An exciting school atmosphere at Eastside revolves around reading.

Elizabeth White
Eastside Elementary School
Douglas, Georgia

B.M.W. (Be a reader, Mull it over, Write about it)

Best for: *Students in all middle school grades*

Implemented by: *Staff and business partner*

Description

B.M.W. (Be a reader, Mull it over, Write about it) is a new type of silent reading program, replacing the well-worn SSR. It is a total school event, allowing students and staff a time to read for pleasure (about 25 minutes), to think about what was read (3-5 minutes), and to write (or diagram) a summary and response to the reading. Often students and staff will share what was written or drawn. Students have a "B.M.W. journal" to use each week. Staff members remind students of a reading skill to try during "start your engines" time as students get set up for B.M.W.

Every classroom and office area shuts down for the 40 minutes of B.M.W. time, and all locations have huge B.M.W. posters on walls (donated by our business partner—a local dealership). This business partner brought a B.M.W. convertible for our first day and donates prizes, which are given away two times a year through a drawing. Each week students receive blue ribbon/B.M.W. raffle tickets for being prepared and making a super effort during B.M.W. time.

Benefits

Because B.M.W. is a new idea, fun and relevant, students and staff enjoy it. Staff model the importance of reading for pleasure and remind students of reading strategies, and students get practice and reinforcement of skills. Students get to read in a variety of settings. For many students, this is the only sustained time for reading what they choose. Time is actually set aside for thinking and writing about what was read, thus ensuring better understanding and retention. Being able to write, draw, or speak allows for use of multiple intelligence. Business and schools have formed a partnership to help students become better learners.

Steven J. Cohen
Mary L. Flood Middle School
Englewood, Colorado

A Sense of Community

Best for: *Students in all elementary grades*

Implemented by: *Principal and all school staff*

Description

Our school's goal of building a sense of community among all students, teachers, staff, and volunteers expanded this year. It became a natural way for us to emphasize our school as a community of readers as well. We looked for opportunities to have the children's classroom reading experiences spill over into the broader community.

As the year started, each child and adult in the school wrote a short statement that expressed our hopes and dreams for Glenridge School. Our morning announcements always end with one of us sharing the hopes we have written. It takes only a minute, but it helps set the tone for the day.

Once a month, all the students and teachers have a multiage team meeting that consists of two or three children from each grade level. This same team has fun participating in community-building games. For the first time this year, we included a time when each child shared his or her favorite book and had time to read to a team member from another class. They were an enthusiastic audience for one another.

Throughout the building during the day, struggling readers or children who don't have many opportunities outside of school to read have a significant adult from the staff who listens to them read and plays a consistent and supporting role. Older adults from our community have now joined us to provide faithful individual reading and T.L.C. to those children at least once a week.

Benefits

Our Sense of Community focus has helped us embrace the commitment that all children can read and provides the students with some compelling reasons for doing so. Watching a little first grader listen raptly to an older student who may not excel in the eyes of his own classmates is a priceless moment for a teacher. The ripple effect of having more appreciative audiences for a reader also helps that child in turn reach out to another.

Integrating our reasons to read into the whole school community and finding ways to provide strong positive responses from other students, the school nurse, the cafeteria worker, and the OASIS volunteer, all reflect how much we value the love of reading and each member of our Glenridge family.

Laura DuPont
Glenridge Elementary School
Clayton, Missouri

First Steps .

Best for: *Teachers in Grades K-7*

Implemented by: *Trained teachers in Grades K-5*

Description

In the past 20 years, we have learned many things about how children learn to read. Much of what we now know has caused us to question our traditional approaches to the way we deliver reading instruction to children. Three years ago, the teachers at Hartwood Elementary School recognized the need to reconsider our basic approach to how we structure and deliver instruction in reading. As a group of adult learners, we analyzed what already existed in terms of what we expected of children as they progressed through the school and how we measured their progress. After working with and analyzing this information over the course of a year, we discovered a resource called First Steps.

First Steps is a developed reading continuum that provides a structure for teachers to analyze the reading development of each child and then design instruction based on the unique needs of learners at that developmental level. Over the course of the past two years, teachers have engaged in formal training and "trial and error" learning as they have challenged themselves to provide more effective, assessment-based reading instruction.

Benefits

The use of the developmental continuum has enabled teachers to effectively plan and deliver instruction to children at various stages of reading development. The staff has become unified in its understanding of reading instruction across grade levels, and we have achieved a level of consistency not previously seen in our school. The continuum is also becoming an effective tool for communicating progress to parents and helping them identify ways they can help their child learn to read.

Ronald J. Korenich
Hartwood Elementary School
Pittsburgh, Pennsylvania

Literary Day Parade

Best for: *Students in all elementary grades*
Implemented by: *Faculty, staff, and students*

Description

During the past 7 years, the reading program at Hillview Intermediate Center has moved from a textbook- to a literature-based approach. Students are reading entire novels, works of nonfiction, and poetry to develop skills in plot development, comprehension, and character analysis.

One way our reading program is extended and enriched is through our annual Literary Day Parade. In lieu of the traditional Halloween parades of witches, pirates, and vampires, our students dress as characters from, or authors of, their favorite books. Students and teachers alike participate, as "Mary Poppins," "Tom Sawyer," and "Pippi Longstocking" join other characters in a parade through our nearby senior citizen high-rise and skilled nursing care facility. Elderly residents of each center look forward to the yearly event.

In preparation for choosing characters, individual teachers pursue a variety of ideas. Students in sixth-grade classrooms read biographies and dressed as the characters. In addition, these students gave oral presentations in class as if they were famous people. A proposed activity for future Literary Days is an author workshop conducted via closed-circuit TV by an established author. As one can see, the possible activities for this theme are limited only by one's creativity!

Benefits

The Literary Day Parade helps to bring books alive for children. By assuming the roles of characters and authors with whom the student has made a connection, a child's love of literature is further solidified.

Literary Day costs little, but the benefits to the students and elderly residents of the parade route are inestimable. The students' enjoyment of this activity is heightened by the smiles, handshakes, and words of praise they receive along the way. Our students and staff are building bridges of communication and sharing that ultimately lead to a sense of a "school/town" community.

Richard Bonnar
Hillview Intermediate Center
Grove City, Pennsylvania

Summer Reading Challenge

Best for: *Students in all elementary grades*

Implemented by: *Students, mentor, and parents*

Description

Students returning to school after the summer break had difficulty in getting their skills back to their peak performance. This was especially true of low-performing students. During the summer, Irmo Elementary used the U.S. Department of Education's Read*Write*Now program. Students are expected to read 30 minutes per day, 5 days per week. Students in Grades 3 through 5 are expected to maintain a log of 30 minutes of writing 5 days per week and a list of vocabulary words. Students are also expected to complete reading of at least 10 books on the suggested list. Students can read these books or have the books read to them by their mentor/adult. The logs, lists of books, library assembly, and book sale are conducted in May. In September the principal visits each classroom and awards each student who meets the summer challenge with a special T-shirt, which reads "I Met the Summer Reading Challenge at Irmo Elementary School 1997."

We contacted our local library about conducting an assembly. This program told about various activities at the library for the summer. They also provided bookmarks for the students to take home with them. The librarian also shared a storytelling experience with the primary- and elementary-age students with age-appropriate stories. This age-appropriate story generated enthusiasm for student attendance at the library during the summer.

Just prior to this assembly, our teachers had created a suggested reading list for the summer. This reading list was composed of Newbery, Caldecott, and other award-winning books. This list also reflected our district's predeveloped suggestions for summer reading. A local bookstore volunteered to bring these books into the Media Center to sell before, during, and after school hours. The profits of this book sale are used to invest back into student incentives and to purchase books for needy students.

Benefits

Students reading daily during the summer months helped to maintain their fluency level when they returned in the fall. By giving out lists of suggested readings by grade level, it helped parents and students know which types of books were grade-level appropriate.

The assembly program by the local library introduced our students to special opportunities for literacy at no cost. This excitement also increased participation at the summer literacy programs.

The incentive of giving T-shirts to students who meet the Summer Reading Challenge has become quite competitive. Each year the logo remains the same except for the year, and by using different colors of the shirts each year, students have begun to take a healthy pride in meeting the reading challenge each summer.

James Shirley
Irmo Elementary School
Irmo, South Carolina

Bringing characters to life.

Books Come Alive!

Best for: *Students in all elementary grades*

Implemented by: *Classroom teachers, aides, and school staff*

Description

Turn to the next story in your reading book? Not at Midland Trail! Our students are surrounded by classic children's literature. Ten years ago, several teachers approached the principal with ideas and research to back up a literature-based reading program.

Teachers bring books alive for students through special activities as well as everyday efforts. A 6-foot-high cardboard Cat-in-the-Hat greeted students on Dr. Seuss's birthday. Students were giggling to the rhymes of *Horton Hears a Who* and *Yertle the Turtle,* and accessing a Dr. Seuss Web site. Even the cooks wore tall, striped hats as they served a "Green Eggs and Ham" breakfast.

Our sixth graders launched into a unit on World War II by reading *The Diary of Anne Frank.* Groups of students read and shared different novels to understand the era.

Students are encouraged to learn about authors. They send letters to their favorites, and several have visited the school, including Cheryl Ware, author of *Flea Circus Summer.* Our students went to hear Phyllis Naylor, a West Virginian, who wrote *Shiloh.* Sixth-grade students nearly missed the bus one day when they received a reply from an author and refused to leave until it was read!

Benefits

We teach our kids to be lifelong learners and lovers of books. Instead of reaching for standard textbooks, our students connect to the world of literature while learning language arts skills. Last year, Midland Trail students read more than 14,000 books, surpassing their goal of 10,000, and our principal kept her promise to read to the whole student body—from the roof of the school! All this from a school of 160 kids.

For the third year in a row, Midland Trail received the state School of Readers award. This year, we were 1 of only 26 schools in the United States and Canada to win the International Reading Association's Exemplary Reading award. More important, our students' test scores and achievement have increased. We know we are successful when traveling bookmobile workers tell us they are impressed when even our young children request specific authors by name.

Joyce Embry
Midland Trail Elementary School
Belle, West Virginia

Instruction in Higher-Order Thinking Skills (HOTS) Improves Critical Reading Skills Across the Curriculum

Best for: *Students in all elementary grades*

Implemented by: *Trained teachers and students*

Description

Through continuous observations, we noted an essential need to further strengthen critical reading skills across the curriculum. After researching well-established educational philosophies, Benjamin Bloom's taxonomy of educational objectives was deemed the best route to pursue. This model involves learning experiences that encourage six levels of thinking: knowledge, comprehension, application, analysis, synthesis, and evaluation.

Teachers received inservice training on implementing these higher-order thinking skills throughout the curriculum. They created teacher-made assessments that would be used in classroom instruction and incorporated into subject area test banks. Alternative assessments and classroom questioning techniques were enhanced through the use of these critical thinking skills.

Students become familiar with the levels of Bloom's taxonomy that are required of their assessments through a coding system. They are also made aware of the levels of thinking through a Bloom's Taxonomy Chart displayed in the classroom and through student work displayed throughout the school. Grade levels have designated areas around the school in which they can display student work that is labeled with the educational objective and level of thinking used.

Benefits

The inclusion of higher-order thinking skills across the curriculum has not only increased students' critical reading skills but also improved comprehension. Students' writing abilities have expanded as they respond to assessments using higher levels of thinking. Our achievement test scores have also risen dramatically, making our school a model school. Thus, we have provided numerous Higher-Order Thinking Skills (HOTS) workshops for teachers as well as welcomed school visitors to examine how we have implemented Bloom's taxonomy across the curriculum and how it has affected our total school climate. This gives us a complete evaluation of the overall success of the implementation of our HOTS program schoolwide. We highly recommend that your school revisit Benjamin Bloom and his taxonomy of educational objectives. It will make a dramatic impact on your students' critical reading and thinking abilities.

Mrs. Charlie Davis Waller
Pauline O'Rourke Elementary School
Mobile, Alabama

Vocabulary Development Program

Best for: Students in Grade K-5 classrooms

Implemented by: Trained teachers and aides

Description

Reading success is a great indicator of future career success. Therefore, Patapsco has embarked on a course of initiatives to boost reading achievement and reading appreciation.

Using data from standardized tests, teacher-made skill-based tests, and teacher observation, an aggressive campaign to implement additional sight works/vocabulary development and phonemic awareness strategies was put in place.

Each teacher has a daily sight work routine. This routine includes schoolwide activities such as Sight Word Bingo and writing using the many words of the Bingo game. Each student on a daily basis uses a copy of the 220 Kucera Francis Briscoe sight word list. The sight words are also a part of the students' weekly spelling list. Because these words are encountered by our students during several periods a day, students are provided with multiple opportunities to interact with these words. Each teacher posts the word of the week on a "Word Wall" that grows as the students' sight vocabulary grows.

In addition, teachers use the Benchmark School Word Identification/Vocabulary Development Program. This system of key spelling patterns emphasizes phonemic-based families. The lists of words that are developed through this program are called "sights and sounds." The students who have participated in the Vocabulary Development Program have demonstrated a great deal of growth as demonstrated by a consistent increase in test scores.

Benefits

Because of the daily schoolwide focus on sight word development as well as phonetic analysis and the integration with writing, Patapsco students' reading achievement has improved.

Yvonne Woods-Howard
Patapsco Elementary School #163
Baltimore, Maryland

A Balanced Approach to Reading Instruction

Best for: *Individual students, small groups, whole class in elementary grades*

Implemented by: *Trained teachers, aides, and parents*

Description

Although Prairie Vista teachers enthusiastically embraced the philosophy and practice of a whole-language approach to reading instruction, phonics has always been a strategy taught to our students since the school opened in 1989. Phonics instruction was delivered, however, through a variety of methods and materials. As new teachers were hired, we noticed that many did not have a strong understanding of phonics.

Two years ago, in an attempt to standardize our phonics instruction, we sent three primary teachers for training in a program that would provide a direct, intensive approach to phonics. These teachers immediately began to implement and share their newly acquired knowledge. Results were dramatic, and teacher enthusiasm was contagious. The remaining kindergarten and first-grade teachers were trained in January and began to build this hands-on phonics instruction into their daily routines. As soon as school started the next year, we brought a trainer to our school, provided primary teachers with a released day, and made it a mandatory initiative for all teachers in kindergarten through third grade to teach phonics in a standardized way. We were amazed and gratified to see a noticeable difference in the way our students began to confidently read, write, and spell.

Benefits

Even before the International Reading Association announced its position on a balanced approach to reading instruction, Prairie Vista students were reaping the benefits of a literacy acquisition philosophy that combined rich, authentic literature; sustained, silent reading; a strong parent component involving take-home books in a bag and reading incentives; and the use of phonics instruction. We find that an eclectic approach allows teachers to offer a variety of experiences for students and to accommodate different learning styles. Strengthening and standardizing the phonics component has proved to be beneficial for our students.

Our plans for the third year of this commitment include (a) training teaching assistants and parent volunteers to reinforce phonics with small groups of students and (b) tracking student progress in reading over time. We feel confident that a balanced approach to reading instruction grows fine, strong readers!

Lorie Garver
Prairie Vista Elementary School
Granger, Indiana

Touching Children Through
Research-Based Reading

Best for: Students in Grades K-5
Implemented by: Entire school

Description

Based on current research in reading education, our reading program is all-encompassing. It includes ideas from Carlene Murphy (a writer and independent consultant for staff development projects) on whole-faculty study groups and Marie Clay's methods stressing reading readiness skills. Components of Success for All, Reading Recovery, and guided reading have been incorporated into the classrooms. Technology and reading are integrated through the use of Accelerated Reader, STAR, WiggleWorks, SmartBooks, reading and writing software, and other computer-based programs.

We start each day with a 90-minute reading block. Staff from all disciplines are paired with classroom teachers. There are at least two adults in each classroom. The ratio of students to adults is 12 to 1 or better. Instruction is based on daily assessment of student needs. A variety of materials, teaching strategies, and groupings are used.

Early release every Wednesday allows for collaboration and staff development. Staff meets in whole-faculty study groups to explore current research, refine our focus, and plan for implementation.

Parents sign contracts agreeing to read 20 minutes per day with their child. Reading Incentive Programs, DEAR (Drop Everything and Read) Days, reading buddies, and family reading nights raise student enthusiasm and encourage community participation.

Benefits

Children are excited about reading, and parents are thrilled that their children share reading with them. The best esteem builder for a child is being able to read. We have seen improvement in behavior and all academic areas. According to SAT 9, our first graders gained 1 full year in reading between October and March. Ninety-four percent of students scored at or above their ability level. Teachers have

seen the "power of two" and have gained professionally from staff
development sessions and whole-faculty study groups. Parents are
happy! Children are reading!

Janet Luce
Rapid Valley Elementary School
Rapid City, South Dakota

Rushmore Support Network

Best for: *Staff development throughout the total school*

Implemented by: *Teachers in the school*

Description

The Rushmore Support Network is a teacher-to-teacher inservice
model that enables teachers to collaboratively review current educational research on reading and writing and share successful teaching
strategies. The support network meets weekly and uses recent literature, including both journal articles and published texts, as a basis
for discussion and self-directed professional growth. Teachers who
participate receive inservice credit.

The Rushmore Support Network is coordinated by the building's
reading specialist, who issues a flyer at the beginning of each semester announcing the text or theme and the dates of that semester's
sessions. The specific literature is chosen cooperatively by the principal, reading specialist, and participating teachers. Teachers meet in
the school library once a week after school for 1½ hours. They collaboratively determine reading assignments from the selected text or
pertinent journal articles. Discussion includes theoretical aspects, as
well as practical considerations for implementing specific strategies
and methods. Attendance records are maintained by the reading specialist, who also serves as a discussion leader. The school district
grants one inservice credit to each teacher who attends 10 of the 12
scheduled sessions. Between 15 and 20 teachers participate each semester, out of a total teaching staff of 30 to 35.

Benefits

The Rushmore Support Network allows teachers to remain current with the research while giving them ownership and control of their professional growth and development. The ongoing nature of the network allows teachers to share ideas and implement new strategies as they feel comfortable and return to the group for additional feedback and support. This sharing of information serves as the basis for improvement of instructional practices throughout the building. Inquiry charts, story boards, cooperative learning techniques, literature circles, discussion webs, and reading and writing workshops, which are now heavily used throughout the building, have all been outgrowths of our support network. Further information is available upon request.

Patricia Sullivan-Kirss
Rushmore Avenue School
Carle Place, New York

Extra! Extra! Read All About it!

Best for: *Students in the primary grade*

Implemented by: *Classroom teachers*

Description

Because we believe reading and writing develop simultaneously through meaningful experiences, teachers prepare a daily letter to inform students about activities in each classroom. Our goal is to help students learn to read for meaning and understand that people use printed words to communicate.

The letter begins with a greeting, is followed by the day and date, and includes special activities for the day. Certain text is repeated each day. It is a multifaceted activity that includes reading apprehension, comprehension, and spelling strategies. Students use closure to complete words with missing letters or fill in missing words in sentences. Depending on the grade, teachers use this introduction as a springboard to language activities. As students become better readers, teachers raise the bar to challenge the learners. We expect them to correct punctuation and read between the lines.

The daily letter is a means of communication, a tool for learning, and an instructional technique.

Benefits

With the implementation of the daily letter in kindergarten, continuity of instruction spirals across the grades. Because the letter is written for a class and incorporates words of praise, students develop a sense of community in this shared reading experience. It fosters risk taking as students naturally engage as active participants in the lesson. It also influences student writing. Vocabulary, grammar, and punctuation improve. When we ask students to "read all about it," we also affect how they "write all about it!"

Lillian A. Augustine
G. Austin Schoenly School
Spotswood, New Jersey

Read-Aloud Lawn Party

Best for: *Entire student body, parents, and community*

Implemented by: *Principal and teachers*

Description

Reading aloud to students is one component of our literacy program. Classroom teachers read aloud to students daily. As students develop reading skills, they practice reading independently through sustained, quiet reading. While they are becoming readers we believe it is important to model good oral reading. Therefore, throughout the year, we have guest readers share books that relate to their careers, were their own childhood favorites, or were written by favorite authors.

In the spring, however, we host a reverse Read-Aloud Lawn Party. On this occasion, each student is allowed to invite one guest to whom he or she will read aloud. This becomes a festive lawn party with clusters of children and guests sitting on blankets on the front lawn, grouped under trees, perched atop the slide, huddled along the sandbox, and engrossed at the picnic tables. Light refreshments are provided, and readers mingle on the lawn discussing books as if they were attending a book-signing event.

Benefits

Community interest in the school grows as the reading program develops. Often an older brother or sister is selected as the guest to whom our students read. Because the spring Read-Aloud is held on our lawn, the community views our students reading. The public becomes more cognizant of our emphasis on reading. Community members, such as the mayor, board members, mail carrier, and so forth, eagerly await their invitations each year. Often they become the guests at the Read-Aloud Lawn Party. This activity engenders a great spirit of enthusiasm from the community and fosters our students' pride as readers.

Lillian A. Augustine
G. Austin Schoenly School
Spotswood, New Jersey

Educational Consultants in the Classroom

Best for: *Students in all elementary grades*

Implemented by: *Administration and teachers*

Description

We recognize a need for more specific training in reading. We needed to find a more efficacious way to empower our students not only with the oral reading skills but also with stronger comprehension skills.

Teachers analyzed teacher-created benchmark tests to determine the strengths and weaknesses of students. Teachers at each grade level worked on specific skills as determined by the benchmarks.

Consultants were brought in to teach teachers and students both separately and together on individual skills as determined by teacher analysis. Student/parent/teacher training was held on Saturdays with breakfast and lunch provided as well as a fun-filled educational experience. Teachers assisted in selecting the consultants and the in-services provided.

Our teachers with specialized training were also used as consultants for the other teachers throughout the grade levels. We used staff development days to work on vertically aligning our curriculum.

Benefits

Through the consultations, our teachers have increased their repertoire of teaching methods. They are better able to determine what individual student needs are and the best way to meet those needs. Dramatic results have been seen not only in the classroom but also in the district benchmarks, ITBS, and TAAS tests as well. The children feel proud of their academic achievements and the recognition that they have brought to their campus. Even the governor recognized their achievement and chose this campus to kick off the Texas Reading Initiative campaign.

Bernard Blanchard
Smith Elementary School
Austin, Texas

Family Night of Reading

Best for: Students in all elementary grades and parents

Implemented by: Resource teacher and some classroom teachers

Description

Research shows that students whose parents show an interest in school activities achieve more than students whose parents do not participate in school activities. To entice parents to become more involved, we created Family Night at Stemley.

On Family Night, the students bring their parents to the school for 1 hour to play games and participate in various activities related to a subject area. One Family Night each year is devoted to reading. Stations are set up around the school and each family receives a schedule of events as they enter the building. Some examples of activities are bingo with vocabulary words, musical chairs with phonics (beginning sounds), computers with favorite reading games, pathfinder for reading comprehension, and make and take a reading game. In our community, paperback books are much sought after prizes. Sometimes books are used as incentives for students to attend.

Family night is held three times a year. The resource teacher coordinates these events with most teachers volunteering to help with at least one. Games are borrowed from classroom teachers to provide a variety of areas and levels.

Benefits

Parents report that attending Family Night is an enjoyable educational experience. Because it is fun, parents feel more comfortable about coming to school. All games and activities reinforce skills taught in the classroom, so students feel successful as they "show off" for parents.

Vicki S. Oliver
Stemley Road Elementary School
Talladega, Alabama

Read-In

Best for: Students in all elementary grades

Implemented by: All teachers, administrators, and instructional assistants

Description

Read-Ins are held twice a year in September and May. The entire day is devoted to reading activities that are planned and coordinated by the Read-In Committee to encourage and celebrate reading. During the fall Read-In, every student sets a reading goal for the year, and the principal and assistant principal are challenged to some outrageous event if the school goal is met (lunch on the roof, human hot dogs, human ice cream sundaes, go-cart race). The spring Read-In is a celebration of the students' and school's meeting their reading goals.

One of the favorite activities is having guest readers. We schedule at least two guest readers, recruited from the business community, for each class during a 30- to 40-minute period.

Other activities include a reading pep rally, skits based on favorite books, paired reading/shared books with partner classes, a book picnic, and an extended DEAR (Drop Everything and Read) time. Students are encouraged to bring their favorite books from home. We try to arrange a special surprise event for the spring Read-In as a reward for meeting the school goal. Some of these surprises have been a hot air balloon demonstration and a performance by David Jack, a children's singer/entertainer.

Benefits

Students are involved in fun activities related to reading for pleasure. The challenge and encouragement from teachers to meet their goals keep students motivated. They are frequently heard to comment to their teachers and administrators about books they are reading.

Vicki S. Oliver
Stemley Road Elementary School
Talladega, Alabama

School Newspaper

Best for: *Total school*

Implemented by: *Students and teachers*

Description

Each classroom, K-5, has a representative who interviews and reports for the school newspaper. The middle school is trained to edit and type and photograph to produce the finished product. They are supervised by the language arts and computer teachers. The 10- to 20-page newspaper is accomplished with the aid of Microsoft Publisher, a color scanner, and color printers. After publication of each of the four yearly issues, students then use the newspaper as part of their reading program.

Our students use the daily community newspapers, the *Indianapolis Star* and the *Indianapolis News*, as part of their regular classroom reading program. Not only do they become familiar with the job of a newspaper, but they learn and study current event issues. Publishing their own newspaper has greatly improved their communication skills and accuracy in reading and writing.

Benefits

The goal of a school newspaper is to enhance reading and writing skills. Students, working as a team, learn to report, write, and edit written copy to publish using technology. Parents lend support to staff by providing them with the latest technology and publishing programs. As the students enter high school, they are ready to continue their knowledge of these skills.

The program is workable in any school. Depending on use of technology, students and faculty have the opportunity to use their knowledge and creativity.

Sister James Michael Kesterson, S. P.
St. Jude Catholic School
Indianapolis, Indiana

Balanced Literacy Program

Best for: Teachers, paraprofessionals

Implemented by: Teachers, principal, paraprofessionals, and parents

Description

To improve student learning, teachers at the Samuel W. Mason Elementary School use a Balanced Literacy Program schoolwide. Daily instruction, from kindergarten to Grade 3, consists of eight strands: shared reading, reading aloud, guided reading, independent reading, shared writing, interactive writing, writers' workshop, and independent writing. Phonics, or word study, an integral part of daily instruction, is interwoven through all reading and writing activities. Grades 4 and 5 teachers use writers' workshop, guided reading, genre study, and independent reading.

The block of time devoted to literacy instruction is 2½ hours each day. To ensure uninterrupted time, subjects such as art, music, and swimming are scheduled in the afternoon. To develop the knowledge and skills needed for the Balanced Literacy approach, everyone in the school—the principal, teachers, and paraprofessionals, as well as the school secretary and custodian—develops a personal professional development plan.

Teachers spend 50 hours in targeted professional development every year. Resources for teachers include a school-based literacy coach for over-the-shoulder mentoring, coaching, and demonstration lessons; study groups; workshops; personal professional development days; model classrooms set up within the school; and time for classroom visits. Parents, as well as the school's business, university, community, and America Reads tutors, channel their efforts to provide extra literacy support for students after school and at home.

Benefits

The Mason School's Balanced Literacy Program has a strong internal accountability system. Assessments for all students in reading and writing, coordinated into a 6-week cycle, ensure teachers are collecting and using data to make decisions about instruction; to recommend tutoring through the school's afterschool, summer school, and America Reads tutoring programs; and/or to use different strategies for teaching. The combination of increased time for reading and writing instruction, consistency in instructional practice, focused professional development, scheduling flexibility, and an internal measurement system have produced steady and significant gains in reading achievement and have earned the school several national reading and school improvement awards.

Mary I. Russo
Samuel W. Mason Elementary School
Boston, Massachusetts

Success for Reading

Best for: Small groups in primary classrooms, also beneficial for ESL and special education students

Implemented by: Trained teachers and instructional aides

Description

Although we are aware of the fact that one-on-one remediation is the most effective form of intervention, many school districts cannot afford the price tag associated with this type of support. Here at our school we went the next best route: intensive, developmentally appropriate, small-group instruction.

We received a $3,000 grant from our local education foundation and matched that amount from our school. This was the beginning of our Success for Reading program.

We sent nine of our primary teachers to a Wright Group Guided Reading workshop. These teachers all came back to inservice as involved personnel. After intensive training in the areas of leveled books, the appropriate strategies to use, and the assessment component (running records), our staff was ready to proceed.

With part of the money from our original grant, money from the school budget, and money from a second grant, we were able to purchase the necessary materials for our program. We now have 20 different titles (in sets of six) for all 20 levels (Reading Recovery-leveled titles).

Benefits

Students are individually assessed to find out their present reading level, which enables us to meet each child at his or her developmentally appropriate reading level and teach strategies that are relevant to that specific level. Through consistent assessment, the instructor is able to decide if a student is at an instructional level and which of the three cueing systems the student uses (or doesn't use) to help determine on-the-spot instruction. Teachers also evaluate if a student is at an independent level and ready to move up to the next level. This gives us happy, successful, independent readers.

Betsy Palmer
G. L. Scarselli Elementary School
Gardnerville, Nevada

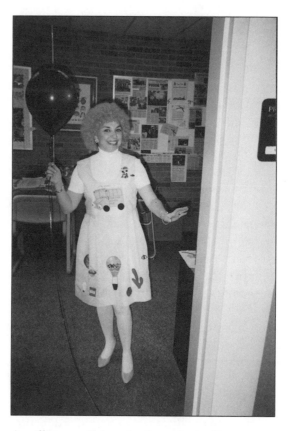

A willing participant—the principal!

Reading Celebration

Best for: *Students in all elementary grades*
Implemented by: *Entire school*

Description

It has been said that when children discover the joy of reading, success is evident. Our approach is one in which the entire school is involved in experiencing the pleasure of reading and then celebrating it with community groups, business partners, government officials, parents, administrators, and school volunteers.

Each class chooses a novel or trade book that ties into the lessons that students are learning across the curriculum. Students thoroughly engage themselves in the process of reading and writing throughout this period. At the end of this thematic unit, a "Reading Celebration" takes place. Community groups, business partners, government officials, and parents are invited to the school to read to the children in their classrooms. On this particular day, students, teachers, and administrators dress up as their favorite character from the novel or trade book they have been reading. After the guests read to the students, all the children, teachers, administrators, and guests parade around the school while the local high school band plays. Children end the celebration by having a picnic lunch outside with their favorite book.

Benefits

The celebration atmosphere present in the school throughout this activity definitely makes an impact on students. Students demonstrate a positive attitude toward reading. They are eager to visit the library and read books just for the fun of reading. Reading is no longer viewed as work. They discover the beauty of reading. Bringing in community members and business partners brings everyone together. In doing so, through unity, we enhance children's perspective on reading. This, in turn, benefits the future generations of our nation.

Maria Teresa Rojas
Sunset Elementary School
Miami, Florida

Schoolwide Plan for Language Arts

Best for: *Students in Grades K-4*

Implemented by: *Teachers, aides, Title I staff, and principal*

Description

Learning to read is critical to future school success as well as after graduation. Even though 2 to 3 hours each day were devoted to language arts, along with Title I push-in and pull-out programs, the rate of success was minimal. In 1995, with 62% of students receiving free or reduced lunch, our school became eligible to develop a Title I Schoolwide Program.

We were able to reschedule the 12½ Title I teachers, include a fourth-grade HOTS classroom, develop three extended-day kindergartens, fund an after-school tutoring program 3 days each week, place one or more computers in every classroom, and continue Reading Recovery.

The greatest impact has been the rescheduling of the Title I teachers. For example, each has been assigned seven to eight students from two classrooms for a 2-hour language arts block. The class sizes for that period have been reduced from 24-27 to 16-18. Teachers are now able to work with individuals, provide higher-interest reading, integrate technology into the curriculum, write and include problem solving, and communicate progress and concerns more effectively with parents. Title I teachers are responsible for reporting progress, meeting with parents, and initiating instructional support when needed.

Benefits

The progress of students has been monitored through the fall, winter, and spring Title I reading assessments. A greater percentage of students are moving from partially proficient than in previous years. Students are not being "singled out" now; all of our 1,000 students in Grades K-4 are able to benefit from the smaller-group atmosphere. A greater amount of reading and writing is going on in our school now.

Paulette Graham
Washington Park Elementary School
Washington, Pennsylvania

O.R.E.O.S.—Outside Reading
Enriches Our Students

Best for: *Students in primary-intermediate grades*

Implemented by: *A team of students, teachers, parents, and community businesses*

Description

Outside Reading Enriches Our Students, or O.R.E.O.S., is an exciting at-home reading program. During the first week of every month, each student is presented with a reading goal of 6 hours of at-home reading to be accomplished by the end of the month. The students are given a record sheet on which we ask the parents/guardians to record their child's progress toward our monthly goal. During the last week of the month, each child returns the completed sheet signed by the parent. Each child will put stickers by his or her name for books (primary) or hours (intermediate) read. Each child will have numerous paper cookie jars to fill with stamped cookies every time he or she completes an entire book.

Our community has been very supportive of our O.R.E.O.S. program. During December, a local grocery store gives students their own individual boxes of Oreo cookies, donated by Nabisco. Award certificates have been obtained from Subway, Pizza Hut, Dairy Queen, Baskin-Robbins, Chicago Bulls, Chicago Bears, Chicago White Sox, and the Chicago Cubs. The first reward for the year comes from the Hunt-Wesson Company, a case of Orville Redenbacher popcorn, to celebrate Valparaiso's annual Popcorn Festival. On Awards Day, all "Stars" who have faithfully turned in a signed O.R.E.O.S. sheet for the whole year receive a trophy engraved with "Star Reader."

Benefits

The partnership developed by O.R.E.O.S. between parent, child, and school is important. My parents are strong O.R.E.O.S. supporters because it ensures that children read regularly. They are active participants in their child's reading development, as well as with reading material selection. As in any endeavor, practice produces proficiency. Reading for enjoyment will help a child become a better reader. Parents are the first and most important teachers of their children. From parents, children learn how to walk, talk, read, write, think, and play. Parents who take time to read to their children and talk about books will reap the rewards of successful children.

Rik Ihssen
Washington Township Elementary School
Valparaiso, Indiana

Try Reading *Month!*

Best for: Students in all grades

Implemented by: Teachers, parents, staff, and administrator

Description

There's too much to do and too little time in which to do it! That's why our annual Reading Week celebration has turned into a Reading Month extravaganza at Western Coventry School.

At the beginning of April, we kick off Reading Month with a book fair organized by our PTA. All students are invited to purchase inexpensive books for their at-home libraries. Next, a Young Authors' Picnic and Book Swap is held one evening. Students who have written original books are invited to an indoor "picnic" to share their writing and to see reaction to their work from family and friends. Our Build a Community of Readers incentive program also begins during the first week and continues throughout the month. During the second week of the month, students are treated to a special "I Don't Know What to Read" assembly by a professional theater group. Each day during the week, students end their day by participating in DEAR (Drop Everything and Read). Following the spring vacation, we conclude our month with a challenge to all students and families to "Dare to Be Free of TV" by finding alternate activities. Participants are eligible to win free T-shirts.

Reading Month gets our kids excited about reading.

Benefits

It is important for students to see other members of the school community as readers and writers. Reading Month accomplishes this by involving students, staff, and the general school community in its varied activities. Whether it's through the purchase of a favorite book, sharing and receiving positive comments about an original publication, participating in the reading incentive program, observing the crossing guard reading during DEAR, attending an entertaining assembly, or participating with family in alternative-to-TV activities, students become excited about the important role reading and writing plays in their lives.

Barry Ricci
Western Coventry School
Coventry, Rhode Island

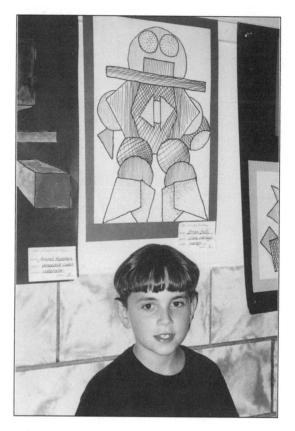

A budding illustrator.

(Photo courtesy of Hillcrest Science and Technology Magnet School, Somerset, New Jersey.)

Reading/Writing Festival

Best for: Students in Grades K-4

Implemented by: Trained teachers and assisting volunteers

Description

Throughout the school year, students write each day in their classroom. All writings are kept in students' portfolios. In the spring, each child selects one favorite piece that is then edited, typed, illustrated, and bound. Many school volunteers assist in typing the books and in doing a sewn library binding. Students do their own illustrations.

At our Reading/Writing Festival that is held at the end of the school year, each student's bound book is displayed for parents, friends, students, and community members to view. Each book contains a "Note to the Author" card where readers can write compliments to the student.

In addition to individual students' bound books, classroom books are also displayed at the festival. Many of these focus on curriculum writings that integrate math, science, and social studies. Even writings in art class and music class, as well as school newspapers, have been displayed.

To encourage reading as well as writing during our festival, a children's author/illustrator visits our school that week, and his or her books are sold as well as others through a book fair. Our Reading/Writing Festival is a weeklong celebration that is a highlight of our language arts program.

Benefits

Students benefit greatly from this program, for writing is now a daily activity. Because students begin to write at a very early age, writing allows for personal expression. Students see themselves as published authors with bound books that are saved for years to come.

The writing process also encourages the integration of writing into other curriculum areas. The entire language arts program is enhanced by this process. As hundreds of parents, students, teachers, and community members crowd the school cafeteria to read the student's books, student smiles of pride abound.

Linnea Gershenberg
Harold H. Wilkins Memorial School/Clark School
Amherst, New Hampshire

1996–1997 Blue Ribbon Elementary and Middle Schools

ALABAMA

George Hall Elementary School
1108 Antwerp Street
Mobile, AL 36605
(334) 476-3299
(334) 478-6393 FAX

Homewood Middle School
1108 Frisco Street
Homewood, AL 35209
(205) 870-0878
(205) 877-4573 FAX

Inverness Elementary School
5251 Valleydale Road
Birmingham, AL 35242-4632
(205) 980-3620
(205) 980-3625 FAX

Pauline O'Rourke Elementary
    School
1975 Leroy Stevens Road
Mobile, AL 36695
(334) 639-9498
(334) 639-1826 FAX

St. Ignatius Catholic School
3650 Springhill Avenue
Mobile, AL 36608-5797
(334) 342-5442
(334) 341-1481 FAX

Stemley Road Elementary School
2760 Stemley Bridge Road
Talladega, AL 35160
(205) 362-9499
(205) 362-7162 FAX

ARIZONA

Andersen Elementary School
1350 N. Pennington Street
Chandler, AZ 85224
(602) 812-7030
(602) 812-6500 FAX

Ganado Primary School
Highway 264
P.O. Box 1757
Ganado, AZ 86505
(520) 755-1020
(520) 755-1085 FAX

Goodman Elementary School
2600 W. Knox Road
Chandler, AZ 85224
(602) 812-7070
(602) 812-7430 FAX

Ramon S. Mendoza Elementary
    School
5831 E. McLellan Road
Mesa, AZ 85205
(602) 396-1730
(602) 985-5576 FAX

St. Thomas the Apostle Catholic
  School
4510 N. 24th Street
Phoenix, AZ 85016
(602) 954-9088
(602) 956-3454 FAX

ARKANSAS

Robert E. Lee Elementary School
400 Quandt Street
Springdale, AR 72764
(501) 750-8868
(501) 750-8870 FAX

Walker Elementary School
1701 S. 40th Street
Springdale, AR 72762
(501) 750-8874
(501) 750-8717 FAX

CALIFORNIA

Alamo Elementary School
250 23rd Avenue
San Francisco, CA 94121
(415) 750-8456
(415) 750-8434 FAX

Barcelona Hills Elementary School
23000 Via Santa Maria
Mission Viejo, CA 92691
(714) 581-5240
(714) 581-6897 FAX

Cadwallader Elementary School
3799 Cadwallader Road
San Jose, CA 95121
(408) 270-4950
(408) 223-4839 FAX

Cedar Grove Elementary School
2702 Sugarplum Drive
San Jose, CA 95148
(408) 270-4958
(408) 270-6856 FAX

Centennial Elementary School
15200 Westdale Drive
Bakersfield, CA 93312
(805) 588-6020
(805) 588-6009 FAX

Cubberley School
3200 Monogram Avenue
Long Beach, CA 90810
(562) 420-8810
(562) 420-7821 FAX

Discovery Elementary School
7500 Vaquero Avenue
Bakersfield, CA 93308
(805) 589-7336
(805) 587-9413 FAX

Dove Hill Elementary School
1460 Colt Way
San Jose, CA 95121
(408) 270-4973
(408) 223-4536 FAX

Emblem Elementary School
22635 Espuella Drive
Saugus, CA 91350
(805) 297-8870
(805) 296-3265 FAX

George L. White Elementary School
25422 Chapparosa Park Road
Laguna Niguel, CA 92677
(714) 249-3875
(714) 495-1871 FAX

H.A. Snow Elementary School
6580 Mirabeau Drive
Newark, CA 94560
(510) 794-2051
(510) 791-8942 FAX

Hebrew Academy
14401 Willow Lane
Huntington Beach, CA 92647
(714) 898-0051
(714) 898-0633 FAX

Holly Oak Elementary School
2995 Rossmore Way
San Jose, CA 95148
(408) 270-4975
(408) 223-4514 FAX

Jefferson Elementary School
1880 Fowler Avenue
Clovis, CA 93611
(209) 299-6868
(209) 299-0161 FAX

Joe Nightingale School
255 Winter Road
Santa Maria, CA 93455
(805) 937-2511
(805) 934-7113 FAX

Liberty Elementary School
1250 E. Liberty Hill Rd.
Fresno, CA 93720
(209) 434-6033
(209) 434-8312 FAX

Linda Vista Elementary School
5600 South Ohio Street
Yorba Linda, CA 92886
(714) 779-2111
(714) 779-2138 FAX

Meadow School
880 Maria Drive
Petaluma, CA 94954
(707) 762-4905
(707) 762-5751 FAX

Meadows Elementary School
2000 La Granada Drive
Thousand Oaks, CA 91362
(805) 495-7038
(805) 374-1160 FAX

Millbrook Elementary School
3200 Millbrook Drive
San Jose, CA 95148
(408) 270-6767
(408) 270-6790 FAX

Monte Vista Elementary School
730 North Hope Avenue
Santa Barbara, CA 93110
(805) 687-5333
(805) 687-0457 FAX

Mt. Woodson Elementary School
17427 Archie Moore Road
Ramona, CA 92065
(619) 788-5120
(619) 788-5353 FAX

The Nueva School
6565 Skyline Boulevard
Hillsborough, CA 94010
(415) 348-2272
(415) 344-9302 FAX

Orangethorpe Elementary School
1400 S. Brookhurst Road
Fullerton, CA 92833
(714) 447-7730
(714) 447-7527 FAX

Pacific Elementary School
1214 Pacific Avenue
Manhattan Beach, CA 90266
(310) 546-8044
(310) 939-1001 FAX

Philip J. Reilly School
24171 Pavion
Mission Viejo, CA 92692
(714) 454-1590
(714) 588-6315 FAX

Pleasant Ridge Elementary School
16229 Duggans Road
Grass Valley, CA 95949
(916) 268-2820
(916) 268-2823 FAX

Rossmoor Elementary School
3272 Shakespeare Drive
Los Alamitos, CA 90720
(562) 799-4520
(562) 799-4530 FAX

Sonoma Elementary School
1325 Sonoma Avenue
Modesto, CA 95350
(209) 576-4683
(209) 569-2725 FAX

South Hillsborough Elementary
    School
303 El Cerrito Avenue
Hillsborough, CA 94010
(415) 344-0303
(415) 548-9443 FAX

St. Joseph School
43222 Mission Blvd.
Fremont, CA 94539
(510) 656-6525
(510) 656-3608 FAX

Vaughn Next Century Learning
  Center
13330 Vaughn Street
San Fernando, CA 91340
(818) 896-7461
(818) 834-9036 FAX

Vista Verde School
5144 Michelson Drive
Irvine, CA 92612
(714) 786-9207
(714) 786-4257 FAX

Will Rogers Learning Community
  School
2401 14th Street
Santa Monica, CA 90405
(310) 452-2364
(310) 452-9035 FAX

COLORADO

Frontier Elementary School
3755 Meadow Ridge Drive
Colorado Springs, CO 80920
(719) 594-0102
(719) 548-8324 FAX

Mary L. Flood Middle School
3695 South Lincoln Street
Englewood, CO 80110
(303) 761-1226
(303) 806-2199 FAX

Rocky Mountain Elementary
  School
800 E. 5th Avenue
Longmont, CO 80501
(303) 772-6750
(303) 772-9507 FAX

CONNECTICUT

The Center School
125 West Street
P.O. Box 110
Litchfield, CT 06759
(860) 567-7510
(860) 567-7518 FAX

East Farms School
25 Wolf Pit Road
Farmington, CT 06032
(860) 674-9519
(860) 677-7915 FAX

Ellen P. Hubbell School
90 West Washington Street
Bristol, CT 06010
(860) 584-7841
(860) 584-3874 FAX

Highland Elementary School
490 Highland Avenue
Cheshire, CT 06410
(203) 272-0335
(203) 272-9003 FAX

The Peck Place School
500 Peck Lane
Orange, CT 06477
(203) 891-8034
(203) 891-8038 FAX

West District School
114 West District Road
Unionville, CT 06085
(860) 673-2579
(860) 675-4103 FAX

DEPARTMENT OF DEFENSE
DEPENDENTS SCHOOLS

Amelia Earhart Intermediate
  School
Unit 5166
APO, AP 96368-5166
(611) 734-1329
(611) 734-7207 FAX

Easterling Primary School
600 Northside Avenue
Marion, SC 29571
(803) 423-8335
(803) 423-8337 FAX

Hood Street Elementary School
5615 Hood Street
Columbia, SC 29206
(803) 787-8266
(803) 782-8863 FAX

Knightsville Elementary School
535 W. Old Orangeburg Road
Summerville, SC 29483
(803) 873-4851
(803) 821-3983 FAX

Roosevelt Roads Elementary School
P.O. Box 420131
Roosevelt Roads Station, PR
   00742-0131
(787) 865-2670
(787) 865-4322 FAX

Valley Creek Elementary School
2800 Valley Creek Trail
McKinney, TX 75070
(972) 569-6460
(972) 569-6465 FAX

DISTRICT OF COLUMBIA

The Lab School of Washington
4759 Reservoir Road, NW
Washington, DC 20007
(202) 965-6600
(202) 965-5105 FAX

FLORIDA

Boca Raton Christian School
315 N.W. 4th Street
Boca Raton, FL 33432
(561) 391-2727
(561) 367-6808 FAX

Diplomat Elementary School
1115 North East 16th Terrace
Cape Coral, FL 33909
(941) 458-0033
(941) 458-1697 FAX

Kendale Elementary School
10693 S.W. 93rd Street
Miami, FL 33176
(305) 274-2735
(305) 274-4792 FAX

Key Largo Elementary School
104801 Overseas Highway
Key Largo, FL 33037
(305) 453-1255
(305) 453-1248 FAX

Palm Springs North Elementary
   Community School
17615 NW 82nd Street
Hialeah, FL 33015
(305) 821-4631
(305) 825-0422 FAX

Saint Michael Lutheran School
3595 Broadway Circle
Ft. Myers, FL 33901
(941) 939-1218
(941) 939-1839 FAX

Sunset Elementary School
5120 SW 72nd Street
Miami, FL 33143
(305) 661-8527
(305) 666-2327 FAX

GEORGIA

Cartersville Primary School
315 Etowah Drive
Cartersville, GA 30120
(770) 382-1733
(770) 387-7493 FAX

Coosa Middle School
5041 Alabama Highway
Rome, GA 30165
(706) 232-1856
(706) 802-6766 FAX

Eastside Elementary School
603 N. McDonald Avenue
Douglas, GA 31533
(912) 384-3187
(912) 383-0520 FAX

Flat Rock Middle School
325 Jenkins Road
Tyrone, GA 30290
(770) 969-2830
(770)969-2835 FAX

Lost Mountain Middle School
700 Old Mountain Road
Kennesaw, GA 30152
(770) 528-6627
(770) 528-6635 FAX

Peachtree Elementary School
5995 Crooked Creek Road, N.W.
Norcross, GA 30092
(770) 448-8710
(770) 417-2451 FAX

Pine Ridge Elementary School
750 Pine Ridge Drive
Stone Mountain, GA 30087
(770) 879-8097
(770) 469-9645 FAX

Samuel Martin Inman Middle
    School
774 Virginia Avenue, N.E.
Atlanta, GA 30306
(404) 853-4017
(404) 853-4085 FAX

HAWAII

Momilani Elementary School
2130 Hookiekie Street
Pearl City, HI 96782
(808) 453-6444
(808) 453-6448 FAX

ILLINOIS

Grayslake Middle School
440 N. Barron Boulevard
Grayslake, IL 60030
(847) 223-3680
(847) 223-0147 FAX

James Hart Junior High School
18211 Aberdeen Avenue
Homewood, IL 60430
(708) 799-5544
(708) 799-1377 FAX

Metamora Grade School
815 E. Chatham Street
Metamora, IL 61548
(309) 367-2361
(309) 367-2364 FAX

Michael Collins Elementary School
407 S. Summit Drive
Schaumburg, IL 60193
(847) 301-2155
(847) 301-7379 FAX

Neil Armstrong Elementary School
1320 Kingsdale Road
Hoffman Estates, IL 60195
(847) 885-6750
(847) 885-8381 FAX

Our Lady of the Wayside School
432 South Mitchell Avenue
Arlington Heights, IL 60005-1894
(847) 255-0050
(847) 253-0543 FAX

Pleasant Hill Elementary School
3040 Linden Avenue
Springfield, IL 62702
(217) 525-3256

Pleasantdale Elementary School
8100 School Street
La Grange, IL 60525
(708) 246-4700
(708) 246-4625 FAX

Westbrook School
1333 Greenwood Road
Glenview, IL 60025
(847) 998-5055
(847) 998-1872 FAX

INDIANA

Allisonville Elementary School
4920 East 79th Street
Indianapolis, IN 46250
(317) 845-9441
(317) 576-5255 FAX

Prairie Vista Elementary School
15400 Brick Road
Granger, IN 46530-8749
(219) 271-0055
(219) 271-0055 x761 FAX

St. Jude Catholic School
5375 McFarland Road
Indianapolis, IN 46227
(317) 784-6828
(317) 780-7592 FAX

Washington Township Elementary
School
383 E. State Road 2
Valparaiso, IN 46383
(219) 464-3597
(219) 465-1753 FAX

IOWA

Hills Elementary School
301 Main Street
P.O. Box 218
Hills, IA 52235-0218
(319) 679-2221
(319) 679-2223 FAX

KANSAS

Broken Arrow Elementary School
5901 Alden Street
Shawnee, KS 66216
(913) 962-3220
(913) 962-3228 FAX

Central Elementary School
324 South Water Street
Olathe, KS 66061
(913) 780-7370
(913) 780-7379 FAX

Kathryn O'Loughlin McCarthy
Elementary School
1401 Hall Street
Hays, KS 67601
(913) 623-2510
(913) 623-2518 FAX

Walnut Grove Elementary School
11800 S. Pflumm Road
Olathe, KS 66062
(913) 780-7710
(913) 780-7719 FAX

KENTUCKY

Catlettsburg Elementary School
3348 Court Street
Catlettsburg, KY 41129
(606) 739-5515
(606) 739-8625 FAX

Dry Ridge Elementary School
275 School Road
Dry Ridge, KY 41035
(606) 824-4484
(606) 824-4924 FAX

Rich Pond Elementary School
530 Rich Pond Road
Bowling Green, KY 42104
(502) 781-9627
(502) 781-9628 FAX

St. Raphael the Archangel School
2131 Lancashire Avenue
Louisville, KY 40205
(502) 456-1541
(502) 456-1542 FAX

LOUISIANA

Dwight D. Eisenhower Elementary
School
3700 Tall Pines Drive
New Orleans, LA 70131
(504) 398-7125
(504) 398-7129 FAX

Henry W. Allen Fundamental
Elementary School
5625 Loyola Avenue
New Orleans, LA 70115
(504) 862-5154
(504) 861-9904 FAX

Our Lady of Prompt Succor
Parish School
2305 Fenelon Street
Chalmette, LA 70043
(504) 271-2953
(504) 271-1490 FAX

Saint Paul's Episcopal School
6249 Canal Boulevard
New Orleans, LA 70124-3099
(504) 488-1319
(504) 482-6893 FAX

Shreve Island Elementary School
836 Sewanee Place
Shreveport, LA 71105
(318) 869-2335
(318) 861-2256 FAX

St. Benilde School
1801 Division Street
Metairie, LA 70001
(504) 833-9894
(504) 834-4380 FAX

MARYLAND

Burning Tree Elementary School
7900 Beech Tree Road
Bethesda, MD 20817
(301) 320-6510
(301) 320-6538 FAX

Kennedy Krieger Lower School
1750 East Fairmount Avenue
Baltimore, MD 21231
(410) 550-9100
(410) 550-9136 FAX

Mayo Elementary School
1152 Central Avenue, East
Mayo, MD 21106
(410) 222-1666
(410) 269-1362 FAX

Middlesex Elementary School
142 Bennett Road
Baltimore, MD 21221
(410) 887-0170
(410) 887-0469 FAX

North Salisbury Elementary School
201 Union Avenue
Salisbury, MD 21801
(410) 742-5150
(410) 341-3920 FAX

Patapsco Elementary School #163
844 Roundview Road
Baltimore, MD 21225
(410) 396-1400
(410) 396-8613 FAX

Plum Point Elementary School
1245 Plum Point Road
Huntingtown, MD 20639
(410) 535-7390
(410) 535-7299 FAX

Ridgely Elementary School
118 North Central Avenue
Ridgely, MD 21660
(410) 634-2105
(410) 634-1789 FAX

St. Camillus Catholic School
1500 St. Camillus Drive
Silver Spring, MD 20903
(301) 434-2344
(301) 431-1442 FAX

MASSACHUSETTS

Johnson Elementary School
99 South Main Street
Natick, MA 01760
(508) 651-7226
(508) 651-7226 FAX

Samuel W. Mason Elementary
   School
150 Norfolk Avenue
Boston, MA 02119
(617) 635-8405
(617) 635-8406 FAX

Steward School
261 Perkins Row
Topsfield, MA 01983
(508) 887-1538
(508) 887-7462 FAX

The Tisbury School
34 West William Street
P. O. Box 878
Vineyard Haven, MA 02568
(508) 696-6500
(508) 696-7437 FAX

MICHIGAN

Anna M. Joyce Elementary School
8411 Sylvester Street
Detroit, MI 48214
(313) 866-7545
(313) 866-8068 FAX

Brace-Lederle Elementary School
18575 West Nine Mile Road
Southfield, MI 48075
(248) 746-8730
(248) 352-8373 FAX

Grand View Elementary School
3701 52nd Street S.W.
Grandville, MI 49418
(616) 530-6830
(616) 530-1655 FAX

Lincoln Park Elementary School
2951 Leon
Norton Shores, MI 49441
(616) 755-1257
(616) 759-2427 FAX

Pine Tree Elementary School
590 Pine Tree Road
Lake Orion, MI 48362
(248) 693-5470
(248) 693-5319 FAX

Roguewood School
3900 Kroes Street
Rockford, MI 49341
(616) 866-2200
(616) 866-7132 FAX

Troy Union Elementary School
1340 E. Square Lake Road
Troy, MI 48098
(810) 879-7576
(810) 689-7483 FAX

MINNESOTA

Farmington Middle School
4200 W. 208th Street
Farmington, MN 55024
(612) 463-6560
(612) 463-6604 FAX

Hillcrest Community School
9301 Thomas Road
Bloomington, MN 55431
(612) 888-7746
(612) 888-0751 FAX

Park Brook Elementary School
7400 Hampshire Avenue North
Brooklyn Park, MN 55428
(612) 561-6870
(612) 561-6871 FAX

Shakopee Junior High School
1137 Marschall Road
Shakopee, MN 55379
(612) 496-5752
(612) 496-5792 FAX

MISSISSIPPI

Oxford Elementary School
1637 Highway 30
Oxford, MS 38655
(601) 234-3497
(601) 236-7942 FAX

MISSOURI

Chesterfield Elementary School
17700 Wild Horse Creek Road
Chesterfield, MO 63005-3799
(314) 532-4882
(314) 532-0614 FAX

Forsyth School
6235 Wydown Boulevard
St. Louis, MO 63105
(314) 726-4542
(314) 726-0112 FAX

Glenridge Elementary School
7447 Wellington Way
Clayton, MO 63105
(314) 726-2355
(314) 862-2497 FAX

Hoech Middle School
3312 Ashby Road
St. Ann, MO 63074
(314) 426-9561
(314) 426-3837 FAX

Lucy Franklin Elementary School
111 NE Roanoke
Blue Springs, MO 64014
(816) 224-1390
(816) 224-1396 FAX

Oak Grove Middle School
501 E. 12th Street
Oak Grove, MO 64075
(816) 690-4154
(816) 690-3976 FAX

Rohan Woods School
1515 Bennett Avenue
St. Louis, MO 63122
(314) 821-6270
(314) 821-6878 FAX

Ross Elementary School
1150 Ross Avenue
St. Louis, MO 63146
(314) 878-8300
(314) 878-4403 FAX

Shepard Accelerated School
3450 Wisconsin Avenue
St. Louis, MO 63118
(314) 776-3664
(314) 664-3708 FAX

Ste. Genevieve du Bois School
1575 N. Woodlawn Avenue
St. Louis, MO 63122
(314) 821-4245
(314) 966-4687 FAX

NEBRASKA

Westside Middle School
8601 Arbor Street
Omaha, NE 68124
(402) 390-6464
(402) 390-6454 FAX

NEVADA

C. C. Meneley Elementary School
1446 Muir Drive
P.O. Box 1150
Gardnerville, NV 89410
(702) 265-3154
(702) 265-7193 FAX

Cyril Wengert Elementary School
2001 Winterwood Blvd.
Las Vegas, NV 89122
(702) 799-8600
(702) 799-0116 FAX

G. L. Scarselli Elementary School
699 Long Valley Road
P.O. Box 1120
Gardnerville, NV 89410
(702) 265-2222
(702) 265-1218 FAX

NEW HAMPSHIRE

Harold H. Wilkins Memorial
    School/Clark School
80 Boston Post Road
P.O. Box 420
Amherst, NH 03031
(603) 673-4411
(603) 672-0968 FAX

NEW JERSEY

Bowne-Munro Elementary School
120 Main Street
East Brunswick, NJ 08816
(908) 613-6810
(908) 257-0029 FAX

Cambridge School
35 Cambridge Road
Kendall Park, NJ 08824
(908) 297-2941
(908) 940-2030 FAX

Cranbury School
23 North Main Street
Cranbury, NJ 08512
(609) 395-1700
(609) 860-9655 FAX

G. Austin Schoenly School
80 Kane Avenue
Spotswood, NJ 08884
(908) 723-5120
(908) 723-5122 FAX

Highland/Godwin School
31 Highland Avenue
Midland Park, NJ 07432
(201) 445-5350
(201) 444-3051 FAX

Hillcrest Science and Technology
    Magnet School
500 Franklin Blvd.
Somerset, NJ 08873
(908) 246-0170
(908) 247-8405 FAX

Memorial School
764 Grant Avenue
Maywood, NJ 07607
(201) 845-9113
(201) 845-0657 FAX

The Midland School
94 Readington Road
P.O. Box 5026
North Branch, NJ 08876
(908) 722-8222
(908) 722-1547 FAX

William F. Halloran School No. 22
447 Richmond Street
Elizabeth, NJ 07207
(908) 558-3423
(908) 351-1761 FAX

NEW MEXICO

Cleveland Middle School
6910 Natalie Avenue NE
Albuquerque, NM 87110
(505) 881-9441
(505) 889-8617 FAX

Susie Rayos Marmon Elementary
    School
6401 Iliff Road NW
Albuquerque, NM 87120
(505) 831-5400
(505) 833-1565 FAX

NEW YORK

Austin Road Elementary School
Austin Road
Mahopac, NY 10541
(914) 628-1346
(914) 628-5521 FAX

Belle H. Waterman Elementary
    School
55 East Street
Skaneateles, NY 13152
(315) 685-8361
(315) 685-0347 FAX

East Middle School
167 East Frederick Street
Binghamton, NY 13904
(607) 762-8371
(607) 762-8398 FAX

Harry B. Thompson Middle School
98 Ann Drive
Syosset, NY 11791
(516) 364-5760
(516) 921-5616 FAX

Herricks Middle School
7 Hilldale Drive
Albertson, NY 11507
(516) 625-6463
(516) 248-3281 FAX

Isaac E. Young Middle School
270 Centre Avenue
New Rochelle, NY 10805
(914) 576-4360
(914) 632-2738 FAX

Lakeview Elementary School
112 Lakeview Drive
Mahopac, NY 10541
(914) 628-3331
(914) 628-5849 FAX

Rushmore Avenue School
251 Rushmore Avenue
Carle Place, NY 11514
(516) 334-1900
(516) 338-0727 FAX

Southgate Elementary School
30 Southgate Road
Loudonville, NY 12211
(518) 785-6607
(518) 783-8878 FAX

St. Joan of Arc School
35-27 82nd Street
Jackson Heights, NY 11372
(718) 639-9020

Thomas J. Lahey Elementary
    School
625 Pulaski Road
Greenlawn, NY 11740
(516) 754-5400
(516) 754-5412 FAX

Thomas O'Brien Academy of
    Science and Technology
Lincoln Park
Albany, NY 12202
(518) 462-7263
(518) 462-7152 FAX

Waterford-Halfmoon Elementary
    School
125 Middletown Road
Waterford, NY 12188
(518) 237-0800
(518) 237-7335 FAX

NORTH CAROLINA

Brentwood Elementary School
3426 Ingram Drive
Raleigh, NC 27604
(919) 850-8720
(919) 850-8728 FAX

Carver Elementary G.T. Magnet
    School
948 Morphus Bridge Road
Wendell, NC 27591
(919) 365-2680
(919) 365-2622 FAX

Charlotte Latin School
9502 Providence Road
Charlotte, NC 28277-8695
(704) 846-1100
(704) 846-1712 FAX

E. E. Miller Elementary School
1361 Rim Road
Fayetteville, NC 28314
(910) 868-2800
(910) 867-1960 FAX

NORTH DAKOTA

Lake Agassiz Elementary School
605 Stanford Road
Grand Forks, ND 58203
(701) 746-2275
(701) 746-2274 FAX

OHIO

Centerville Kindergarten Village
    School
6450 Marshall Road
Centerville, OH 45459
(937) 438-6062
(937) 438-6076 FAX

Cincinnati Hills Christian Academy
Edyth B. Lindner Elementary
11312 Snider Road
Cincinnati, OH 45249
(513) 247-9944
(513) 247-0125 FAX

Crosby Elementary School
8382 New Haven Road
Harrison, OH 45030
(513) 738-1717
(513) 738-1718 FAX

Fairbrook Elementary School
260 N. Fairfield Road
Beavercreek, OH 45430
(937) 429-7616
(937) 429-7687 FAX

Gesu Catholic School
2450 Miramar Boulevard
University Heights, OH 44118
(216) 932-0620
(216) 932-8326 FAX

Reading Central Community
    School
1301 Bonnell Avenue
Reading, OH 45215
(513) 554-1001
(513) 483-6754 FAX

Royalview Elementary School
31500 Royalview Drive
Willowick, OH 44095
(216) 944-3130
(216) 943-9965 FAX

Shawnee Elementary School
9394 Sterling Drive
Cincinnati, OH 45241-5107
(513) 779-3014
(513) 779-3494 FAX

St. Martin of Tours School
14600 Turney Road
Maple Heights, OH 44137
(216) 475-3633
(216) 475-2484 FAX

St. Peter's Elementary School
63 South Mulberry Street
Mansfield, OH 44902
(419) 524-3351
(419) 522-2553 FAX

W. M. Sellman School
6612 Miami Avenue
Cincinnati, OH 45243
(513) 561-5555
(513) 985-6072 FAX

OKLAHOMA

Almor West Elementary School
6902 SW Delta Avenue
Lawton, OK 73505
(405) 536-6006
(405) 536-0385 FAX

Coronado Heights Elementary
School
5911 N. Sapulpa Avenue
Oklahoma City, OK 73112
(405) 942-8593
(405) 948-9014 FAX

Pershing Elementary School
301 N. 54th Street
Muskogee, OK 74401
(918) 684-3830
(918) 684-3701 FAX

Pioneer Park Elementary School
3005 NE Angus Place
Lawton, OK 73507-1400
(405) 355-5844
(405) 585-6453 FAX

Saint Pius X School
1717 South 75th East Avenue
Tulsa, OK 74112-7703
(918) 627-5367
(918) 622-1239 FAX

PENNSYLVANIA

Enders-Fisherville Elementary
School
791 Enders Road
Halifax, PA 17032
(717) 362-9259
(717) 896-3976 FAX

George D. Steckel Elementary
School
2928 MacArthur Road
Whitehall, PA 18052
(610) 435-1521
(610) 435-0124 FAX

Hartwood Elementary School
548 Saxonburg Boulevard
Pittsburgh, PA 15238
(412) 767-5396
(412) 967-2487 FAX

Hillview Intermediate Center
482 E. Main Street
Grove City, PA 16127
(412) 458-7570
(412) 458-0444 FAX

Ingomar Middle School
Ingomar Heights Road
Pittsburgh, PA 15237-1699
(412) 369-5471
(412) 366-4487 FAX

Mary C. Howse Elementary School
641 West Boot Road
West Chester, PA 19380
(610) 436-7335
(610) 436-7336 FAX

Nether Providence Elementary
  School
410 Moore Road
Wallingford, PA 19086
(610) 874-5235
(610) 874-3561 FAX

New Eagle Elementary School
507 Pugh Road
Wayne, PA 19087
(610) 688-0246
(610) 341-9324 FAX

Pennypack Elementary School
130 Spring Avenue
Hatboro, PA 19040
(215) 956-2922
(215) 957-9720 FAX

Washington Park Elementary
  School
801 East Wheeling Street
Washington, PA 15301
(412) 223-5150
(412) 223-5056 FAX

PUERTO RICO

Colegio Catolico Notre Dame
  Elementary School
Box 967
Caguas, PR 00726
(787) 743-2524
(787) 744-6464 FAX

RHODE ISLAND

Mercymount Country Day School
Wrentham Road
Cumberland, RI 02864
(401) 333-5919
(401) 333-5150 FAX

Western Coventry School
4588 Flat River Road
Coventry, RI 02816
(401) 397-3355
(401) 822-9406 FAX

SOUTH CAROLINA

Bethel Elementary School
111 Bethel School Road
Simpsonville, SC 29681
(864) 967-1866
(864) 967-1874 FAX

Forest Lake Elementary School
6801 Brookfield Rd.
Columbia, SC 29206
(803) 782-0470
(803) 738-7365 FAX

Heathwood Hall Episcopal School
3000 South Beltline Boulevard
Columbia, SC 29201-5199
(803) 765-2309
(803) 343-0437 FAX

Irmo Elementary School
7401 Gibbes Street
Irmo, SC 29063
(803) 732-8275
(803) 732-8035 FAX

Lonnie B. Nelson Elementary
  School
225 N. Brickyard Road
Columbia, SC 29223
(803) 736-8730
(803) 699-3672 FAX

Nursery Road Elementary School
6706 Nursery Road
Columbia, SC 29212
(803) 732-8475
(803) 732-8474 FAX

Oakland Elementary School
2728 Arlington Drive
Charleston, SC 29414
(803) 763-1510
(803) 769-2598 FAX

Pelham Road Elementary School
All Star Way
Greenville, SC 29615
(864) 281-1234
(864) 281-1236 FAX

Pelion Elementary School
1202 Pine Street
Pelion, SC 29123
(803) 894-2000
(803) 894-0580 FAX

Taylors Elementary School
809 Reid School Road
Taylors, SC 29687
(864) 292-7655
(864) 292-7337 FAX

SOUTH DAKOTA

Rapid Valley Elementary School
2601 Covington Street
Rapid City, SD 57701
(605) 393-2221
(605) 393-1973 FAX

TEXAS

A. H. Meadows Elementary School
1600 Rigsbee Drive
Plano, TX 75074
(972) 519-8810
(972) 424-1529 FAX

Dr. Joey Pirrung Elementary School
1500 Creek Valley
Mesquite, TX 75181
(972) 222-0034
(972) 289-6105 FAX

Eanes Elementary School
4101 Bee Cave Road
Austin, TX 78746
(512) 327-0337
(512) 327-0784 FAX

Grace School
10219 Ella Lee Lane
Houston, TX 77042
(713) 782-4421
(713) 267-5056 FAX

John Paul II Catholic School
1400 Parkway Plaza Drive
Houston, TX 77077
(713) 496-1500
(713) 496-2943 FAX

L. L. Campbell Elementary School
2613 Rogers Avenue
Austin, TX 78722
(512) 414-2056
(512) 476-9248 FAX

Lorenzo de Zavala Elementary
   School
310 Robert Martinez Jr. Street
Austin, TX 78702
(512) 414-2318
(512) 477-2361 FAX

Mary Hull Elementary School
7320 Remuda Drive
San Antonio, TX 78227-2899
(210) 678-2910
(210) 678-2917 FAX

Maureen Connolly Brinker
   Elementary School
3800 John Clark Parkway
Plano, TX 75093
(972) 519-8827
(972) 403-7013 FAX

Memorial Drive Elementary School
11202 Smithdale
Houston, TX 77024
(713) 365-4960
(713) 365-4967 FAX

Michael Kennedy Elementary
   School
10200 Huntington Place Drive
Houston, TX 77099
(281) 983-8338
(281) 879-9380 FAX

O. C. Taylor Elementary School
5300 Pool Road
Colleyville, TX 76034
(817) 358-4870
(817) 540-3940 FAX

Pine Tree Middle School
P.O. Box 5878
Longview, TX 75608
(903) 295-5160
(903) 295-5162 FAX

Pond Springs Elementary School
7825 Elkhorn Mountain Trail
Austin, TX 78729
(512) 464-4200
(512) 464-4290 FAX

Prestonwood Elementary School
6525 La Cosa Drive
Dallas, TX 75248
(972) 448-2860
(972) 448-2870 FAX

Smith Elementary School
4209 Smith School Road
Austin, TX 78744
(512) 385-5121
(512) 389-3688 FAX

Spring Shadows Elementary School
9725 Kempwood Drive
Houston, TX 77080
(713) 329-6470
(713) 329-6480 FAX

St. Clement's Episcopal Parish
   School
605 E. Yandell Drive
El Paso, TX 79902
(915) 533-4248
(915) 544-1778 FAX

St. Patrick School
3340 S. Alameda Street
Corpus Christi, TX 78411
(512) 852-1211
(512) 855-7552 FAX

St. Thomas Aquinas Catholic
   School
3741 Abrams Road
Dallas, TX 75214
(214) 826-0566
(214) 826-0251 FAX

T. A. Brown Elementary School
505 West Anderson Lane
Austin, TX 78749
(512) 414-2047
(512) 452-6097 FAX

Terrell W. Ogg Elementary School
208 Lazy Lane
Clute, TX 77531
(409) 265-2090
(409) 265-5231 FAX

Valley View Elementary School
1201 Loop 360 South
Austin, TX 78746
(512) 327-7420
(512) 328-5351 FAX

Walnut Creek Elementary School
401 West Braker Lane
Austin, TX 78753-3038
(512) 414-4499
(512) 837-6789 FAX

Walnut Glen Academy for
   Excellence
3101 Edgewood Drive
Garland, TX 75042
(214) 494-8330
(214) 494-8330 FAX

UTAH

Ferron Elementary School
115 West Mill Road
Ferron, UT 84523
(801) 384-2383
(801) 384-2550 FAX

VIRGINIA

Beaverdam Elementary School
15485 Beaverdam School Road
Beaverdam, VA 23015
(804) 449-6373
(804) 449-6510 FAX

George F. Baker Elementary School
6651 Willson Road
Richmond, VA 23231
(804) 226-8755
(804) 226-8769 FAX

George J. McIntosh Elementary
School
185 Richneck Road
Newport News, VA 23608
(757) 886-7767
(757) 989-0326 FAX

Kingston Elementary School
3532 King's Grant Road
Virginia Beach, VA 23452
(757) 431-4015
(757) 431-4017 FAX

Northampton Middle School
7247 Young Street
P.O. Box 370
Machipongo, VA 23405
(757) 678-5383
(757) 678-7645 FAX

Riner Elementary School
4069 Riner Road
Riner, VA 24149
(540) 382-5165
(540) 382-6157 FAX

WASHINGTON

Camelot Elementary School
4041 South 298th Street
Auburn, WA 98001
(206) 839-4450
(206) 839-6863 FAX

Chief Kanim Middle School
32627 S.E. Red-Fall County Road
P.O. Box 639
Fall City, WA 98024
(206) 222-6686
(206) 222-4937 FAX

Holy Rosary School
4142 42nd Avenue, SW
Seattle, WA 98116
(206) 937-7255
(206) 935-4303 FAX

Juanita Elementary School
9635 132nd Street NE
Kirkland, WA 98034
(206) 823-8136
(206) 820-2312 FAX

Morgan Owings Elementary School
401 East Woodin Street
P.O. Box 369
Chelan, WA 98816
(509) 682-4031
(509) 682-3373 FAX

Mountain View Elementary School
5780 Hendrickson Road
P.O. Box 935
Ferndale, WA 98248
(360) 384-9270
(360) 384-9201 FAX

WEST VIRGINIA

Academy Primary School
2 College Avenue
Buckhannon, WV 26201
(304) 472-3310
(304) 472-0258 FAX

Arthur I. Boreman Elementary
School
Route 18
P.O. Box 299
Middlebourne, WV 26149
(304) 758-2152
(304) 758-2148 FAX

Harrisville Elementary School
1201 E. Main Street
Harrisville, WV 26362
(304) 643-2220
(304) 643-2710 FAX

Madison Elementary School
91 Zane Street
Wheeling, WV 26003
(304) 243-0367
(304) 243-0368 FAX

Midland Trail Elementary School
200 Ferry Street
Belle, WV 25015
(304) 949-1823
(304) 949-1016

Norwood Elementary School
Kidd Avenue
Stonewood, WV 26301
(304) 624-3262
(304) 624-3286 FAX

Pleasant Hill School
Route 16 North
HC 68 Box 2
Grantsville, WV 26147
(304) 354-6022
(304) 354-7420 FAX

WISCONSIN

Cushing Elementary School
227 Genesee Street
Delafield, WI 53018
(414) 646-6700
(414) 646-6730 FAX

Dousman Elementary School
341 E. Ottawa Avenue
Dousman, WI 53118-9703
(414) 965-6550
(414) 965-6559 FAX

1996-1997 SPECIAL EMPHASES WINNERS

Technology

Walker Elementary School
Springdale, AR

Joe Nightingale School
Santa Maria, CA

Diplomat Elementary School
Cape Coral, FL

Key Largo Elementary School
Key Largo, FL

Eastside Elementary School
Douglas, GA

Flat Rock Middle School
Tyrone, GA

Pine Tree Elementary School
Lake Orion, MI

Chesterfield Elementary School
Chesterfield, MO

Glenridge Elementary School
Clayton, MO

Westside Middle School
Omaha, NE

Thomas O'Brien Academy
Albany, NY

Pershing Elementary School
Muskogee, OK

Dr. Joey Pirrung Elementary School
Mesquite, TX

Northampton Middle School
Machipongo, VA

Chief Kanim Middle School
Fall City, WA

Juanita Elementary School
Kirkland, WA

Professional Development

Stemley Road Elementary School
Talladega, AL

Meadows Elementary School
Thousand Oaks, CA

Amelia Earhart Intermediate
    School
Okinawa, Japan

Department of Defense Dependents Schools

Easterling Primary School
Marion, SC

Knightsville Elementary School
Summerville, SC

Valley Creek Elementary School
McKinney, TX

School Safety, Discipline, and Drug Prevention

Momilani Elementary School
Pearl City, HI